Breaking Feminist Waves

Series Editors
Alison Stone
Philosophy and Religion
Lancaster University
Lancaster, UK

Linda Martin Alcoff
Department of Philosophy
Hunter College
New York, NY, USA

"This series promises to invite feminist thinkers from a variety of disciplinary backgrounds to think theoretically about feminism's history and future - work that needs to be done. I look forward to incorporating titles from this series into my women's and gender studies teaching." —Alison Piepmeier, Director, Women's and Gender Studies Program, The College of Charleston

For the last thirty years, feminist theory has been presented as a series of ascending waves. This picture has had the effect of deemphasizing the diversity of past scholarship as well as constraining the way we understand and frame new work. The aim of this series is to attract original scholars who will offer unique interpretations of past scholarship and unearth neglected contributions to feminist theory. By breaking free from the constraints of the image of waves, this series will be able to provide a wider forum for dialogue and engage historical and interdisciplinary work to open up feminist theory to new audiences and markets.

Proposals are encouraged from a range of disciplines including but not confined to women's and gender studies, philosophy, English, religious studies, history, cultural studies, and ethnic studies. We welcome proposals for projects that re-examine feminism and its history in ways that question, complicate, or challenge the wave image.

LINDA MARTÍN ALCOFF is Professor of Philosophy at Hunter College and the City University of New York Graduate Center, USA. Recent books include *Rape and Resistance, The Future of Whiteness*, and *Visible Identities: Race, Gender and the Self*. She is past President of the American Philosophical Association, Eastern Division.

ALISON STONE is Professor of European Philosophy at Lancaster University, UK. She is the author of books on feminist philosophy, Hegel and German idealism, Irigaray, motherhood and psychoanalysis, popular music, and nineteenth-century philosophy. She co-edited the *Routledge Companion to Feminist Philosophy* (with Ann Garry and Serene J. Khader) and is co-editing the *Oxford Handbook of American and British Women Philosophers in the Nineteenth Century* (with Lydia Moland).

Palgrave Contact: Amy Invernizzi, amy.invernizzi@palgrave-usa.com

Emily Cousens

Trans Feminist Epistemologies in the US Second Wave

Emily Cousens
London School of Economics
London, UK

ISSN 2945-6991   ISSN 2945-7009   (electronic)
Breaking Feminist Waves
ISBN 978-3-031-33730-7   ISBN 978-3-031-33731-4   (eBook)
https://doi.org/10.1007/978-3-031-33731-4

This Palgrave Macmillan imprint is published by the registered company Springer Nature Switzerland AG.
The registered company address is: Gewerbestrasse 11, 6330 Cham, Switzerland

PREFACE

This book about feminism's intellectual development has its own intellectual and embodied history. I came to the topic of trans feminist epistemologies in the US second wave as a feminist philosophy student, first and foremost interested in gender and increasingly turning to trans feminist texts - first Julia Serano, then Kate Bornstein—in order to make sense of my own experiences of gender, and to address the elisions that seemed to permeate much of the dense feminist theory I was being assigned. My initial teenage forays into feminist theory had been into the second wave texts of Andrea Dworkin and bell hooks. Here was a feminism that seemed set out to change the world. These writers offered clear critiques of capitalism, racism and patriarchy and seemed to propose nothing less than we wake up to the problems and do something about them! Whilst my teenage impatience and quest for crystal clear visions waned, and I became more comfortable with the ambivalence and unknowability that infused the work of post-structuralist thinkers like Judith Butler, the experience of encountering trans feminism, with its manifesto-like urgency, once again made me alive to the pleasures of experientially accountable theory that sought to peel back the skin and expose structures (this time cis-sexism and trans misogyny) for what they are. The affective experience of reading trans feminist and second wave feminist texts for the first time was clarifying, motivating and gave the sense of being life changing. So my initial encounters with "transgender" were with the assumption that "transgender" *is* gender. Whilst there is no one "trans" experience, "transgender", translated as "not assigned gender", can tell us *something* about how gender works through how it is policed, shedding light on gender's compulsory, chosen and culturally overdetermined dimensions equally. "Cisgender" by contrast is gender's mystification.

It was my search for second wave trans feminist texts that led me to the archive, to carefully documented and intimately shared experiences. The second wave feminism that has reached academically authored books remains relatively selective. However, once you make the switch from library shelves to archival catalogues - many of which can be found thanks to the immense resource that is the Digital Transgender Archive - it doesn't take much to be captivated by the abundance of trans community periodicals that were circulating at the time of the second wave, both in tandem with, and occasionally in dialogue with, the wider feminist movement. Through sharing experiences and survival information and creating networks and social spaces, these publications are so clearly doing the work of feminism: discussing and theorising sex and gender, and making more inhabitable worlds for those who lived some or all of the time as women. Indeed, if second wave feminism was principally a period of grappling with what it meant to be a "woman", and how to protect and empower those who travelled under that sign, then those on the trans feminine spectrum were doing vital feminist work simply through articulating what it felt like to be themselves. Moreover, exploring these archives quickly highlights not only the conversations that trans individuals were having with one another, but also the influence that these communities had on the development of clinical understandings of "sex" and "gender" at the time.

Writing about trans identities, as a queer person who—whilst not identifying as, or probably qualifying for, "cisgender"—is not trans, is a careful balancing act, and one that requires the exercise of humility. This need to avow the intellectual expertise of my interlocutors is compounded by the fact that many of the identities I discuss, those of self-identified "crossdressers", "transvestites", and "transsexuals" in the 1970s, are in less wide circulation in the UK and the US today than the umbrella term "transgender"—and often carry negative, pathologised overtones. Working with lived experiences which are not my own, I am aware that my interpretations will be imperfect acts of translation. I do believe, however, that it is important to revise philosophy so that those who have been excluded have their contributions to knowledge production recognised and incorporated. As such, through engaging with trans community periodicals and foregrounding the contributions of trans individuals to the debates within feminism, and within the scientific community, I treat these contributions as philosophical texts, worthy of critical engagement and cross-disciplinary dialogue.

Foregrounding trans individuals' involvement in and contribution to second wave feminism is important for countering the violences that circulate under the banner of feminism in the present. I urge all readers to pick up where I leave off—to read first-hand the journals I discuss, to create your own interlocutors by exploring those journals and contributors that I do not, and to open up history and theory to those whose investments and labour have the capacity to transform our present-day dialogues and ontologies for better.

London, UK   Emily Cousens

ACKNOWLEDGEMENTS

Behind every first book there is an immense network of care that provides its fragile conditions of possibility, and it would take hundreds of pages to do justice to each and every person, conversation and moment that made this book possible. So here, I want to acknowledge Sarah Pine. You have been there from day one thought one, to the final misplaced comma. For twelve years of vital feminist friendship and hand-holding, thank you.

There are also a few individuals and networks to whom I am immensely grateful. First, I want to thank the MSt. Women's, Gender and Sexuality Studies cohorts at the University of Oxford between 2018 and 2022 for your conversations, confidence and care. And, second, this project was enabled by the archivists whose love, labour and expertise have preserved and made accessible many of the materials included here- and who have facilitated my own explorations and enquiries. Thanks, in particular, to Isaac Fellman and Sy Auerbach at the GLBT Historical Society, Ms. Bob Davis at the Louise Lawrence Transgender Archive, Dr Aaron Devor and Lara Wilson at the University of Victoria Transgender Archives, Philip Virta for your work with the Gale Archives and K.J. Rawson for envisaging and establishing the Digital Transgender Archive.

I am grateful to the British Academy and the Leverhulme Trust for the research grant which enabled the archival research in this project.

CONTENTS

CHAPTER 1

Introduction: Second Wave Trans Feminism

> Bringing trans and feminist together, making them hold hands, as it were, is a quest to radicalise them both
> —Marquis Bey, Black Trans Feminism

If feminism is, according to the current shelf life for ideologies, old, and trans people are even older—gender being "one of our oldest systems of classification of embodied experience" (Long in Bychowski et al. 2018, 672)—then trans feminism should be old news. Yet trans feminism has been characterised as "a 'third wave' feminist sensibility" (Stryker and Bettcher 2016, 11)- even as the longstanding feminist roots of trans

© The Author(s), under exclusive license to Springer Nature Switzerland AG 2023
E. Cousens, *Trans Feminist Epistemologies in the US Second Wave*, Breaking Feminist Waves, https://doi.org/10.1007/978-3-031-33731-4_1

1

studies are more widely recognised.[1] Second wave feminism, on the other hand, has been historicised as both epistemically and demographically "cis"- mired in biologically essentialist philosophies and trans-exclusionarity politics. Second wave feminism is associated with elaborating the social construction of gender whilst remaining attached to a biologically fixed and binary understanding of sex—and, in turn, using this sex/gender distinction to justify exclusions from activist spaces and support services. If not ideologically opposed (fighting the patriarchy vs fighting the gender binary) then temporally out of sync (first second wave feminism, then trans feminism) the coexistence of second wave feminism with trans feminism is rarely taken for granted.

These understandings are so embedded in the grammar of western feminist theory's storytelling (Hemmings 2011), that they often proceed as given—with little by way of citational support. As Finn Enke writes, "In less than one generation, the 'second wave' became aka 'white feminism' and 'trans-exclusionary feminism'" (2018, 10) with the effect that alliances between trans feminism and second wave feminism are rarely sought. When second wave feminism is uncritically accepted as hostile to trans, non-binary and intersex experiences and knowledges (which, for the

---

[1] Stephen Whittle, for example, describes "trans studies" as "a true linking of feminist and queer theory" in the foreword to the first edition of the *Transgender Studies Reader* (2006, xii). Susan Stryker writes that "Transgender feminism [...] had its roots in the feminist radicalism of the late 1960s" (2008a, 3). When looking at the history of trans activism in the US, the wave metaphor has also been applied. Suzy Cooke, a trans feminist activist in the 1970s, describes the activism of trans people in the feminist and liberation movements of the 1960s and 1970s as part of a "second wave" of trans liberation; a more radical movement who were "influenced by the pop culture of the sixties, who were influenced by feminism, who were influene (sic) by [...] Stonewall and the whole gay liberation thing. Because that first generation, that first wave, they would not even consider interacting with the gays. They just would not" (Stryker 1998, 29). The explosion of trans theory and activism in the 1990s, which influenced and was influenced by postmodern and post structuralist approaches- Sandy Stone (1992), Kate Bornstein (1994) and Leslie Feinberg (1996)—could qualify as a "third wave" and this is what is usually indexed by the notion of trans feminism's "third wave" sensibility. For more on trans feminism being narrated as closely/more closely aligned with third wave feminism see Edward Burlton Davies: Third Wave Feminism and Transgender (2019). Karine Espinera and Marie-Hélène/Sam Bourcier (2016) also tie trans feminism to third wave feminism. Meanwhile, Paisley Currah describes the third wave as "more politically ecumenical third wave" (2016, 2).

purpose of this book, will be collected under the umbrella of "trans epistemologies")[2] the very presence of trans, non-binary and intersex feminists in US feminism's second wave gets overlooked.

This association of second wave feminism with trans exclusion has been give further weight due to the mobilisation of the label of "second wave radical feminism" by trans-exclusionary feminists. Among the endorsements on the cover of Julie Bindel's book *"Feminism for Women: The Real Route to Liberation"* (2021), which presents transgender rights as a threat to "women's liberation", is the following extract from *The Times* newspaper's review: "Bindel is a rock star of second-wave feminism... an important, courageous book" (2021, cover). Bindel proudly takes up what she presents as the beleaguered mantle of second wave feminism, presenting it as a long-lost project of women's liberation. Sheila Jeffreys, another

---

[2] I am mindful that grouping all challenges to sex/gender dimorphism under the umbrella "trans feminist" risks "categorical conflation" (Meyers 2022, 200) between trans and intersex embodiments, a conflation that has the potential to overlook the distinctly different political constituencies and needs of trans and intersex communities. However, in contesting naturalised and immutable dimorphic sex categories, there are important overlaps between trans and intersex epistemologies- and it is these that I take forward. Whilst feminist, queer and trans theories have often proceeded with insufficient attention to the lived experiences of intersex individuals, I understand that "refusing medically originating separations between trans and intersex may be a way to resist divisiveness that exemplifies medicine" (Swarr in Wolff et al. 2022, 148). In what follows, I seek harness the coalitional potential of challenges to cisnormativity. I am using the category of "trans feminism" capaciously, then, to designate sexed and gendered embodiments and subjectivities that deviate from the cisgendered norm. Cisgenderism (the ideology that proposes that sex and gender are distinct, binary and immutable, and that gender follows from sex) excludes not only gender variance, but intersex embodiments. According to Erica Lennon and Brian Mistler, "cisgenderism refers to the cultural and systemic ideology that denies, denigrates or pathologises self-identified gender identities that do not align with the gender assigned at birth as well as resulting behaviour, expression and community" (2014, 63). My focus however is on the norm that this produces; the norm of gendered identification aligning with the sex one is assigned at birth- where sex is a fixed, rather than a historical, political and cultural category.

In the UK and US contexts, the contexts I am writing from and about, gender normativity and therefore cisnormativity are approximated by, if not dependent on, whiteness, able-bodiedness and thinness. See Marquis Bey *Cistem Failure* (2022b) for the interaction of cisnormativity with whiteness, Francis White "Fucking Failures" (2016) on the entanglement of cisnormativity with thinness and the de-gendering of fat bodies, and Jasbir K. Puar's "Bodies with New Organs" (2015) for an analysis of the interrelation between biopolitical discourses of disability and gender normativity.

trans-exclusionary British feminist, also posits second wave feminism as the truly political, radical version of feminism against which queer and trans feminists have departed (2014). This alignment with second wave feminism bolsters the arsenal of trans-exclusionary radical feminists (TERFS) who position themselves [cis, white women] as the original and authentic heroine of feminism, and present "trans" as both new and threatening (Bassia and LaFleur 2022).

Trans-exclusionary feminisms, however, under whatever banner they choose to operate, have always been on the defensive. As Susan Stryker and Talia Mae Bettcher point out, anti-transgender rhetoric always emerges in *reaction* to gains for transgender human and civil rights and greater support of trans lives—no matter "however haltingly or unevenly" these developments proceed (2016, 5). Resisting the appropriation of the label "second wave" by a minority of embattled yet highly networked feminists is a necessary historiographical, political, and philosophical move. The reality is that it is impossible to understate, let alone separate, the longstanding importance of trans people to feminist political liberation (Bassia and LaFleur 2022, 327) and, as this book will argue, second wave feminism's philosophical conditions of possibility were created by trans individuals. Revisiting the influences on and investments in second wave feminism by trans people deauthorises the weaponisation of feminism's recent past and enables us to revisit "women" and "liberation" as open, collective, and ultimately ambitious categories.

In the UK, trans-exclusionary feminists are currently self-styled as "gender critical feminists", although a more precise description would be "chromosome-reductivism" or "sex-essentialism" feminists (Lewis 2022, para 26).[3] I proceed with the acronym TERF in this book as the most descriptive and widely recognised category available.[4] It also indexes the histories of radical feminism and second wave feminism with which this

---

[3] I find the label "gender critical" to be misleading because it conflates trans-exclusionary feminism with gender abolitionism. As such, it positions the goal of trans-exclusionary feminism to be the abolition of "gender", when in fact it is the abolition of trans existences (and, therefore, the very careful policing and maintenance of [cis]gender). By contrast, gender abolition, when understood as resistance to the coercive gender binary or a commitment to the universality of gender as self-fashioning- is, for many, the goal of trans feminism (e.g. Bey 2022a; Bornstein 2012).

[4] I use "TERFist" to refer to a person or collective who ascribes to these core elements of TERFism.

book is concerned. As Judith Butler (in Ferber 2020) has argued, "trans-exclusionarity" is a straightforward, descriptive- rather than necessarily pejorative- nomenclature for a group of people whose politics is directed at excluding trans people from feminist spaces, public spaces, and who claim the authority and legacy of radical feminism to do so.[5] Trans-exclusionary radical feminism, or TERFism is also an ideology of whiteness (Tudor 2020; Bassia and LaFleur 2022), committed to gender essentialism and therefore depending on a non-intersectional understanding of "women" as a unified group, where their shared "sex" is all that matters. Whilst one available response to the co-optation of feminist discourses by trans-exclusionary coalitions is to argue that TERFs are *not* radical feminists, they advance forms of essentialism incompatible with the key principles of radical feminism—I propose that the lines between what is or what isn't radical feminism are not so clear cut. Indeed, all language is vulnerable to being reworked and that the banner of radical feminism is being claimed, is cause for acknowledgement- and resistance.

In the conclusion, I adapt Cassius Adair, Cameron Awkward-Rich and Amy Marvin's argument that we are "before trans studies" (2020) into a methodology which contests the positing of trans epistemologies as feminism's modifier rather than the other way round. "Before: trans studies" enquires into the trans epistemologies that were circulating before key moments in feminism's intellectual development and asks how these trans knowledges shaped and informed the direction and development of feminism. One clear application of this methodology is to Janice Raymond's *The Transsexual Empire*. Published in 1979, at the end of the decade most closely associated with US feminism's second wave, this text put in motion the ideological contours of trans-exclusionarity in the name of feminism,

---

[5] Butler's full comment was: "I am not aware that terf is used as a slur. I wonder what name self-declared feminists who wish to exclude trans women from women's spaces would be called? If they do favour exclusion, why not call them exclusionary? If they understand themselves as belonging to that strain of radical feminism that opposes gender reassignment, why not call them radical feminists? My only regret is that there was a movement of radical sexual freedom that once travelled under the name of radical feminism, but it has sadly morphed into a campaign to pathologise trans and gender non-conforming peoples. My sense is that we have to renew the feminist commitment to gender equality and gender freedom in order to affirm the complexity of gendered lives as they are currently being lived" (Ferber 2020, para 9).

the influence of which is increasingly felt today.[6] Yet taking Raymond's text as the teleological expression of a factious and increasingly exclusionary women's movement not only overlooks the contributions of trans activists in the period—but makes it possible to tell a history of second wave feminism without them.

The questions that motivate this study are as follows: How do dominant perceptions of second wave feminism impact our understandings of the period's conceptual and theoretical output? What does trans studies have to

[6] *Trans feminist epistemologies* argues that whilst transphobia was present throughout much of the second wave, these sentiments did not become widespread until the end of the decade, and they received their first ideological accounting in Raymond's *The Transsexual Empire*. The following discussion between Gayle Rubin and Judith Butler, in their important conversation "Sexual Traffic" (Rubin [1994] 2011) locates the emergence of TERFism as a late 1970s phenomenon. Rubin recalls that when "the debate on transsexuality…hit print toward the late 1970s, the discussion really flipped me out because it was so biologically deterministic. When it finally erupted into print over the hiring of Sandy Stone, a male-to-female transsexual, by Olivia Records, there were a number of articles in the lesbian press about how women were born and not made, which I found rather … " and Butler joins in "[in unison] distressing" (2011, 285). Sandy Stone also presents Raymond's attack on her as ushering in a new period of transphobia within feminism. In an interview with Cristan Williams, in response to the question: "Can you tell me how you first became aware of the TERF movement?" Stone answers "That would have been the Janice Raymond incident. That came in the context of my work with Olivia Records […] what happened with Raymond was so betraying, so bizarre and so completely unexpected" (Williams 2020, paras 4–7).

"Transsexuality" had first become a "question", particularly among white feminists and lesbian feminists, in the early 1970s and Beth Elliot, a self-identified lesbian transsexual, was on the receiving end of much of the transphobia that this "debate" spawned. Her membership of the San Francisco Chapter of lesbian feminist organisation Daughters of Bilitis (DofB), for which she had been the Vice-President and served on the editorial collective for their newsletter *Sister* was debated in 1972. Elliot was voted out, prompting the resignation of many members. The Los Angeles Chapter of DofB responded by issuing a statement welcoming her, should she wish to join. Elliot's participation in lesbian feminist spaces was then "debated" again at the West Coast Lesbian conference in 1973, when lesbian separatist group, Gutter Dykes, protested her participation, Despite a vote among those in attendance going in favour of Elliot's presence and participation, the following day Robin Morgan delivered a transphobic keynote speech (see Bettcher 2016). I discuss how Elliot's experiences with Daughter of Bilitis and the wider feminist movement have been claimed both as evidence of the era's trans-exclusionarity and trans-inclusivity later in this chapter. However, Elliot's own arguments in response to the transphobia she experienced remain politically valuable. She writes: "I distrust speakers whose idea of a rousing speech is a trashathon" (1973, 15) and makes a prescient link between trans exclusionary feminism and fascism: "And doesn't feminism say that we are not what we are conditioned to be? And that we can overcome our conditioning? […] I will concede you one point on conditioning. Having grown up in Nixon's America, you make a damned good fascist: (1973, 26).

offer received readings of second wave feminism? And does second wave feminism have anything to offer trans studies? Whilst associations of the second wave's trans-exclusionarity would suggest otherwise, what happens if we ask the question: do second wave feminism and transgender studies need one another? As Marquis Bey's epigraph to this chapter submits, "bringing trans and feminist together, making them hold hands, as it were, is a quest to radicalise them both" (2022a, 56). Can trans studies radicalise *second wave* feminism too? Which bodies or identities are positioned outside the frame when the second wave is overdetermined as exclusively cisgendered? And how can we read the second wave otherwise? Moreover, I am interested not only in how these approaches might inform one another in the present, but in what different views of history come to the fore when second wave and trans feminism no longer read as mutually exclusive epistemologies and are made to converge theoretically and temporally. What if second wave feminism has always needed trans studies? How does the influence of trans individuals on the science of sex and gender in the mid-twentieth-century impact the idea that we can ever have had second wave feminism without trans feminism? And if a central element of second wave feminism was a contest over the meaning of the word "women", how did trans women shape these debates?

Each of the chapters is organised in relation to a different aspect of the influence of trans feminism during the US second wave. Chapter 2 starts with the exchanges between trans women and the wider feminist movement that were taking place "on the ground" so to speak—in the feminist and gay presses. It focusses on radical trans feminist Margo Schulter's contributions to the underground print culture from the period in which she aims to educate the rest of the feminist movement about sex, gender, and the centrality of countering transphobia as part of a coherent feminist, and lesbian feminist, strategy. The following two chapters then consider the philosophical articulations of trans feminism that were being developed during the second wave, outlining a "trans" and "feminist" set of arguments in turn. Chapter 3 explores the *Journal of Male Feminism*, an independently produced newsletter for a community of cross-dressers who identified as "male feminists" and invoked—both earnestly and strategically—discourses and politics of women's liberation in order to argue for the normalisation of feminine expression in bodies assigned male at birth. Chapter 4 undertakes a trans feminist reading of archetypical second wave feminist Andrea Dworkin's extensive corpus. It argues that when read outside of a presumption of cisness (the idea that sex and gender are strictly binary, immutable, and aligned such that from sex, gender follows), her philosophy presents both sexuality and biological sex as equally constructed as gender. Moreover, the trans feminist priority of countering the violence of binary sex categorisation emerges as inseparable from her well known, regularly weaponised, politics of countering violence against women. Chapter 5 explores the role of citation conventions in creating an intellectual environment in which we have come to presume that second wave feminism was "cis"- attached to a binary and biological understanding of sex as the immutable foundation upon which gender is constructed. It argues that the concepts of "sex" and "gender" that feminists were adapting from the US sexological literature of the 1960s and 1970s were developed as a direct result of the labour and influence of trans individuals in the mid-twentieth century. Therefore, not only were trans people involved in second wave feminist activism, but it was trans-led epistemologies that provided second wave feminism with its intellectual and philosophical foundations. The conclusion then takes up these discussions in the present moment, arguing that the trans feminist epistemologies circulating in the US second wave are not only valuable academically, they also serve as important counters to the weaponisation of second wave anti-violence politics by trans-exclusionary radical feminists today.

SECOND WAVE FEMINISM

There are many well placed criticisms of the concept of "second wave feminism". Kimberly Springer points out that the wave metaphor excludes feminists of colour whose activism didn't ebb and flow in the ways the metaphor evokes, noting that if we "consider the first wave as that moment of organising encompassing woman suffrage and the second wave as the women's liberation/women's rights activism of the 1960s, we effectively disregard the race-based movements before them that served as precursors, or windows of political opportunity, for gender activism" (2002, 1061). Beverly Guy-Shefthall agrees that Black women "have been concerned with gender issues for well over a hundred and fifty years" (2002, 1093). Sheila Radford-Hill (2002) builds on Springer's argument to highlight the importance of intergenerational ties between black feminists that get overlooked in the oppositional, reactionary imaginary of the wave. Meanwhile, not only does the temporality evoked by the logic of the wave fall foul of much maligned liberal logics of progress, but as Mridula Nath Chakraborty highlights, the "very idea of a phase/stage/wave-based consciousness is an ideological construct of the Eurocentric subject that seeks to subsume and consume the challenges posed to it through notions of 'inclusion' and 'solidarity'" (2007, 101–2).[7]

Heeding these criticisms regarding the racialised and colonial temporality of the wave narrative and recognising the internal diversity collecting under the sign "second wave", I employ it here not to signal a linear story of western feminism's development. Rather, I am invested in the banner of "second wave feminism" for two reasons. First, to counter the idea that feminism can be categorised into discrete decades; I prefer the notion of a "wave"- with its associations of motion, resurgence and even potential destruction—to the more descriptive term "1970s feminism" (e.g. Havlin 2015; Enke 2018). And second, my appeal to idea of "the second wave" is underscored by a contention that the banner is saturated with negative affect and that wrestling with these affects might itself be a politically and philosophically generative move. "Second wave feminism" is not a neutral designation. It is perceived to be over, embarrassing, a container for whatever third wave, fourth wave, queer and post- feminists seek to disavow.[8] The label regularly functions not only a description, but a prescription; a shorthand for not just what feminists did, but what they did wrong, and as such comes with a series of negatives attached: what not to read, what not think, what not to do.[9]

If it is the injunction to dismiss anything that is characterised as "second wave" that has, as I am arguing, led to the baby of revolutionary aspirations being thrown out with the bathwater of political infighting and philosophical essentialism, then animating the spectre of the second wave is necessary for reconsidering the texts and arguments that get regularly overlooked. Indeed, the wave metaphor is itself a disciplining device; Dworkin, whose theorisation of the social construction of "sex" is the

---

[7] For a further overview of the wave metaphor debates, see Kathleen Laughlin et al. "Is It Time to Jump Ship? Historians Rethink the Waves Metaphor" (2010).

[8] See Victoria Hesford, *Feminism and its ghosts* (2005) and Clare Hemmings, *Why Stories Matter* (2011) on the place of second wave feminism within western feminist storytelling.

[9] Lisa Marie Hogeland discusses the elisions that shorthand dismissals of the second wave give rise to: "It's become a truism that second wave feminism was racist, for instance, no matter that such a blanket argument writes out of our history the enormous and important contributions of women of color in the 1970s […] it's become a truism that second wave feminism enshrined middle-class women's experience as universal […] The absolutism of both these views reinforces young(er) feminists' sense of themselves and their politics as distinct from earlier feminist movement, and from old(er) feminists as well; to explore continuities would be to admit to racism and classism" (2001, 118).

subject of Chap. 4, is firmly consigned to "second wave feminism" despite the fact that she published regularly until her death in 2005. Meanwhile, contributions from the period that have become more canonical, Laura Mulvey's 1975 essay *Visual Pleasure and Narrative Cinema* for example, Sylvia Federici's 1975 *Wages against Housework* or the 1977 Combahee River Collective's Statement, for example, are rarely hailed as second wave feminist texts. When second wave feminism attaches then, it attaches to *bad* objects; Betty Friedan's white middle-class centrism and Andrea Dworkin's anti-sex, anti-porn extremism, or to historical relics; Kate Millett's theory of "patriarchy", but rarely to our enduring philosophical theories and frameworks. Describing a text or thinker as "second wave", says more about how we *feel* about said text or thinker, than necessarily specifying when or what they were writing.

In re-reading the second wave, this book seeks to harness the negativity evoked by that banner; encouraging readers to sit with the discomfort of the idea of "second wave feminism", which is only sometimes motivated by considered engagement and intellectual disagreement. Whilst recent years have corrected the historical record that the women's liberation movement in the US second wave was exclusively white and middle class (Berger Gluck (1998), Thompson (2002), Roth (2003), Springer (2005) and Potter (2018)), such a reassessment has not extended to the intellectual contributions of the period. More often than not, second wave texts are presented as "abjected and taboo—not even worthy of being read or debated" (Downing and Cox 2018, 263). Like Robyn Wiegman, I believe that there's a rich archive of theorising on sex and gender stretching across the 1970s that gets lost in dismissals of second wave feminism as always already over, and I can similarly "confess to wanting contemporary scholars to spend more time reading and studying it, which is quite different from the way so many of us assume that we already know it or, worse, that we do not have to" (Wiegman 2007, 508). Second wave feminism was a product of the civil rights movement, the anti-war movement, the sexual revolution and the student organising of the 1960s. Its knowledge production was as diverse as the movements that gave rise to it. Yet it has become readily overdetermined on account of its whiteness, exclusionarity, fragmentation, separatism and universalism. In such associations, which prepare readers and students for the more sophisticated arguments of the present, is an absence of engagement with the ambitions and multiplicity of investments in "women's liberation" and an elision of the complex intellectual history that emanated from the idea that sex and gender roles could be abandoned and new ways of living, expressing and relating realised.

I employ the term "second wave feminism" capaciously, then, to index the generic qualities of the period's politics and philosophy; coalitional, pre-figurative and utopian. Moreover, when reconceived as a genre, second wave feminism is more readily aligned with trans feminist perspectives than conventionally presumed. In the second half of the 1960s, inspired by their involvement in the civil rights movement and the New Left and anti-Vietnam war organising of the previous years, the women that labelled themselves feminism's "second wave" really did believe that anything was possible and that "economic and social justice could be achieved, the family reorganised, and all hierarchies based on gender, race, or class erased" (Echols 1989, 19). As Barbara Smith recalls, "because I came out in the context of black liberation, women's liberation and- most significantly- the newly emerging black feminist movement that I was helping to build, I worked from the assumption that all of the 'isms' were connected" (1998, para 4). Whilst not a heterogenous entity, and despite not delivering on its ambition to end all forms of dominance, many feminists in the second wave began the prefigurative process of asking what such a world might look like, and how we might get there. In its desire to imagine otherwise, to hold out the possibility of a horizon of structural change within the "quagmire of the present" (Muñoz 2009, 1), I propose that there may be overlooked elements of second wave feminism, particularly regarding the diversity of engagements with the complex entanglement of sex and gender, that are worth revisiting today. At its best, second wave feminism was characterised not by its answers, but its asking. To write it off is to "miss some of the grappling of that era, and the way that the grappling itself offers useful lessons" (Enke 2018, 10).

By focussing on the second wave as a style, rather than set of political commitments or a temporally bound collection of arguments, I am consciously resisting clear boundaries between radical, liberal, socialist or cultural feminism. Indeed, I am more interested in reading for the overlaps; a critique of patriarchy and a belief that it could be dismantled, a critique of the family and its perpetuation of compulsory heterosexuality, and a critique of [cis, white] masculinity and its propensity to violence: a vision of liberation from sex/gender roles and an end to all forms of dominance. I read second wave feminism as a period characterised by "sweeping, radical, revolutionary thinking that marked major breaks with traditionalism and incremental, slow, steady change" (Fahs 2020, 5).[10] In focussing on the trans feminist epistemologies in this period, I am also interested in the way that trans feminism in particular crosscut conventional distinctions between different "branches" of feminism. As we will see, trans feminists in the second wave were socialist: calling for nothing less than human liberation and highlighting the role of capitalism in the perpetuation of sex/gender fictions.[11] Trans feminists in the second wave were liberal: aligning with the state as a means of securing legitimacy and vital protections. Trans feminists in the second wave were radical: calling for an end to patriarchy and sexism in all its forms: traditional sexism, heterosexism and cis-sexism. And trans feminists in the second wave were cultural feminists: celebrating and revaluing femininity in all bodies over and against long histories of misogynistic devaluation. Unsurprisingly, there was no one second wave trans feminism.

I run the risk of romanticising second wave feminism, and this is not my intention. In many segments of the movement, as theory moved from action to ideology, an increasingly divided and divisive politics took hold (Ryan 1992). By the end of the 1970s in both the UK and the US, the reactionary right-wing social, economic and political agendas of Thatcher and Reagan were establishing themselves and, in the process, many of the

---

[10] This quote is in reference to the genre of the feminist manifesto. An argument I don't pursue here, is that the manifesto condenses many of the features of second wave feminism that I am exploring here: urgent, insurgent and improvisational. As such, the manifesto is a genre that is (and has been) essential to the world-building character of both second wave feminism and trans feminism.

[11] An example of the socialist leaning of [some] second wave trans feminisms can be found in Sylvia Rivera and Marsha P. Johnson's S.T.A.R. manifesto which reads: "We want a revolutionary peoples' government, where transvestites, street people, women, homosexuals, Puerto Ricans, Indians, and all oppressed people are free, and not fucked over by this government who treat us like the scum of the earth and kills us off like flies, one by one, and throws us into jail to rot. This government who spends millions of dollars to go to the moon, and lets the poor Americans starve to death" (S.T.A.R 1970). Susan Stryker has highlighted how Shulamith Firestone also advances a socialist trans-positive second wave feminism, quoting Firestone's argument in the *Dialectic of Sex* that "just as the end goal of socialist revolution was not only the elimination of the economic class privilege but of the economic class distinction itself, so the end goal of feminist revolution must be, unlike that of the first feminist movement, not just the elimination of male privilege but of the sex distinction itself" (2008a, 108).

liberal feminist gains that had taken place in the last decade were undone.[12] At the beginning of these "backlash years" (Snitow 2015, 7) the equal rights amendment lost its momentum as Phyllis Schlafly's "pro-family values" politics mobilised conservative women to oppose it and the first Hyde Amendment was passed in 1976 by the House of Representatives to override the use of Medicaid funding for abortions (Echols 1989, 289). Against the backdrop of political losses, consciousness-raising groups became increasingly factious, and the many lesbian groups clung to an essentialist notion of "lesbian" as an identity uniquely under siege, embracing separatism and rejecting coalitional politics. As Asa Seresin and Sophie Lewis write, there are fascistic currents in "the euphoria of the womanhood-as-suffering worldview, in the wounded attachment undergirding same-sex cis separatism" (Lewis and Seresin 2022, 463)- and these endure in TERF discourses today. As with any political movement, second wave trans feminism is an ambivalent archive and the perspectives I consider here are not immune from exclusions, elisions and errors.

This book doesn't seek to counter the existing stories of second wave feminism's failures. It does affirm, however, that, for those who have been set up to fail, there can be much to be salvaged from the epistemology of resistance itself. For many, the fantasy of utopia remains the purview of the privileged, where escapism not survival is the dominant epistemology. Yet, as *José Esteban Muñoz* distinguishes, "concrete utopias are relational to historically situated struggles" (2009, 3) and the hope which animates them can be both affective and illuminating, enabling a cartography of possibilities to be built from the binds of the present. In this book then, I seek to animate the affective currency of second wave feminism, a feminism of resistance which cannot be reduced to its worst excesses and, alongside its anachronisms, contains hopes, desires and radical trans feminist longings that remain epistemically valuable today.

[12] Following Zillah Einstein, liberal feminism in the second wave can be "defined as support for the Equal Rights Amendment (ERA), abortion rights, and economic equity in the market" (1987, 237). Liberal feminism is closely aligned with white feminism, as it is based on a gendered private/ public divide that never accurately characterised black women's lives, which have always involved working "outside the home in disproportionate numbers to white women, whether in slave society or in the free labour market" (ibid., 239).

Trans Women and Men in the US Second Wave

Recent retrievals of trans women's involvement with US second wave feminism have tended to focus on what the participation of individual trans people in lesbian feminist spaces indicates about the histories of trans inclusion within the feminist movement (Heaney 2017; Enke 2018). The leading role played by Beth Elliot as Vice President of the San Francisco Chapter of lesbian feminist organisation Daughters of Bilitis has been offered as a reminder of the important participation of trans women in lesbian feminist groups (Enke 2018; Heaney 2017).[13] However, Elliot's experience at the West Coast Lesbian Conference in 1973, when her performance at the opening concert was protested (although quickly overturned by an audience vote in Elliot's favour), is regularly cited as exemplary of the long history of feminist transphobia.[14] Sandy Stone's employment at lesbian feminist record label, Olivia Records, has also split the historical record. On the one hand, she was an active and highly valued member of the feminist recording collective.[15] However, when "the news" [that Stone was trans] hit the feminist press in 1977, Stone's employment with Olivia prompted an open letter in the West Coast feminist newspaper *Sister* penned by twenty two feminist musicians, sound technicians, radio women, producers and managers who articulated a biologically essentialist feminism that refused to recognise Stone as a woman and saw her employment as taking a job away from [cis] women sound technicians.[16] To the

[13] As mentioned in footnote 6, in 1972, the collective voted to oust Elliot, which led to the entire staff of the chapter's journal *Sisters* resigning, and the Los Angeles collective issuing a statement making clear that Elliot was welcome in the LA Chapter. See The Tide Collective, "A Collective Editorial" in TSQ (2016) for a re-publication of the collective's pro-inclusion/ anti-inclusion arguments.

[14] This altercation was amplified the following day by Robin Morgan's keynote address where she referred to Elliot using male pronouns and played the "transsexual rapist" trope (Koblin 1973).

[15] Olivia Records had been started by a few disbanded members of The Furies—a radical separatist feminist group based in Washington D.C (Valk 2008, 154). For more on The Furies see Anne Valk Living a Feminist Lifestyle: The Intersection of Theory and Action in a Lesbian Feminist Collective (2002).

[16] The response by Olivia, educating the writers about what a "transsexual" person is, and highlighting that living "as a woman and a lesbian, [Stone] is now faced with the same kinds of oppression that other women and lesbians face. She must also cope with the ostracism that all of society imposes on a transsexual" demonstrates that transphobia, whilst gaining traction- particularly in the radical separatist parts of the movement- was not a foregone conclusion. In fact, Stone, who had been an active member of the lesbian community in Santa Cruz prior to joining Olivia Records in 1976, says that she didn't encounter many transphobic radical separatists until the publication of Raymond's book (Drucker 2018).

extent that second wave feminism's trans history has been explored then, much of the focus has been on the existence of trans individuals in the activist groups of the day.

This book argues that not only were trans people *included* in feminist spaces, a term which gives agency and power to the rest of the feminist movement, but that trans feminist epistemologies are an indispensable component of feminism's intellectual history. "Debates" over trans inclusion during US feminism's second wave are a depressingly familiar *drag*, to use Elizabeth Freeman's (2010) term for the pull of the past on the present. They also function to narrate the history of feminism from the vantage point of the ostensibly cisgender, white woman, reinstalling her as the central subject of feminism.[17] Yet, as historians have highlighted, in the mid-twentieth-century trans labourers shaped a great deal of knowledge production—the medical archive in particular (Meyerowitz 2004, Gill-Peterson 2018). The archive of second wave feminism is no exception.[18] If, as Emma Heaney writes, "to revisit the trans-feminist solidarities of the 1970s is to restore trans women's claims to feminism and women's autonomy to historical memory" (Heaney 2016, 140) my intention is to revisit trans feminist influences, and, in doing so, contest any idea that those who consider themselves cisgender have a monopoly on feminist thought.

Who gets considered as an intellectual, rather than an activist, is a political question (Hill Collins 2018) and trans feminists, like Black feminists,

---

[17] I use the term "ostensibly cisgender" following Shanna Carlson's description of "*ostensibly* 'non-transsexual' subjects" (Carlson 2013, 311, italics original) as a way of challenging the ontological basis of "cisgender" and also to recognise the potential fluidity of gender identity in all subjects. Whilst it is too clunky to refer throughout to "cisgender" subject positions as "ostensibly cisgender", when using the term "cisgender", I am using it as a placeholder for a subject position situated, either politically, epistemically, or subjectively as "non-trans". I do not mean by cisgender that it is possible to be born a gender and stay that way.

[18] This book builds on the significant number of re-readings of second wave feminism that have emerged in recent years. Lisa Downing's 2018 special issue of *Paragraph*, Queering the second wave: Anglophone and Francophone contexts, offers important reconsiderations of canonical second wave themes and thinkers. Articles explore Monique Wittig, Shulamith Firestone, Andera Dworkin, Marilyn Frye, Donna Haraway, Gloria Anzaldúa, and Cherríe Moraga as precursors to ideas that would become widely associated with queer theory. The women's liberation movement in both the UK and the US has been revisited, and charges of homogeneity- particularly white, middle-class homogeneity- complexified. For the US context see: Kimberley Springer (2005), Anne Valk (2008), Stephanie Gilmore (eds.) (2008), Angie Maxwell and Todd Shields (eds.) (2018) and SaraEllen Strongman (2016). For the UK context see: D-M Withers (2019), Natalie Thomlinson (2016). For reconsiderations of trans people's involvement with US second wave feminism see: Finn Enke (2018) and Emma Heaney (2016).

have been more often read as the latter. The influence that trans-led discourses had on the development of feminism is important, given that prevailing histories naturalise divisions between cisgender and transgender people in the history of feminism. Not only where there plenty of trans feminist epistemologies circulating throughout the US second wave, but, in important ways, trans feminism can be read as possessing a second wave feminist sensibility. In other words: these two categories, which are conventionally presumed to have little in common, in fact have theoretical and temporal overlaps.

Trans Feminist Epistemologies

There are two dimensions to what I am terming "trans feminist epistemologies". The first is an explanation of what I mean by epistemology in this case. If "feminist epistemology", as Linda Alcoff and Elizabeth Potter contend (1993, 1) "marks the uneasy alliance of feminism and philosophy, an alliance made uneasy by this contradictory pull between the concrete and the universal", I propose that a trans feminist epistemology foregrounds the bearing of trans experiences on universal issues.[19] Epistemology asks questions about who counts as a knower (Code 1981) and what gets considered as knowledge (Hill Collins 2000). A trans feminist epistemology departs from the understanding that trans people are knowledge producers, and that recognition of this is a matter of political and social justice. Trans feminism develops feminist contributions to the idea that knowledge is embedded to foreground the notion that knowledge is also *embodied*. However, the body itself is also made and mutable, both the source and site of subjectivity, and the location of often violent and violating cultural interpretations.

Foregrounding experiential and embodied knowledge underscores a key conviction of this book: that the self-authored subjectivities collected in second wave texts that circulated outside the academy are philosophically valuable. Like Blas Radi, I intend a trans epistemology "to level the

---

[19] For feminist epistemology see: bell hooks ([1984] 2015); Sandra Harding (1986); Lorraine Code (1981); Linda Alcoff and Elizabeth Potter (eds.) (1993); Patricia Hill Collins (2000). For trans feminist epistemology see Viviane Namaste (2008) and Tey Meadow (2016). The aspects of feminist epistemology I am interested in are the situatedness of knowledge and its critique of androcentrism (Alcoff and Potter 1993, 2). Building on this, I understand a transfeminist epistemology to involve a critique of the ciscentrism of knowledge construction.

epistemological playing field, opening a space at the philosophical banquet for those who have historically not been invited- or who have been on the menu" (2019, 45). A trans feminist epistemology is profoundly philosophical and political, challenging the fabric of received wisdom and exposing the relations of domination, exclusion, and extraction through which such knowledge has been generated.

Secondly, I will expand on what I mean by "trans feminism" and briefly state the key convictions that I understand a trans feminist perspective to advance.[20] First, drawing on Marquis Bey, I argue that trans feminism can be characterised by "an assault on the genre of the binary" (Bey 2022a, 53). I pursue the idea of an assault on the genre of the binary to involve a contestation of the power of the coercive sex/gender binary, its ontological foothold and mutually exclusive mystification. Thus, whilst someone might assume a binary identification, to do so wilfully rather than following an imperative, is to resist the genre of automatic subjective identification on the basis of the interpretation of various body parts within a binary sex/gender frame.[21] This also extends to critiquing the binary of cisgender/transgender, which has the potential to erase the gender variance among all people while dangerously extending the practical reach and power of multiple normativities (Enke 2013, 113). Instead, this book departs from Enke's contention that "transgender" "is about everyone in so far sit offers insight into how and why we *all* 'do' gender" (2012, 2). A second central tenet of trans feminism that I take forward here is the twofold priority of self-definition and bodily autonomy. As Emi Koyama writes, "each individual has the right to define her or his own identity and to expect society to respect it" and "we have the role right to make

---

[20] See Stryker and Bettcher (2016) for a discussion of the origins and development of "transfeminism" as a term. The authors write that "US activists Diana Courvant and Emi Koyama are generally credited with coining the term transfeminism itself circa 1992, in the context of their intersectional work on trans, intersex, disability, and survivorship of sexual violence" (2016, 11).

[21] I use sex/gender here when referring to the historically and (often) politically intertwined system of sex and gender and refer to "sex" and "gender" separately when highlighting their different ideological, subjective or political reach. I understand "sex" following Susan Stryker, to be a category which "is not one" and includes "chromosomal sex, anatomical sex, reproductive sex, morphological sex- that can, and do, form a variety of viable bodily aggregations that number far more than two" (2006, 9). Chromosomal sex is the only one of these which cannot change. I understand "gender" as a subjective and social category, historically associated with the attributes of "man" and "woman" in the English speaking Global North, but encompassing a wide and proliferating potential of non-binary categories.

decisions regarding our own bodies, and that no political, medical, or religious authority shall violate the integrity of our bodies against out will or impede our decisions regarding what we do with them" (2003, 245). Finally, as Julia Serano (2007) has elucidated, trans feminism advances a resistance to the cultural devaluation of the feminine. These three priorities are clearly interrelated and deceptively straightforward. What is at stake, however, as I will develop, is a radical rethinking of the subject and solidarities of feminism.

Finally, I have chosen to keep the words trans and feminism separate for the following reasons.[22] Although I understand there to be clear overlaps between trans epistemologies and feminist ones, I also recognise that these cannot be assumed in advance. "Trans" and "feminism" do come apart and, even though it is tempting to reject the notion that trans-exclusionary feminism is feminism at all, much of feminism's history is decidedly ambivalent. I understand reckoning with feminism's less ideal elements to be an important part of negotiating its more insurgent potential. "Trans" and "feminism", despite our better wishes, are not always aligned and to keep them separate is a reminder that we need to do political work to make feminism trans positive. "Trans", then, is an adjectival modifier for feminism that disrupts the assumption of cisness that I am arguing is a common dimension of feminist philosophies and historiographies. Moreover, feminism has a rich history of modifiers: socialist, radical, Black, Chicana, lesbian and postcolonial, to name just some. I see trans feminism's

---

[22] Alternative formulations of "trans feminism" include: "trans/feminism" (Stryker and Bettcher 2016), with the slash intended "to mark a break between the two halves of the neologistic portmanteau transfeminism" and to make space for a wider range of work that explores the many ways that transgender and feminist work can relate to one another" (ibid.,12); the most common "transfeminist" which- in Finn Enke's formulation- is a compound that "arises out of a desire to see both "trans" and "feminist" do more flexible work; we would like to see them not only opening each to the other but opening broadly in all directions, as though they are both potential prefixes and suffixes that may modify and be modified by participants whose names we may not even yet know" (2012, 3). For discussions of transfeminism in France see: Karine Espineira and Marie-Hélène/Sam Bourcier (2016). For Spain see Aitzole Araneta and Sandra Fernández Garrido (2016). For Brazil see Joseli Maria Silva and Macio Jose Ornat (2016) and Hailey Kaas (2016). For trans activism around abortion rights in Argentina, see Romero F. Fernández (2020). This is far from a comprehensive list, and it is also important to note that decolonial critiques of transgender (and by implication trans feminism) have noted the term's "colonial operation, spreading western ontologies and logics such as western medicine; the idea of the individual unchanging self; and the binary gender system" (cárdenas in Boellstorff et al. 2014, 434).

potential as working alongside, in dialogue with, and in coalition with, these equally longstanding currents of feminist thought.

Therefore, my use of both "trans" and "feminism" remains fairly descriptive. Although I am sympathetic to projects which engage the figurative, metaphorical and deconstructive potential of "trans", and "trans*" harnessing the fact it is "open-ended and resists premature foreclosure by attachment to any single suffix" (Stryker et al. 2008, 11), rather than engaging "trans" as a category of potentiality, I am concerned with "trans" as a relation to gender that is lived. This book therefore takes a fairly straightforward interpretation of what trans feminist epistemologies clarify: that it is not only gender that is non-dimorphic and mutable, but sex too. That "the meaning attached to bodies is not an inherent result of bodies themselves" (Skidmore 2017, 9) and therefore the category "woman" is multiple, unable to be delineated in advance, and "women" and "trans" are not discrete categories (Malatino 2015, 399). I agree that "trans" can be a methodology for thinking more broadly outside of the hegemony of western, masculinist, binaristic and bordered logics (although equally, it can reinscribe these),[23] however, this more flexible work is not my focus.[24] I am interested in the second wave feminist thinking that didn't start from a presumption of cisnormativity, and the philosophical contributions contained therein.

SECOND WAVE FEMINISM, TRANS FEMINISM AND THE EVIDENCE OF EXPERIENCE

One of the themes running throughout this book is that experience is valuable epistemology, and that to revisit the experientially derived knowledges contained within the print culture of the 1970s is to access a wealth of feminist theory. Within much Black feminism, the idea that experience and subjectivity are part of the knowledge creation process has been paramount, accompanied by the important contention that theorising has

---

[23] For the colonial politics of "transgender" see Yv E. Nay (2019) and Tom Boellstorff et al. (2014).

[24] Moreover, I am not convinced that "trans" is necessarily the best methodology for thinking through the specificities of all forms of violence. There is much longstanding feminist work that addresses the violence of the border (e.g. Mohanty 2003), of coloniality (e.g. McClintock 1995; Scott and Wynter 2000; Lugones 2007, 2010), and of the prison system (e.g. Davis 2003)—the distinctiveness of which would be flattened by an umbrella of "trans*" to index transnational *and* transborder *and* transformative justice.

happened, and continues to take place, outside the walls and restrictive language of the academy: in stories, riddles, proverbs and poetry (Christian 1988; Lorde 2017). Sara Ahmed writes about encountering the work of Black and Chicana feminists, including Audre Lorde, bell hooks and Gloria Anzaldúa: "here was writing in which an embodied experience of power becomes the basis for knowledge" (2017, 10). This insight, that to make the body speak is to access epistemology, and therefore not only marginalised subjectivities, but also marginalised embodiments, can bear on universality, is central to this project.[25]

The evidence of experience is another undertheorised dimension of second wave feminism, embedded throughout the print culture of the period. Using the particular to challenge the universal was one ambition of the well-known phrase "the personal is political". Second wave feminism contested the false objectivity of the white-patriarchal academy, through the centring of embodied and experiential knowledges. This gestures towards one of the methodological overlaps between much second wave feminism and trans feminism given that "epistemological concerns lie at the heart of transgender critique" and "transgender phenomena… point the way to a different understanding of how bodies mean, how representation works, and what counts as legitimate knowledge" (Stryker 2006, 8–9). Both second wave feminist and trans feminist epistemologies have constructed an embodied materialism out of experience, which contests ontological operations of power and begins with the idea that subjectivity can be the starting place for an assault on structures.

Whilst some white second wave feminists appealed to what I will call an "essentialism of experience"—the idea that there was one thing that all women shared that could form the foundation of feminist politics and theorising—this was far from the case in Black feminist contributions where constitutive exclusion from white, patriarchal meanings of womanhood and femininity were the foundation for resistance.[26] Rather than

---

[25] For a concise overview of the relationship between epistemology and marginality see Mary Evans and Sumi Madhok "Epistemology and Marginality" (2014).

[26] This is evident throughout black feminist print culture (e.g. *Triple Jeopardy* 1971–1975), academically consulted texts such as Toni Cade Bambara (eds.) *The Black Woman* ([1970] 2005), and in widely anthologised publications such as the Combahee River Collective's statement which states: "Although we are feminists and lesbians, we feel solidarity with progressive black men and do not advocate the fractionalisation that white women who are separatists demand. Our situation as black people necessitates that we have solidarity around the fact of race, which white women of course do not need to have with white men, unless it is their negative solidarity as racial oppressors. We struggle together with black men against racism, while we also struggle with black men about sexism" (2014, 274).

using experience to create a politics around sameness, "what was being asked for was the ability to work with and mobilise around difference" (Green in Green and Bey 2017, 450). Black feminism extended the focus on the personal as political to develop the insights that have become crucial to transgender studies. Namely, that the personal is theoretical (Ahmed 2017), that pre-existing delimitations of thought cannot do justice to the complexity of experience and, crucially, that the self is a valid entry point to knowledge: one can be bruised by a structure, undone by a name. As Audre Lorde writes, "The white fathers told us, I think therefore I am; and the black mothers in each of us—the poet—whispers in our dreams: I feel therefore I can be free" (2017, 10). The trans feminist discussions I consider here take forward this idea that sensing and feeling are the point of access to our categories, rather than our accomplishment of their hegemonic varieties. Both the contributions in the *Journal of Male Feminism* and Andrea Dworkin's sense of authority which she derived from her own experiences are, far from an attempt to codify what exists, an attempt at using embodied and felt experience to expose and intervene in the world as it is. One of the biggest contributions of second wave feminism was a phenomenological interpretation of the category of "woman"—what it *feels* like to be a woman or to inhabit a sexed and gendered body—and lived experience provides a vital entry point onto such a world.

Taking up these this focus on embodied and experiential knowledge motivates my exploration of community produced print culture from the second wave, which is reader generated, and a significant proportion is made up of life experiences. The self-identified "transvestites", "transsexuals" and "cross-dressers" (to list just some of the identities that contributors assumed) writing in the journals and newsletters of underground membership organisations, often encountered other gender variant people on the pages of such publications for the first time. A concern with experience also influences my choice of Andrea Dworkin as an example indication of trans feminist epistemologies in the "canon" of second wave feminism, as it was her—at the time pioneering—appeals to her own experiences of sexual violence that became the source of her epistemic discrediting.[27]

---

[27] See Tanya Serisier (2015) "How Can a Woman Who Has Been Raped Be Believed?" for more on the relationship between Dworkin's experiences of sexual violence and her epistemic credibility.

Enabling marginalised groups to speak for themselves is an important means of accessing alternative epistemologies; one which entails a challenge to institutionalised knowledges as the only, or best, authorities.[28] This is separate to an argument according to which marginalised groups are *only* allowed to speak from experience, an endemic feature of the contemporary news, media and publishing landscapes which repeatedly consign trans individuals to only "tell their own stories", and then employ "experts" to interpret and theorise these. Chela Sandoval cautions in *Methodology of the Oppressed*, that there is a distinction between minoritised knowledge being "translated as a demographic constituency only" or as a "theoretical and methodological approach in its own right" (2000, 171). This is certainly applicable to trans epistemologies. Whilst the genre of autobiography enabled self-acknowledged subjectivity to provide the basis for the formation of linguistic and social communities (Whittle 2006, 199), when mainstreamed it has been critiqued for its essentialising, reductive, and frequently sensationalised scripts directed at cisgender audiences (Chu 2017; Pellegrini 2020). Moreover, as Viviane Namaste notes, "when we restrict ourselves to the *identity* of sex change, we simultaneously limit our understanding of social change" (Namaste 2011, 23). In turning to the autobiographical in trans community print culture, I take the subjectivities articulated to have both particular and universal significance. The contributions to the *Journal of Male Feminism* outline the personal experiences of individuals within a small, underground social group. Yet, at the same time, they also speak to the everyday violence of a coercive sex/gender system for all those whose interiority cannot be captured by restrictive categorisations.

Susan Stryker writes that "one important task of transgender studies is to articulate and disseminate new epistemological frameworks, and new representational practices, within which variations in the sex/gender relationship can be understood as morally neutral and representationally true" (2006, 10). Enabling life stories to speak to our present moment without requiring translation or interpretation is one means of establishing new epistemes and destabilising prevailing ones. As such, I reproduce the

---

[28] This also runs against Foucault's discursive method which, as Henry Rubin's comments on the value of phenomenology for trans studies note, can "undermine the authority of individual speaking subjects and thereby plays into patterns of domination that work against the possibility of marginalized subjects using their own knowledge of their own subject positions to speak counterdiscursively" (1998, 264).

language and monikers that contributors carefully chose when constructing and sharing their own identities. Whilst "the ascendency of transgender and then trans has periodised trans identity, life and appearance so that the transsexual and the transvestite are seen as relics of the past" (Gill-Peterson 2021, 414), such a linear approach to identity formation overlooks the often entangled and enduring character of these subject positions. Moreover, from the vantage point of a second wave trans feminism, given that the popularisation of "transgender" as an identity category took place in the 1990s, granting epistemic value to the subcultural adoptions of, occasionally short-lived, but subjectively held, identities such as "crossdresser", "femmiphile", "male woman", "transvestite" and "transsexual", resists the "progress-oriented notion of transness" from "sad transvestite pasts" to "open-ended trans presents and futures" which "renders these identities and embodiments backward or anachronistic" (Harsin Drager and Platero 2021, 418).

At the same time, "gender only arrives in any language as a result of a difficult translation" (Butler 2021, 18) and avoiding translation completely is impossible and irresponsible. For some readers, terms like "transvestite" and "transsexual" may be jarring at best, pathologising at worst. Moreover, for many of the trans feminists I consider here, "transgender" and "trans", as they subsequently circulated within the English-speaking Global North did become preferred identifications. As such, whilst it is appropriate to attend to the self-authored subjectivities on the page and to allow autobiography and self-narratives to contribute to a pedagogical tapestry of lived experiences, these are historically specific and contextually situated. Therefore, when describing people's subject positions in my own words, I use the umbrella language more widely circulated in English-speaking trans communities today: of "trans woman", "transfeminine", "trans man", "transmasculine" and "trans" to avoid relying on or reproducing diagnostic categories, and to minimise distinctions between different forms of transness for the purpose of making broader claims about how people who were not cis contributed to feminism in the second wave.

At times, there is an incommensurability of language across historical periods. For example, the idea that "transgender" was a 1990s invention, and a necessarily more politically expedient category to those I engage here, is contested by a 1976 issue of the newsletter *Hose and Heel*, the forerunner to *Journal of Male Feminism*, where "transgender" is understood as more reliant on binary gender than it is today: "Several years ago 'transgenderism' may have been selected as the best alternative designation. Today however, the idea of two genders increasingly appears dated as the success of Women's Liberation Movement carries us toward a unigender ("the unisex movement" is really a "unigender movement"), or gender free society" (Hose and Heel 1976, 2). For a few years, concepts such as "unigender" were popular within the 1970s cross-dressing community and indexed an investment in an androgynous future. By contrast, "trans" was a prefix that some of my interlocutors expressly resisted on account of its medicalised connotations and "transgender" was understood to be invested in the continuation of binary gender possibilities. I use "trans" here as a shorthand for transgender understood, following Stryker, as a referent for "people who move away from the gender they were assigned at birth, people who crossed over (*trans-*) the boundaries constructed by their culture to define and contain that gender" (2008a, 1, italics in original). Importantly, "trans" reflects the open-endedness of many of the gender identities being articulated in the publications I discuss, which were often in the process of becoming.

Finally, the value of trans-led experiential knowledges for feminism is an important aspect of the broader argument of this book, which is the two-fold insistence that feminism needs trans epistemologies and that trans epistemologies have already been central and essential to the development of feminism. Thus, feminism in its academic instantiations: gender studies, women's studies and gender and sexuality studies, needs to recognise its already heavy indebtedness to the contributions of trans knowledges. This book proposes that by exploring the trans perspectives that were self-avowedly feminist, and the feminist perspectives that were already trans, re-reading second wave feminism for its trans feminist insights offers new potential alliances for feminism and trans studies in the future. Such a project also contests the marginalising of "transgender" as a "topic" for feminist enquiry, rather than an epistemological foundation, and reconsiders not just trans feminist solidarities but trans feminist influences that shaped the development of feminist theory from the start.[29]

Print Culture in the Second Wave

Revisiting second wave feminism as epistemically valuable in the present already necessitates a theory of history; one which problematises linear progress narratives (Wiegman 2012) academic feminism's "presentism"

---

[29] For more on the relationship between Women's Studies, feminism and trans perspectives see Gayle Salamon "Transfeminism and the Future of Gender" in *Assuming a Body* (2010).

(Newman 2002) and modernist logics of advancement. Foregrounding second wave trans feminists as an entry point into a period that has become so heavily overdetermined facilitates a softening of rigidified temporal and disciplinary boundaries. Expanding the canon of second wave feminism to include grassroots, community produced print culture is just one of the necessary ways of incorporating trans feminist knowledges that existed outside of the rarefied walls of the academy and an essential means by which its hegemonic histories can be decentralised.

In addition to being a somewhat more diverse archive, I also propose that print culture is at least as good, if not a better, source of second wave feminist knowledge production than academically authored books. Given that universities and traditional publishing houses were likely to reject books by women, [openly] trans women were excluded from the majority of mainstream knowledge production processes, and that book writing was a resource and time intensive process, only a narrow group of women could find their way into monographs or journals. Books were also far too slow and too convoluted for the ambitious dissemination of radical ideas that second wave groups sought. The changes that many second wave feminists envisioned required mass mobilisation, quickly! Therefore, much second wave theory circulated in community produced journals and news-letters, not in reputed academic publications, making these a particularly valuable source of theory that was developing in real time and alongside feminist strategy.

Alma Garcia has highlighted how the Chicana feminist discourse which developed throughout the US at this time can be "traced in the speeches, essays, letters, and articles published in Chicano and Chicana newspapers, journals, newsletters, and other printed materials" (1989, 217). As femi-nist consciousness-raising groups were forming at speed across the coun-try, many crafted collective identities and developed distinct political philosophies which were co-created and disseminated through the group's print publication.[30] On one count, between March 1968 and August 1973 over 560 new publications produced by feminists appeared in the United

[30] These include: The Combahee River Collective, Boston's Cell 16, bread & roses, the Chicago Women's Liberation Union, DC Women's Liberation, The Feminists, The Furies, New York Radical Women, Redstockings, Seattle Radical Women, and Women's International Terrorist Conspiracy from Hell (witch), as well as the network of chapters of the National Organization for Women (NOW). For more on second wave feminism's different consciousness-raising groups see Echols (1989) and Norman (2007).

States (Mather quoted in Flannery 2005, 24).[31] From the Third World Women's Alliance's *Triple Jeopardy* (1971–1975) to *Black Belt Woman: The Magazine of Women in the Martial Arts and Self Defence* (1975–1976), each collective had its own magazine, newsletter or newspaper. The sheer ubiquity of print culture produced during feminism's second wave makes it "a dynamic and important source of feminist knowledge production" (Enszer and Beins 2018, 22).

Despite varying levels of editorial (or editorial collective) discretion, there is no ideological consensus within publications, let alone across publications and therefore print culture traces the emergence of ideas as they were forming for feminists with different social contexts and political priorities. Newsletters, manifestoes, zines, periodicals and independently produced journals were an essential source of idea generation and transmission for different feminist groups, each crafting distinct ideologies, co-developing political priorities and offering updated interpretations of "women's liberation".[32] Moreover, within trans community publications, these texts (some of which were explicitly feminist, many of which were not) provided the space where gender variant people could craft their own collective identities and negotiate, and begin to articulate, diverse gendered subjectivities and embodiments.

By arguing for the value of print culture as an expression of second wave feminist theory and politics, *Trans feminist epistemologies* provides the building blocks for a deep dive into the sex/gender knowledges that were being produced throughout the 1970s that contest a cisnormative

---

[31] See also Myra Marx Ferree and Beth B Hess *Controversy and Coalition: The New Feminist Movement across Three Decades of Change* (2000, 78) for a discussion of the value of print for individual consciousness-raising groups.

[32] For more on the affect and optimism of the early women's movement, Alix Kates Shulman has a lovely description from a conference on the occasion of the 10th anniversary of Kate Millett's Sexual Politics. She explains: "I'd like to talk about the characteristic of that moment that seems to me in the greatest danger of being forgotten, the part of lived history that too often escapes written history- namely, the emotional part; the passion, excitement, and high energy of those days which consciousness-raising, the chief movement tool of organizing and discovery, so effectively fostered and tapped; the anger, love, sense of upheaval, community, and exhilaration that exploded into a powerful movement" (in Stimpson et al. 1991, 32–33).

frame.[33] I echo Rachel Corbman's desire to reconsider the "informal networks of feminist researchers who worked inside and outside of universities" who are "central to the development of feminism as a field of study" (2015, 52). Part of this book's aspiration is therefore to open the doors to a recovery project: what gets lost when we take second wave feminism's contribution to knowledge production as identical with the academically authored texts that a newly institutionalised women's studies was gradually beginning to produce?

Because my intervention takes as one of its targets field-formation and disciplinary origin stories, I have focussed on the contributions taking place in the US. This might seem like a strange move for an academic located in the UK—especially given that many of the events that I discuss here had parallels in the UK context too. Sex wars also took place in UK, trans community and feminist print culture was also thriving in the UK during the 1970s, and radical feminism in the UK contained trans feminist epistemologies. My decision to focus on the US is because I am interested in how trans individuals were shaping the development of academic

---

[33] This is distinct from the anti-normative impulse in queer theory, which positions itself against the structure of the norm (see Wiegman and Wilson 2015). The formulation of trans feminism I take forward here holds that a critique of or challenge to cisnormativity can go hand-in-hand with the stabilisation or pursuit of other norms; heteronormativity, homonormativity, chrononormativity…. To resist cisnormativity is to resist the binarisation of sex and gender and to contend that all gendered identification's must be self-determined. Beyond this, a challenge to the "cis" norm has no necessary bearing on relations to other norms, especially when being undertaken from within whiteness. Whilst, as Roderick A. Ferguson notes, black people in America may have been "heterosexual but never heteronormative" (2004, 87), as Chap. 3 develops, many white, middle-class, heterosexual, transfeminine individuals in the 1970s- especially those who had and wanted to maintain well paid jobs and families, actively pursued heteronormativity. Moreover, even whilst blackness and transness have been conceptualised together as fugitive phenomena (e.g. C. Riley Snorton 2017; Marquis Bey 2022a), the *pursuit* of heteronormativity can be undertaken by anyone regardless of race. Therefore, there is no direct or presumed relationship between "trans" and "queer". This is in keeping with the trans identities I explore in this book and is consistent with the circulation of "transgender" in 1970s. At this time, "transgenderist" and "transgenderal" named "a conceptual middle ground between transvestism (merely changing one's clothing) and transsexualism (changing one's sex)" (Stryker 2008b, 146) and was sometimes asserted within a liberal, identity based logic of inclusion, where gender fluidity (unlike homosexuality or transsexuality) was presented as normal and non-pathological.

feminism during the second wave, and the UK was much slower to institutionalise identity knowledges than the US.[34]

METHODOLOGY AND ORGANISATION

This is an unruly book in a number of ways. It doesn't stake its position within any one philosophical tradition, and it seeks to contribute to contemporary philosophical discussions via those who wrote from outside the rarefied world of institutionalised academic knowledge production. It draws on seemingly divergent critical approaches; ideology critique, postmodernism and affect theory, and it takes as its objects "sex" and "gender" without explicitly staking out a position on how these two are related. Following Amia Srinivasan (2022, xi–xii), I understand sex to be an act (sexuality) and an assignment. Moreover, as an assignment there is no final understanding of what "sex" signifies. Indeed, as Chap. 5 explores, "sex" is eternally messy. "What biological 'facts' determine sex have been the subject of much debate: chromosomes, hormones, gonads (ovaries/testes), internal reproductive structures and genitalia have variously been seen as the basis for defining a person's sex" (Richardson and Robinson 2008, 12) and adjudicating on this matter is not my intention.[35] To the contrary, I receive both "sex" and "gender" to be political and contestable categories and one of the insights of bringing trans perspectives to bear on

[34] Whilst Women's Studies degrees and departments were being incorporated into university's in the US throughout the 1970s, it took until 1980 for the first degree in Women's Studies to be offered in the UK. (See Kelly Coate (2000) for a discussion of the development of Women's Studies in the UK). Moreover it still remains the case that whilst Gender Studies, and identity knowledges such as Critical Race Studies, Transgender Studies have been widely institutionalised across North America and Canada, the UK has not witnessed the same formalisation of these disciplines. There are only a handful of Gender Studies departments, and it remains taught at postgraduate level- with no BA degrees in women's or gender studies available. Critical Race and Transgender Studies tend to get taught as modules, or even "weeks" in social science and humanities MA courses, receiving very little independent institutional recognition or funding. This is despite, of course, the sensationalised political and media narratives which position Critical Race Theory as one of the many threats to national stability and identity in a highly racialised importation of Donald Trump's "culture wars".

[35] See Catherine Duxbury "Of Monkeys, Men and Menstruation: Gendered Dualisms and the Absent Referent in Mid-Twentieth Century British Menstrual Science" (2019) for a discussion of the gendered construction of sex, and its relationship to the mid-century treatment of both women and non-human animals as Other. This article is particularly insightful for its detailing the history of how hormones became classified as gendered.

second wave feminist ones, is a complication of the idea that we can ever tell the story of gender without exploring its complex enmeshment with the category of sex.

I see the contributions of the book as somewhat open. Transness is "a project of undoing (gender, disciplines, selves) a project that… never tries to build a house" (Awkward-Rich 2017, 853) and likewise, whilst I see to undo dominant associations of second wave feminism with trans-exclusionary feminism, it is not altogether clear what will emerge in its place. Moreover, just as "transgender" unsettles dominant categories through the proliferation of new ones, the trans feminist epistemologies I consider do not have to agree to do important philosophical work. What I think is relevant however, and somewhat consistent among the perspectives I consider, is the theoretical ease with which the ontological absoluteness of sex and gender binaries were challenged in the second wave. An ease which in turn offers utopian possibility. Finally, I wish to re-create what I see as the "spirit" of the second wave; improvisational, coalitional and world-building. Rather than stake myself to one discipline or one "proper" mode of inquiry, the approach here mirrors the collaging style of second wave feminist and trans community print publications. Selecting, repurposing, and resignifying already existing ideas in the name of a whole new mode of social relationally and an end to structural oppressions.

This book, in that spirit of second wave feminism then, is not intended to have found the answer to questions (what *is* sex, what *is* gender). Neither does it seek to offer a comprehensive or definitive account of the trans feminist perspectives circulating in and amongst second wave feminism's knowledge production. To the contrary, whilst I want to make a case for print culture as part of an expanded canon of second wave feminist theory, the voices that made their way into the trans community publications are still those of largely white, middle-class activists and individuals. These are the groups for whom the dialogical character and relative formality of print made it an appropriate site of politics and knowledge sharing. By contrast, for poor or racialised trans people, many of whom worked as sex workers—shelter, safety and survival were far more of a priority than textual community and exchange. Outside of print, trans people—particularly working-class, Latinx and Black trans people were using direct action and protest in their confrontations with second wave feminist transphobia. A well-documented example is Sylvia Rivera's speech at the 1973

Christopher Street Liberation Day Parade. In protecting the women that
women's liberation groups were ostracising, fighting for bodily autonomy,
and advocating for gendered self-determination, Rivera also did the work
of second wave trans feminism. However, her intellectual contributions
are more ephemeral and the S.T.A.R. manifesto (1970) is one of the few
archived examples of street queen's organising.[36]

Susan Stryker and Paisley Currah write that "the 'transgender archive'
as it now exists, imperfect as it is, powerfully attests to the persistent, long-
term presence of transgender people within society. Some kinds of trans
people at least" (Stryker and Currah 2015, 542) and it is the presence of
self-identified feminists during the second wave, who would now fall
under the umbrella term "trans", that I am interested in here. Whilst
much of the archival turn, particularly in trans studies, has sought to estab-
lish a counter archive or a subversive archive, resisting regulatory power
and constitutive exclusions, my intention is more modest: I share Victoria
Hesford's ambition: "to open up the complexity of the movement's emergence as an event of second wave feminism and to lay bare some of the
processes of elision, reduction and displacement through which we have
come to know of that event and those feminists" (Hesford 2013, 24).
However, in partaking in a specific recovery project, this book participates
in the "residual silencing of others" (Rawson 2014, 25) that archival practices have been critiqued for—and, in particular, the elision here of transmasculine second wave feminists and trans feminists of colour is notable.
Bearing this in mind, I proceed with the hope that if we can begin to pay

[36] Rivera took to the stage to protest lesbian feminist Jean O'Leary's phobic representation
of trans women and drag queens as part and parcel of the "exploitation of women by men for
entertainment and profit". Rivera, one of the founders of Street Transvestite Action
Revolutionaries (S.T.A.R), denounced the women's movement for failing to protect its most
marginalised, trans members: "Have you ever been beaten up and raped and jailed? Now
think about it. They've been beaten up and raped after they've had to spend much of their
money in jail to get their hormones, and try to get their sex changes. The women have tried
to fight for their sex changes or to become women, on the women's liberation. And they
write "S.T.A.R.", not to the women's groups, they do not write women, they do not write
men, they write "S.T.A.R." because we're trying to do some- thing for them. (Rivera [1973]
2017)". Rivera expresses her anger at how, despite claiming rape as one of their key priorities,
the women's movement had offered nothing to trans women, particularly those in poverty
and making a living through sex work, who have been raped and forced to endure the most
intolerable conditions. In forcing feminists to confront the narrowness of their understandings of who deserved protection under the sign "woman", Riviera's speech mirrors the trans
feminism that was taking place in print.

attention to what is already in the archive and refuse to let received and firmly established wisdoms constrict our ability to see, then a host of possibilities for re-narrating not only second wave feminism, but the history of feminism more broadly, may be possible.

My choice of Dworkin, a queer, Jewish, cisgender writer as an example of trans feminist epistemologies in more well-known second wave feminist texts further clarifies that this is not a representative archive. The picture of patriarchy that she presents is ultimately one of white, American patriarchy, and her analysis of gendered dynamics often presume an unmarked whiteness.[37] However, it is her reputation as *quintessentially* second wave, as well as the fact that her arguments about violence against women are inseparable from her arguments about the violence of cisnormativity, that makes her a valuable theorist to reconsider in this book. That Dworkin is taken to be emblematic of second wave feminism makes her an important figure to (re)consider, as her trans positive arguments demonstrate that trans feminist epistemologies were not exceptional within second wave feminist arguments. Moreover, her critiques of male violence are regularly weaponised within trans-exclusionary feminist circles, which overlook the

---

[37] Dworkin was an anti-racist feminist and, as with many feminists of her generation, her first experiences of activism were opposing the Vietnam war. Her ultimate vision was nothing sort of an end of every form of violence, inequality and oppression. She is quickly let down by the white middle-class privileges endemic within the mainstream women's liberation movement, criticising that "most of the women involved in articulating the oppression of women were white and middle class... Because of our participation in the middle-class lifestyle we were the oppressors of other people, our poor white sisters, our Black sisters, our Chicana sisters" (1974, 21). She reminds them that "One cannot be free, never, not ever, in an unfree world, and in the course of redefining family, church, power relations, all the institutions which inhabit and order our lives, there is no way to hold onto privilege and comfort. To attempt to do so is criminal and intolerable" (1974, 22–3). She also argues that "the fate of every individual woman—no matter what her politics, character, values, qualities—is tied to the fate of all women whether she likes it or not" (1983, 220)—directly indicting liberal feminism. However, whilst she acknowledges what she calls "the nexus of sex and race" (1989, 157), her analysis as a whole does not take seriously the constant imbrication of sex and gender with race and class. For example, Dworkin writes that: "the feminist aim is to end male domination—to obliterate it from the face of this earth. We also want to end those forms of social injustice which derive from the patriarchal model of male dominance-that is, imperialism, colonialism, racism, war, poverty, violence in every form" (1981, 61) demonstrating that although she understood that feminism needs to take seriously all forms of oppression, she also reifies gender as the privileged axis of oppression, reflecting a white feminist standpoint which views gender oppression as universal and invisibilises race and class in order to make gender visible (Mohanty 2003).

fact that Dworkin regards violence against cisgender women to be a subset of "gender violence" understood more capaciously to include the violence of *all* coercive gender categorisations. Demonstrating that Dworkin sees feminism as equally a fight for women's bodily autonomy, and more fluid, less restrictive ways of inhabiting gender and sexuality for everyone, contests discourses which position cisgender women's protection and trans people's protection as a necessary battleground.

My argument proceeds as follows. Chapter 2 picks up where much of the existing literature has left off, looking at the participation of trans women in the feminist consciousness-raising groups being formed across the United States during the 1970s. It highlights the exchanges between the trans and ostensibly cisgender feminists that were taking place in the pages of print, demonstrating that trans women were not only present in the movement, but pushing the wider movement to expand their understanding of "womanhood" to include the lives of trans, intersex and queer people. On the basis of the discussions taking place in the early 1970s, it argues that "women's liberation" is better historicised as a coalitional politics where "woman" was a collective identity to be fought for, not an ontological foundation to be protected. This move decentres cisness in the history of the movement and foreground the contributions of trans feminists and feminists of colour for whom the unity of "woman" was never an available fantasy.

Chapter 3 then explores what exactly gets lost when we propose that trans feminism arrived after second wave feminism? What subject positions and philosophical contributions are overlooked? It explores the *Journal of Male Feminism*, the communications method for an organisation of self-identified cross-dressers on the transfeminine spectrum, as just one example of the kind of embodied, experiential knowledge generation taking place during this period that remains worthy of consultation today. I have chosen this journal on the basis of the directness of its alignment with the women's liberation movement discourses and goals. Contributors identify as "male feminists", using male to signify assigned male at birth, and "feminists" to index feminine identification on an either part-time or more full-time basis. However, the appeal to feminism extends beyond simply a neologism for femininity. The journal demonstrates key second wave feminist aspirations, resembles the style of much second wave feminist print, yet also can be read as partly strategic in its appeal to the respectability of the liberal women's liberation movement when making claims for citizenship.

I propose that in addition to containing valuable trans feminist epistemologies, and re-signifying key second wave feminist concepts such as "sexism" and "liberation" in the process, a discourse of "femonormativity" can be observed where the respectability of the liberal, white feminist movement is appealed to as a means of securing group-based protections.

A very different archive containing trans feminist epistemologies is Chap. 4's deep dive into the work of Andrea Dworkin. Dworkin is a divisive figure, who until recently was consigned to the dustbin of embarrassing, man-hating radical feminism. However, she has been revived in recent years both as an example of radical feminism's trans inclusive history and as a weapon in the arsenal of trans-exclusionary radical feminists. This chapter argues that her arguments clearly evidence important dimensions of a trans feminist epistemology: she rejects biological determinism, contests the idea that either sex or gender are binary, argues for free gender affirmative healthcare as a community function and the anti-pornography ordinances that she wrote with friend and colleague, the legal scholar Catherine MacKinnon, designate "transsexuals" as a specific category deserving legislative protection. I do not intend revisiting Dworkin's corpus to be a straightforward rescue project. I am sensitive to the fact that her involvement in the feminist sex wars and attacks on sex-positive feminists were highly damaging and whilst many of her arguments about misogyny and woman hating as the causes of sexual violence (which are inseparable from her arguments about the social construction of sex and gender) I believe have stood the test of time, her contention that representation *causes* reality and that attacking all representations of sexualised inequality was necessary, have not. Dworkin is not an easily assimilable figure then, and I engage her here without trying to clean her up first.[38] What I take forward from her work, however, is an understanding of how the violence of compulsory heterosexuality and the violence of compulsory gender are all part of the same system. This is the masculinist (she largely overlooked that, as María Lugones (2007) has higlighted, the hierachical gender binary is distinctly western and colonial) culture of male-female discreteness. This means that ending violence against women entails ending a commitment to male and female as biologically based categories.

---

[38] I borrow the idea of wanting to "clean-up" an ambivalent feminist figure from Clare Hemmings' discussion of Emma Goldman's ambivalent archive (2018, 6).

The book ends by looking at the role of trans individuals in shaping the intellectual foundations of second wave feminism. Asking how it is that we have come to know in advance that second wave feminism was "cis", this chapter highlights the vital contributions that a network of influential trans individuals had in shaping the scientific developments that would provide the conceptual architecture for second wave feminism. Louise Lawrence, Virginia Prince, and Reed Erickson are just three of the influential individuals without whom the sexologists that second wave feminists sourced their concept of "gender" from, would not have been able to get their research off the ground.

Reproducing received wisdoms about feminism's recent past enables established narratives to take the place of close readings and despite being an era which witnessed widescale transformations in relations of gender, race, sexuality, and nation, much of the feminist output from the period has been side-lined, "consigned to the 'dustbin of history' and frequently dismissed without even being read" (Browne 2014, 10). The "canon" of feminist theory is constantly up for renewal and very few reading lists grant equal weight to texts written in the 1970s, as they do those in the 1990s and 2000s (Hemmings 2011). As the old, misogynistic saying goes, women age badly. Resisting disciplinary orthodoxies and the citation conventions that scaffold them, *Trans feminist epistemologies* takes up the adage that women age badly as a provocation to expand the canon of usable second wave feminism and to consider those voices who were never included in annuls of feminist theory in the first place. Avowing humility with respect to our engagements with the past reminds us both that contemporary discussions have historical precedents and that disciplinary distinctions are as historical and constructed as the objects they explore.

The "second wave" lingers as an object lesson in what *not* to do, rarely of theoretical value in itself (Wiegman 2012). As such, this book is an argument for reconsidering the temporality of feminist citation. It is an argument for endurance within feminist philosophy, for granting overlooked archives a staying power and a continued capacity to speak to and inspire resistance. If my intervention has been successful, it will no longer be possible to tell the history of second wave feminism without telling the history of the trans women, trans men and gender variant individuals who shaped the meaning of women's liberation and made feminism's theoretical developments possible.

BIBLIOGRAPHY

Adair, Cassius, et al. 2020. Before Trans Studies. *TSQ: Transgender Studies Quarterly* 7 (3): 306–320.

Ahmed, Sara. 2016. An Affinity of Hammers. *TSQ: Transgender Studies Quarterly* 1 (1–2): 22–34.

———. 2017. *Living a Feminist Life*. Durham: Duke University Press.

Alcoff, Linda Martín, and Elizabeth Potter. 1993. *Feminist Epistemologies*. New York: Routledge.

Araneta, Aitzole, and Sandra Fernández Garrido. 2016. Transfeminist Genealogies in Spain. *TSQ: Transgender Studies Quarterly* 3 (1–2): 35–39.

Awkward-Rich, Cameron. 2017. Trans, Feminism: Or, Reading Like a Depressed Transsexual. *Signs: Journal of Women in Culture and Society* 42 (4): 819–841.

Bambara, T.C., ed. 2005. *The Black Woman : An Anthology*. New York: Washington Square Press.

Bassia, Serena, and Greta LaFleur. 2022. Introduction: TERFs, Gender-Critical Movements, and Postfascist Feminisms. *TSQ: Transgender Studies Quarterly* 9 (3): 311–333.

Berger Gluck, Sherna. 1998. Whose Feminism, Whose History. In *Community Activism and Feminist Politics: Organizing across Race, Class, and Gender*, ed. Nancy Naples, 31–56. New York; London: Routledge.

Bettcher, Talia M. 2016. A Conversation with Jeanne Córdova. *TSQ: Transgender Studies Quarterly* 3 (1–2): 285–293.

Bey, Marquis. 2022a. *Black Trans Feminism*. Durham: Duke University Press.

———. 2022b. *Cistem Failure: Essays on Blackness and Cisgender*. Durham: Duke University Press.

Bindel, Julie. 2021. *Feminism for Women the Real Route to Liberation*. London: Constable.

Boellstorff, Tom, et al. 2014. Decolonizing Transgender: A Roundtable Discussion. *TSQ: Transgender Studies Quarterly* 1 (3): 419–439.

Bornstein, Kate. 1994. *Gender Outlaw: On Men, Women, and the Rest of Us*. New York: Routledge.

———. 2012. *A Queer and Pleasant Danger: A Memoir*. Boston: Beacon Press.

Browne, Victoria. 2014. The Persistence of Patriarchy. *Radical Philosophy* 188. https://www.radicalphilosophy.com/article/the-persistence-of-patriarchy.

Butler, Judith. 2021. Gender in Translation: Beyond Monolingualism. Chapter. In *Why Gender?* ed. Jude Browne, 15–37. Cambridge: Cambridge University Press.

Bychowski, M.W., et al. 2018. Transhistoricities: A Roundtable Discussion. *TSQ: Transgender Studies Quarterly* 5 (4): 658–685.

Carlson, Shanna. 2013. Transgender Subjectivity and the Logic of Sexual Difference. In *The Transgender Studies Reader 2*, ed. Susan Stryker and Aren Z. Aizura, 302–315. New York: Routledge.

Chakraborty, Mridula Nath. 2007. Wa(i)ving It All Away: Producing Subject and Knowledge in Feminisms of Colours. In *Third Wave Feminism: A Critical Exploration*, expanded second edition, ed. Stacey Gillis et al.: 101–114. Basingstoke: Palgrave Macmillan.

Christian, Barbara. 1988. The Race for Theory. *Feminist Studies* 14 (1): 67–79.

Chu, Andrea Long. 2017. The Wrong Wrong Body. *TSQ : Transgender Studies Quarterly* 4 (1): 141–152.

Coate, Kelly. 2000. *The History of Women's Studies as an Academic Subject Area in Higher Education in the UK, 1970–1995*. ProQuest Dissertations Publishing.

Code, Lorraine B. 1981. Is the Sex of the Knower Epistemologically Significant? *Metaphilosophy* 12 (3–4): 267–276.

Collins, Patricia Hill. 2018. Pauli Murray's Journey toward Social Justice. *Ethnic and Racial Studies* 41 (8): 1453–1467.

Combahee River Collective. [1978] 2014. A Black Feminist Statement. *Women's Studies Quarterly*, 42 (3/4): 271–280.

Corbman, Rachel. 2015. The Scholars and the Feminists: The Barnard Sex Conference and the History of the Institutionalization of Feminism. *Feminist Formations* 27 (3): 49–80.

Currah, Paisley. 2016. General Editor's Introduction. *TSQ: Transgender Studies Quarterly* 3 (1–2): 1–4.

Davies, Edward Burlton. 2019. *Third Wave Feminism and Transgender: Strength Through Diversity*. New York: Routledge.

Davis, Angela Y. 2003. *Are Prisons Obsolete?* New York, NY: Seven Stories Press.

Downing, Lisa, and Lara Cox. 2018. Queering the Second Wave: Anglophone and Francophone Contexts. *Paragraph. A Journal of Modern Critical Theory*, 41 (3, Nov.). Edinburgh: Edinburgh University Press.

Drucker, Zackary. 2018. Sandy Stone on Living among Lesbian Separatists as a Trans Woman in the 70s. *VICE*. 19 December. https://www.vice.com/en/article/zmd5k5/sandy-stone-biography-transgender-history.

Duxbury, Catherine. 2019. Of Monkeys, Men and Menstruation: Gendered Dualisms and the Absent Referent in Mid-Twentieth Century British Menstrual Science. *Journal of Historical Sociology* 32 (1): 94–107.

Dworkin, Andrea. 1974. *Woman Hating*. New York: Dutton.

———. [1976] 1981. Our Blood: Prophecies and Discourses on Sexual Politics. New York: Perigee Books.

———. 1983. *Right-Wing Women: The Politics of Domesticated Females*. New York: Pedigree Books.

———. 1989. *Pornography: Men Possessing Women*. New York: E.P. Dutton.

Echols, Alice. 1989. *Daring to Be Bad: Radical Feminism in America: 1967–75*. Minneapolis: University of Minnesota Press.

Eisenstein, Zillah. 1987. Liberalism, Feminism and the Reagan State. *Socialist Register* 23: 236–262.

Elliott, Beth. 1973. Of Infidels and Inquisitions. *The Lesbian Tide*, 15 (June): 26. Accessed 7 January 2023. https://revolution.berkeley.edu/of-infidels-and-inquisitions/.

Enke, Finn. 2012. *Transfeminist Perspectives in and Beyond Transgender and Gender Studies*. Philadelphia: Temple University Press.

———. 2013. The Education of Little 'CIS'. In *The Transgender Studies Reader*, ed. Susan Stryker and Aren Z. Aizura. New York: Routledge.

———. 2018. Collective Memory and the Transfeminist 1970s: Toward a Less Plausible History. *TSQ: Transgender Studies Quarterly* 5 (1): 9–29.

Enszer, Julie R., and Agatha Beins. 2018. Inter- and Transnational Feminist Theory and Practice in Triple Jeopardy and Conditions. *Women's Studies* 47 (1): 22.

Espineira, Karine, and Marie-Hélène/Sam Bourcier. 2016. Transfeminism: Something Else, Somewhere Else. *TSQ: Transgender Studies Quarterly* 3 (1–2): 84–94.

Evans, Mary, and Sumi Madhok. 2014. Epistemology and Marginality. In *The SAGE Handbook of Feminist Theory*, ed. Mary Evans, Clare Hemmings, Marsha Henry, Hazel Johnstone, Sumi Madhok, Ania Plomien, and Sadie Wearing, 1–8. London: SAGE Publications Ltd.

Fahs, Breanne. 2020. *Burn It Down! Feminist Manifestos for the Revolution*. London: Verso Books.

Federici, Sylvia. 1975. *Wages Against Housework*. Bristol: Falling Wall Press [for] the Power of Women Collective.

Feinberg, Leslie. 1996. *Transgender Warriors Making History from Joan of Arc to Dennis Rodman*. Boston, MA: Beacon Press.

Ferber, Alona. 2020. Judith Butler on the Culture Wars, JK Rowling and Living in 'Anti-Intellectual Times.' *New Statesman*. 22 September. https://www.newstatesman.com/long-reads/2020/09/judith-butler-culture-wars-jk-rowling-living-anti-intellectual-times.

Ferguson, R.A. 2004. *Aberrations in Black : Toward a Queer of Color Critique*. Minneapolis: University of Minnesota Press.

Fernández Romero, F. 2020. 'We Can Conceive Another History': Trans Activism Around Abortion Rights in Argentina. *International Journal of Transgender Health* 22 (1–2): 126–140.

Ferree, Myra Marx, and Beth B. Hess. 2000. *Controversy and Coalition: The New Feminist Movement across Three Decades of Change*. 3rd ed. New York: Routledge.

Flannery, Kathryn Thomas. 2005. *Feminist Literacies, 1968–75*. Urbana: University of Illinois Press.

Freeman, Elizabeth. 2010. *Time Binds: Queer Temporalities, Queer Histories*. Durham: Duke University Press.

Garcia, Alma M. 1989. The Development of Chicana Feminist Discourse, 1970–1980. *Gender and Society* 3 (2): 217–238.

Gill-Peterson, Jules. 2018. *Histories of the Transgender Child*. Minneapolis: University of Minnesota Press.

———. 2021. General Editor's Introduction. *TSQ: Transgender Studies Quarterly* 8 (4): 413–416.

Gilmore, Stephanie. 2008. *Feminist Coalitions: Historical Perspectives on Second-Wave Feminism in the United States, Women in American History*. Urbana: University of Illinois Press.

Green, Kai M., and Marquis Bey. 2017. Where Black Feminist Thought and Trans Feminism Meet: A Conversation. *Souls* 19 (4): 438–454.

Guy-Sheftall, Beverly. 2002. Response from a 'Second Waver' to Kimberly Springer's 'Third Wave Black Feminism?'. *Signs* 27 (4): 1091–1094.

Harding, Sandra. 1986. *The Science Question in Feminism*. New York: Cornell University Press.

Harsin Drager, Emmett, and Lucas Platero. 2021. At the Margins of Time and Place: Transsexuals and the Transvestites in Trans Studies. *TSQ: Transgender Studies Quarterly* 8 (4): 417–425.

Havlin, Natalie. 2015. 'To Live a Humanity Under the Skin': Revolutionary Love and Third World Praxis in 1970s Chicana Feminism. *Women's Studies Quarterly* 43 (3/4): 78–97.

Heaney, Emma. 2016. Women-Identified Women: Trans Women in 1970s Lesbian Feminist Organizing. *TSQ: Transgender Studies Quarterly* 3 (1–2): 137–145.

———. 2017. *The New Woman: Literary Modernism, Queer Theory, and the Trans Feminine Allegory*. Evanston, IL: Northwestern University Press.

Hemmings, Clare. 2011. *Why Stories Matter: The Political Grammar of Feminist Theory*. Durham: Duke University Press.

———. 2018. *Considering Emma Goldman: Feminist Political Ambivalence and the Imaginative Archive*. Durham: Duke University Press.

Hesford, Victoria. 2005. Feminism and Its Ghosts. *Feminist Theory* 6 (3): 227–250.

———. 2013. *Feeling Women's Liberation*. Durham: Duke University Press.

Hill Collins, Patricia. 2000. Black Feminist Epistemology. In *Black Feminist Thought: Knowledge, Consciousness and the Politics of Empowerment*, 2nd ed., 251–271. New York: Routledge.

Hogeland, Lisa Maria. 2001. Against Generational Thinking, or, Some Things That 'Third Wave' Feminism Isn't. *Women's Studies in Communication* 24 (1): 107–121.

hooks, bell. 2015. *Feminist Theory: From Margin to Center*. London: Routledge.

Hose and Heel. 1976. Issue 3. In Francine Logandice Collection, Carton 1 Collection Number 2002-04, *The Gay and Lesbian Historical Society Archives*. San Francisco, CA.

Jeffreys, Sheila. 2014. *Gender Hurts: A Feminist Analysis of the Politics of Transgenderism*. London: Routledge.

Kaas, Hailey. 2016. Birth of Transfeminism in Brazil: Between Alliances and Backlashes. *TSQ: Transgender Studies Quarterly* 3 (1–2): 146–149.

Koblin, Helen. 1973. 1500 Women at UCLA hold Lesbian Conference. *Los Angeles Free Press,* 10 April: 3–5.

Koyama, Emi. 2003. In *The Transfeminist Manifesto. In Catching a Wave: Reclaiming Feminism for the 21st Century,* ed. Rory Cooke Dicker and Alison Piepmeier, 244–262. Boston: Northeastern University Press.

Laughlin, Kathleen, et al. 2010. Is It Time to Jump Ship? Historians Rethink the Waves Metaphor. *Feminist Formations* 22 (1): 76–135.

Lennon, Erica, and Brian J. Mistler. 2014. Cisgenderism. *TSQ: Transgender Studies Quarterly* 1 (1–2): 63–64.

Lewis, Sophie. 2022. Serf 'n' Terf. *Salvage.* https://salvage.zone/serf-n-terf-notes-on-some-bad-materialisms/.

Lewis, S., and Seresin, A. 2022. Fascist Feminism: A Dialogue. *TSQ: Transgender Studies Quarterly.* [Online] 9 (3), 463–479.

Lorde, Audre. 2017. *Your Silence Will Not Protect You.* London: Silver Press.

Lugones, María. 2007. Heterosexualism and the Colonial/Modern Gender System. *Hypatia* 22 (1): 186–219.

———. 2010. Toward a Decolonial Feminism. *Hypatia* 25 (4): 742–759.

Malatino, Hil. 2015. Pedagogies of Becoming: Trans Inclusivity and the Crafting of Being. *TSQ: Transgender Studies Quarterly* 2 (3): 395–410.

Maxwell, Angie, and Todd G. Shields, eds. 2018. *The Legacy of Second-Wave Feminism in American Politics.* Cham: Palgrave Macmillan.

McClintock, Anne. 1995. *Imperial Leather. Race, Gender and Sexuality in the Colonial Contest.* New York: Routledge.

Meadow, Tey. 2016. Toward Trans* Epistemology: Imagining the Lives of Transgender People. *WSQ: Women's Studies Quarterly* 44 (3–4): 319–323.

Meyerowitz, Joanne J. 2004. *How Sex Changed: A History of Transsexuality.* Cambridge, MA: Harvard University Press. ProQuest Ebook Central.

Meyers, Quincy. 2022. Strange Tensions. *TSQ: Transgender Studies Quarterly* 9 (2): 199–210.

Mohanty, Chandra Talpade. 2003. *Feminism Without Borders: Decolonizing Theory, Practicing Solidarity.* Durham: Duke University Press.

Mulvey, Laura. 1975. Visual Pleasure and Narrative Cinema. *Screen* 16 (3): 6–18.

Muñoz, José Esteban. 2009. *Cruising Utopia : the Then and There of Queer Futurity.* New York: New York University Press.

Namaste, Viviane. 2008. Undoing Theory: The 'Transgender Question' and the Epistemic Violence of Anglo-American Feminist Theory. *Hypatia* 24 (3): 11–32.

———. 2011. *Sex Change, Social Change: Reflections on Identity, Institutions, and Imperialism.* Toronto: Women's Press.

Nay, Yv E. 2019. The Atmosphere of Trans Politics in the Global North and West. *TSQ: Transgender Studies Quarterly* 6 (1): 64–79.

Newman, Jane O. 2002. The Present and Our Past: Simone de Beauvoir, Decartes, and Presentism in the Historiography of Feminism. In *Women's Studies on Its Own: A Next Wave Reader in Institutional Change*. Durham, N.C. Duke University Press: 141–173. Wiegman, Robyn.

Norman, Brian. 2007. 'We' In Redux: The Combahee River Collective's Black Feminist Statement. *Differences* 18 (2): 103–132.

Pellegrini, Chiara. 2020. The I in Trans Genre: An Interview with Juliet Jacques. *TSQ: Transgender Studies Quarterly* 7: 105–113.

Potter, Claire. 2018. Not in Conflict, But in Coalition: Imagining Lesbians at the Center of the Second Wave. In *The Legacy of Second-Wave Feminism in American Politics*, ed. A. Maxwell and T.G. Shields, 207–232. Cham: Palgrave Macmillan.

Puar, Jasbir K. 2015. Bodies with New Organs. *Social Text* 33 (3): 45–73.

Radford-Hill, Sheila. 2002. Keepin' It Real: A Generational Commentary on Kimberly Springer's 'Third Wave Black Feminism?'. *Signs* 27 (4): 1083–1190.

Radi, Blas. 2019. On Trans Epistemology: Critiques, Contributions, and Challenges. *TSQ: Transgender Studies Quarterly* 6 (1): 43–63.

Rawson, K.J. 2014. Archive. *TSQ: Transgender Studies Quarterly* 1 (1–2): 24–26.

Raymond, Janice G. 1979. *The Transsexual Empire: the Making of the She-Male*. Boston: Beacon Press.

Richardson, Diane, and Victoria Robinson. 2008. *Introducing Gender and Women's Studies*. 3rd ed. Basingstoke: Palgrave Macmillan.

Rivera, Sylvia. [1973] 2017. Y'all Better Quiet Down Now. Video 5:28, Posted by LoveTapesCollective on Vimeo. https://vimeo.com/234353103.

Roth, Benita. 2003. *Separate Roads to Feminism: Black, Chicana, and White Feminist Movements in America's Second Wave*. Cambridge: Cambridge University Press.

Rubin, Henry S. 1998. Phenomenology as Method in Trans Studies. *GLQ: A Journal of Lesbian and Gay Studies* 4 (2): 263–281.

Rubin, Gayle. 2011. Sexual Traffic: Interview with Gayle Rubin by Judith Butler. In *Deviations: A Gayle Rubin Reader*, 276–309. Durham, NC: Duke University Press.

Ryan, Barbara. 1992. *Feminism and the Women's Movement: Dynamics of Change in Social Movement, Ideology and Activism*. New York: Routledge.

S.T.A.R. 1970. *Manifesto*. NYPL Digital Collections, The New York Public Library.

Salamon, Gayle. 2010. *Assuming a Body Transgender and Rhetorics of Materiality*. New York: Columbia University Press.

Sandoval, Chela. 2000. *Methodology of the Oppressed*. Minneapolis, MN: University of Minnesota Press.

Scott, David, and Sylvia Wynter. 2000. The Re-Enchantment of Humanism: An Interview with Sylvia Wynter. *Small Axe*, 8 September: 119–207.

Serano, Julia. 2007. *Whipping Girl: A Transsexual Woman on Sexism and the Scapegoating of Femininity*. Emeryville, CA: Seal Press.

Serisier, Tanya. 2015. How Can a Woman Who Has Been Raped Be Believed?: Andrea Dworkin, Sexual Violence and the Ethics of Belief. *Diegesis* 4 (1): 68–87.

Silva, Joseli Maria, and Marcio Jose Ornat. 2016. Transfeminism and Decolonial Thought: The Contribution of Brazilian *Travestis*. *TSQ: Transgender Studies Quarterly* 3 (1–2): 220–227.

Skidmore, Emily. 2017. *True Sex: The Lives of Trans Men at the Turn of the Twentieth Century*. New York: New York University Press.

Smith, Barbara. 1998. Where's the Revolution? *The Nation*. 21 August. https://www.thenation.com/article/activism/wheres-revolution/.

Snitow, Ann Barr. 2015. *The Feminism of Uncertainty: A Gender Diary*. Durham, North Carolina: Duke University Press.

Snorton, C. Riley. 2017. *Black on Both Sides: A Racial History of Trans Identity*. Minneapolis, MN: University of Minnesota Press.

Springer, Kimberly. 2002. Third Wave Black Feminism? *Signs* 27 (4): 1059–1082.

———. 2005. *Living for the Revolution: Black Feminist Organizations, 1968–1980*. Durham: Duke University Press.

Srinivasan, Amia. 2022. *The Right to Sex: Feminism in the Twenty-First Century*. London: Bloomsbury Publishing.

Stimpson, Catharine R. et al. 1991. Sexual Politics: Twenty Years Later. *Women's Studies Quarterly* 19 (3/4): 30–40.

Stone, Sandy. 1992. The 'Empire' Strikes Back: A Posttranssexual Manifesto. *Camera Obscura* 10 (29): 150–176.

Strongman, SaraEllen. 2016. The Sisterhood: Black Women, Black Feminism, and the Women's Liberation Movement. PhD dissertation, University of Pennsylvania.

Stryker, Susan. 1998. *Suzan Cooke Interview*. GLBT Historical Society.

———. 2006. (De)Subjugated Knowledges: An Introduction to Transgender Studies. In *The Transgender Studies Reader*, ed. Susan Stryker and Stephen Whittle, 1–18. London: Routledge.

———. 2008a. *Transgender History: The Roots of Today's Revolution*. New York: Seal Press.

———. 2008b. Transgender History, Homonormativity, and Disciplinarity. *Radical History Review* 100 (1 Jan.): 145–157.

Stryker, Susan, and Talia M. Bettcher. 2016. Introduction: Trans/Feminisms. *TSQ: Transgender Studies Quarterly* 3 (1–2): 5–14.

Stryker, Susan, and Paisley Currah. 2015. General Editors' Introduction. *TSQ: Transgender Studies Quarterly* 2 (4): 539–543.

Stryker, Susan, et al. 2008. Introduction: Trans-, Trans, or Transgender? *Women's Studies Quarterly* 36 (3/4): 11–22.

The Tide Collective. 2016. A Collective Editorial. *TSQ: Transgender Studies Quarterly* 3 (1–2, 1 May): 276–277.

Thomlinson, Natalie. 2016. *Race, Ethnicity and the Women's Movement in England, 1968–1993*. Hampshire: Palgrave Macmillan.

Thompson, Becky. 2002. Multiracial Feminism: Recasting the Chronology of Second Wave Feminism. *Feminist Studies* 28 (2): 337–360.

———. 2020. Terfism Is White Distraction: On BLM, Decolonising the Curriculum, Anti-Gender Attacks and Feminist Transphobia. *Engenderings*. 19 June. https://blogs.lse.ac.uk/gender/2020/06/19/terfism-is-white-distraction-on-blm-decolonising-the-curriculum-anti-gender-attacks-and-feminist-transphobia/.

Valk, Anne. 2002. Living a Feminist Lifestyle: The Intersection of Theory and Action in a Lesbian Feminist Collective. *Feminist Studies* 28 (2): 303–332.

Valk, Anne M. 2008. *Radical Sisters: Second-Wave Feminism and Black Liberation in Washington, DC*. Urbana: University of Illinois Press.

White, Francis Ray. 2016. Fucking Failures: The Future of Fat Sex. *Sexualities* 19 (8): 962–979.

Whittle, Stephen. 2006. Foreword. In *The Transgender Studies Reader*, ed. Susan Stryker and Stephen Whittle, xi–xvi. New York: Routledge.

Wiegman, Robyn. 2007. Un-remembering Monique Wittig. *GLQ: A Journal of Lesbian and Gay Studies* 13 (4): 505–518.

———. 2012. *Object Lessons*. Durham, NC: Duke University Press.

Wiegman, Robyn, and Elizabeth A. Wilson. 2015. Introduction: Antinormativity's Queer Conventions. *Differences* 26 (1): 1–25.

Williams, Cristan. 2020. Terf Hate and Sandy Stone. TransAdvocate. Accessed 28 June 2022. https://www.transadvocate.com/terf-violence-and-sandy-stone_n_14360.htm.

Withers, D.M. 2019. Laboratories of Gender: Women's Liberation and the Transfeminist Present. *Radical Philosophy* (204). Accessed 7 June 2021. https://www.radicalphilosophy.com/article/laboratories-of-gender.

Wolff, Michelle, David A. Rubin, and Amanda Lock Swarr. 2022. The Intersex Issue: An Introduction. *TSQ: Transgender Studies Quarterly* 9 (2): 143–159.

CHAPTER 2

The "Women" of Women's Liberation

The instability of the categories of "woman" and "women" is the condition of possibility for feminism as a transformative politics
—Sara Ahmed (1998), Differences that Matter

Central to much of second wave feminism was a contest over the meaning of the word "women". How did trans women shape these debates? In this chapter, I start with the assumption that trans people were central to second wave feminism. How do the histories of second wave feminism, the women's liberation movement, and academic feminism read differently if we foreground the dependence of the feminist movement on trans feminist epistemologies, rather than presuming that trans women and the rest of the feminist movement had nothing in common?[1]

[1] This approach to rewriting the history of the women's liberation movement mirrors Claire Potter's approach to historicising the place of lesbians in second wave feminism. Potter asks: "what would the history of the women's movement look like if we put lesbians, rather than conflicts over lesbianism, at the center [*sic*] of Second Wave Feminism? What if, instead of using "lesbian" as a modifier for feminism's most destructive political tendencies- lesbian feminism, lesbian separatism, lesbian culture- we also understood lesbians as agents of, and advocates for, feminism's most potent social justice agendas? What would this history look like if we scrutinised what lesbians- despite their frequent difficulties functioning as feminist insiders- wanted, and continued to want, from feminism after the founding of the National Organization for Women (NOW) half a century ago? Or if we extended that history to how lesbians linked feminism to gay liberation?" (Potter 2018, 206).

© The Author(s), under exclusive license to Springer Nature Switzerland AG 2023
E. Cousens, *Trans Feminist Epistemologies in the US Second Wave*, Breaking Feminist Waves,
https://doi.org/10.1007/978-3-031-33731-4_2

43

This chapter explores the exchanges between trans feminists and the wider feminist movement that were taking place in the feminist and gay presses during the 1970s. Recent correctives to the historical amnesia regarding trans women's involvement in US feminism during the 1970s by scholars such as Finn Enke (2018) and Emma Heaney (2017) have foregrounded the participation of trans women in the feminist activist groups of the day. Heaney and Enke have urged historians to resist one-dimensional readings of the hostility towards trans feminists Beth Elliot, Sylvia Rivera and Sandy Stone in the 1970s by vocal swathes of the women's movement as *proof* of trans-exclusionarity. Beth Elliot after all, had been Vice President of the San Francisco chapter of lesbian feminist organisation Daughters of Bilitis from 1971–1972 and remained committed to the "women's community" despite the vitriol that parts of that community threw at her.[2] Sandy Stone's employment at feminist recording label Olivia Records was emphatically defended by the collective—despite TERFist protests. And Sylvia Rivera's challenge to Jean O'Leary's transphobic speech at the 1973 Christopher Street Liberation Day Gay Parade is part of the history of trans-of-colour led resistance to lesbian feminist transphobia.[3] Focussing only on exclusion, then, overlooks the important influence that many trans individuals had in second wave feminist groups and buttresses defences of trans-exclusionary feminism in the present as shaped by precedent.

Documenting the very presence of trans women, and men, in second wave feminist groups is an important contribution in itself.[4] The 1970s in the US witnessed widescale transformations in relations of gender, race

---

[2] See Beth Elliot, *Mirrors; Portrait of a Lesbian Transsexual* (2011) for Elliot's own recounting of her relationship to feminism, and the women's movement.

[3] O'Leary later regretted this stance- see Martin Duberman (1994, 236).

[4] My focus in this chapter is on trans women, and the work they did reconfiguring the boundaries of "womanhood" through their participation in women's liberation movement groups and discussions. However, there were also many trans men and trans masculine feminists in the movement who did important work challenging the gendered essentialism of the category "feminist". In addition to well-known trans men including Patrick Califia and Lou Sullivan, and self-identified "transgender, lesbian, female revolutionary communist" Leslie Feinberg, there is a substantial presence of trans men writing into feminist journals at the time to educate the rest of the movement, highlighting their own commitments to feminism as trans men. See for a good example, see Mike Curie "Becoming A Man" in *Echo of Sappho*, vol. 1, no. 5, June 1973.

and sexuality.[5] That trans people would have had no investments in this moment of historical rupture is highly unlikely. Reading beyond dominant dismissals of the women's liberation movement as concerned with securing protections for an already relatively privileged group of white, middle-class women reminds us that, as Finn Enke points out, "feminism reached far beyond its most explicit proponents" and "trans people ... across sexuality, race, class and political inclination built vehicles for this truly vast movement" (Enke 2007, 256). Highlighting the diverse political constituencies of second wave feminism is an important corrective to the historical record.

Beyond acknowledging the presence of trans people in the feminist movement however, in this chapter I am interested in the intellectual contributions made by trans people's involvement with second wave feminism, exploring how trans women's participation in the debates and discussions taking place in the 1970s shaped the direction of feminism. Kimberly Springer (2005), Stephanie Gilmore (2008), Anne Valk (2008), Benita Roth (2003), Sherna Berger Gluck (1998), Winifred Breines (2006) and Becky Thompson (2002) have noted that the political and epistemic contributions of the women's liberation movement have been underestimated, due to the lack of attention given to the activism of Black feminists, Chicana feminists, working-class and incarcerated feminists. These authors have highlighted how "woman", far from the basis of exclusionary identity politics, was, for many, a generative site of contest against patriarchally imposed expectations. I will argue that a trans feminist reading of the women's liberation movement needs to start from a similar place as a feminist of colour reading; that the category of woman, far from being universal, its contents decided in advance, was a potentially insurrectionary category, a right to be claimed, and a horizon of resistance against white, cis, patriarchally imposed expectations (e.g. Davis 1983; Dotson 2014; hooks 2015). In this I follow Talia Mae Bettcher who argues that "trans uses of 'woman' can be seen as resistant uses that emerge out of and respond to a form of oppression that is, in some sense, prior to the resistant identities" (Bettcher 2016, 420). In short, in this

---

[5] Most of these movements were also closely linked with anti-imperialism and New Left reckonings with US national identity in the face of the war in Vietnam- opposition to which was the largest and most organised anti-war movement in the country's history.

chapter, I am interested in the work that trans activists did in redefining the "woman" of women's liberation, urging white, cisgender and middle-class feminists in the movement to expand their concept of womanhood beyond violent, exclusionary and essentialist operations. Indeed, whilst third wave feminism argued that the instability facing the category of "women" was part of second wave feminism's failure (Snyder 2008; Tong 2009), this narrative already presumes a white, cisgender subject of feminism.[6] By contrast, if we begin with "woman's" operative exclusions as the centrepiece of feminist activism and resistance, the illumination of the category's instability in the second wave is no longer the movement's downfall, but rather its most enduring contribution.

FEMINISM'S SCHOLARLY STORY

Trans women are absent from the well-rehearsed narratives of the US women's liberation movement. According to the movement's "scholarly story", it emerged out of the civil rights movement at the end of the 1960s, started off with radical, if naive, ambitions, but became increasingly divided on issues such as sexual freedom and lesbianism. The strand that prevailed by the end of the 1970s was an essentialist, predominantly white, cultural feminism, concerned with women's distinct values and moral superiority. The nails in the coffin of the movement then came with the ascendency of anti-pornography and its alignment with the right-wing Moral Majority at the beginning of the 1980s. On such typical accounts, the second wave feminist movement is represented as being primarily white, middle class and cisgender (Buechler 1990; Curthoys 1997; Ferree and Hess 2000).

Yet "the scholarly story of feminism was the production of feminist activists who entered the academy" (Gilmore 2008, (1). In fact, this hegemonic history which documents the supplanting of (white) radical feminism by (white) cultural feminism has gained ascendency on the basis of a few key texts (e.g. Echols 1989; Evans 1979; Freeman 1975). Chief

---

[6] At the same time as arguing against the political utility of a universal category of woman, academic feminism in the 1990s departed from a critique of the category of woman's theoretical fragmentation. See Elizabeth Spelman (1990) and Natalie Stoljar (1995).

among them, Alice Echols' *Daring to be Bad*, a riveting story of the rise and fall of radical feminism in the US, has become the canonical history of the women's liberation movement's activist groups. Echols documents how the politicisation and revolutionary character of the early years of the women's liberation movement was soon compromised by divisions within the movement. She narrates how the loss of momentum that the escalation in feminist factionalism produced was matched, at the turn of the 1980s, by an increasingly hostile political environment and defeats on key political issues. The second half of the 1970s according to this story, saw radical feminism mutate into cultural feminism, a decidedly less political version of feminism according to Echols—where utopian revolutionary ambitions were replaced by "lifestyle politics", understood by Echols as "a solipsistic preoccupation with self-transformation" (1989, 17). The effect of such a teleological narrative, then, is that the failure of the movement becomes in-built from the start.

The idea that there was a unified origin of the movement which only later gives way to difference, however, reifies the participation of white, middle-class, cisgender activists at the beginning of the women's liberation movement, and cements the exclusion of second wave lesbian, Black, Chicana and—as I will demonstrate—trans feminists from the frame. From its origins, the women's liberation movement was precisely that: a movement, not an organisation (Forster 2016). A proliferation of local and interest-based feminist organisations were formed and "separate groups of women engaged in the work of the movement, in one form or another, for any or all of the stated goals of contemporary feminism" (Ferree and Hess 2000, xix). Decentralised, non-hierarchical and diffuse, the women's liberation movement was splintered from the start. If we dismiss the period on the basis of its hegemonic history, we overlook the "ways that feminist, lesbian, and queer of color and trans activists grappled hard to develop critical insights and knowledges that move us today" and acquiesce to the monopolisation of the narrative by a few (Enke 2018, 11). Many of feminism's philosophical and political gains owe a great deal of debt to the second wave trans feminists who were spearheading the decades developments in sex and gender knowledges. Yet their presence is still rarely acknowledged in dominant histories of the movement.

WOMEN'S LIBERATION IN PRINT

Turning to print culture from the 1970s provides an important source of counter-histories to the mainstream, academically authored narratives that have assumed centre stage. Second wave feminist journals were central sites where movement theory and ideas were debated and developed. The sheer ubiquity of zines, newspapers and independently produced journals from the second half of the 1960s—on one count between March 1968 and August 1973 over 560 new publications produced by feminists appeared in the United States (Ann Mather quoted in Flannery 2005, 24)—make them "a dynamic and important source of feminist knowledge production" (Enszer and Beins 2018, 22). The mimeograph had made self-publishing and duplicating extremely quick and cost effective and therefore newspapers and newsletters- cheap to produce, cheap to share and amenable to creative presentations of ideas, were the communications methods of activist ideas. As such, much second wave theory circulated in print, not reputed academic publications.

These newsletters, journals and pamphlets exemplify how different groups of women were catalysed to articulate the specificities of these terms; Black womanhood, Chicana womanhood and lesbian womanhood for example.[7] They highlight the cross-fertilisation between different movements; trans liberation, gay liberation, women's liberation, Black liberation and Chicana liberation. The discussions in print also track in real time the priorities, concerns and debates that were taking place in different feminist communities throughout the 1970s.

MARGO SCHULTER'S LESBIAN TRANS FEMINISM

Margo Schulter's essays in feminist journals, and other underground newspapers such as *Gay Community News* are good examples of the trans feminist knowledges that were being shared in these spaces as part of a

---

[7] Emma Heaney makes a similar argument to my own which is that the materialist trans feminist writing that can be observed in trans liberation publications such as *Moonshadow* "decenters cis experience to more accurately theorise the political category of woman" (2017, 255). My argument proposes how these insights were also being advanced on the pages of feminist print culture, with the explicit aim of decentering cis experience in the women's liberation movement. However, decentering cisness does not necessarily make the category of "woman" inclusive, and many of the trans feminist writers contributing to second wave periodicals allowed their whiteness to go unmarked.

broader project of consciousness-raising.[8] According to Susan Stryker and Talia Mae Bettcher, Schulter was "a self-proclaimed lesbian feminist transsexual living in Boston in the late 1960s and early 1970s" (Stryker and Bettcher 2016, 10). She is listed as "News Staff" and then "Features Staff" in issues of *Gay Community News* between 1974–1975 (GCN 1974; Tholander 1975), and contributed important trans feminist articles to the paper. Schulter co-authored an article titled: "Lesbian/ feminist orientation among male-to-female transsexuals" that was published in *The Journal of Homosexuality* in 1976.[9] She continues to contribute to discussions at the intersection of radical lesbian feminism and trans femi-

---

[8] For further examples see: lesbian newsletter *Mother* vol.1 iss.2 (1971) which contains an informational article titled: "Transsexuality *as discussed by* Laura Cummings *and* Jo, *a female transsexual*"[*sic*]. Laura is described as a "male transsexual"- and "female" and "male" are being used to index the sex assigned at birth. In the piece, Laura and Jo explain the difference between sex and gender as they understand it and educate readers on what "gender identity" means (1971, 4). Another example is the June 1972 issue of *Sisters,* the magazine of the San Francisco chapter of Daughters of Bilitis, which had Beth Elliot as its Vice President. The issue includes an informational article with an anonymous "male-to-female transsexual member" educating the rest of the organisation on fairly straight-forward questions: "The male-to-female transsexual is considered a woman. Should she be attracted to other women, she would therefore be a Lesbian" (1972, 23) Elliot was one of the editors and may have written the piece herself, however the author remains anonymous. Angela Douglas wrote a long three page informational in feminist newspaper *Everywoman,* titled "Letter From A Transsexual" in the "fervent hope" that "some of the clouds of ignorance scouring the transsexual experience will be dispelled by the magic of truth and understanding, and that this letter will inspire other transsexuals to write similar letters or do other things to help end the oppression of transsexuals" (1971, 13). She talks extensively about the violence of prisons and being let down by the misogyny and transphobia of the Gay Liberation Front. Whilst the next couple of years would see Douglas lose her faith in feminism and women's liberation, the presence of these dialogues early in the 1970s points to the trans-feminist exchanges that were taking place during the second wave. (Douglas would later fuel the trans-exclusionary feminist fire when she responded to the transphobic attack on Sandy Stone's hire with a letter to *Sister: West Coast Feminist Newspaper* titled "Phew!!" in which she turns the "lesbian under threat" logic on its head: "Genetic women are becoming quite obsolete which is obvious and the future belongs to transexual women. We know this and perhaps some of you suspect it. All you have left if your ability to bear children, and in a world which will groan to feed 6 billion by the year 2000, that's a negative asset" (1977, 34). Whilst Douglas' letter reads in the same manner as Valerie Solans' *SCUM Manifesto,* an emblem of subversive irony- caustic? Yes. Literal? No.- It became regurgitated within trans-exclusionary feminist circles as the "told-you-so" expression of trans women's id).

[9] "Male-to-female transsexuals" was the term commonly used for transwomen. It is an outdated, biologically essentialist formulation and I reproduce it here for reasons of historical accuracy.

nism today.[10] Margo was (and still is) also a blues musician and composer who, according to an early review of a performance, specialises in "an area of music never before conceptualised, pre-sixteenth Century Western Medieval Modal and Asian Blues" and plays an array of instruments "the organ, the xylophone, kalimba and melodica" (Rose 1974). Schulter herself has made links between her "genre defining" approach to lesbian blues, and her "genre defining" approach to gender, describing herself as: "enjoying medieval music, which has scales in between major and minor. Reflecting that even in classical music you are permitted to modulate, to change key" (1973, 41).[11] Both music and writing can be approached as forms of expression, that if done differently, offer the experience of new modalities that eclipse categorisation.

Whilst there is much that could be explored about Schulter's trans feminism, in what follows I will focus on the significance of two of her articles. The first: "Notes of a Radical Transsexual" in a 1973 edition of the feminist journal *The Second Wave*, and the second: "The Transsexual/Lesbian Misunderstanding" in a 1975 issue of *Gay Community News*. I propose that these are valuable both for their placement in central underground community journals, the intended audience being radical feminists and lesbian feminists, and for the robust and distinctively trans feminist theorisations of second wave concepts: patriarchy, sexism and cisnormativity (termed "two-genderism") that they contain. I will also draw on a third article written by Schulter for *Gay Community News* in 1974 "Transsexophobia: Old Arguments Against New People". Whilst not directly addressing the women's liberation movement, this is a remarkably prescient and lucid refutation of the arguments used to justify trans people's oppression and illuminates the sophisticated radical trans feminism articulated in Schulter's other articles.

In "Notes of a Radical Transsexual" Schulter advances a radical trans feminist critique of "two-genderism", which she self-effacingly describes as "a rather clumsy term upon which I hope someone will improve"

---

[10] Schulter has contributed to online publication the *TransAdvocate's* "The Conversations Project" which describes itself as "committed to bringing attention to a decades old inclusive radical feminist tradition through inspiring informed critical discourse rooted in an intersectional trans and radical feminist perspective" (Williams 2015).
[11] See Margo Schulter (2004) "Medieval polyphony" for a discussion of Schulter's approach to music as "polyphony" and trans-genre.

(Schulter 1973, 40)[12] and which can be translated as cisnormativity. Both the gay movement and the feminist movement are chastised for their failures to address the discrimination that stems from the belief that that there are two mutually exclusive sexes: "the feminist and gay movements have been challenging some basic assumptions about human sexuality and expression" (Schulter 1973, 40) i.e. for feminists—that women are inferior, and for the gay movement—that monogamous, coupled, heterosexuality exhausts sexual possibilities. Schulter argues that whilst gender and sexuality as expressions of sexism have been addressed, there remains "a third aspect of sexism which has not been challenged" (ibid.)—the commitment to a sex binary, fixed from birth. Schulter (ibid.) outlines the following:

> Two-genderism can be summed up in the following assumptions: (1) human beings are divided into two distinct and mutually exclusive biological pigeonholes, male and female; (2) human beings are divided into two distinct and mutually exclusive psychological and social pigeonholes, men and women; (3) biological sex, subjective identity, and social assignment always coincide and (4) none of these facts can change as a person grows and develops.

This rejection of not only gender binaries but sex binaries, along with a theorisation of sexism as discrimination faced by people forced to live within the binary sex classification system, is an important contribution of trans feminism in the 1970s.[13] It is present in the opening line of the S.T.A.R. manifesto, for example, where the collective write: "The oppression against Transvestites of either sex arises from sexist values and this oppression is manifested by heterosexuals and homosexuals of both sexes in the form of exploitation, ridicule, harassment, beatings, rapes, murders" (S.T.A.R. 1970). It is operationalised too in submissions to the *Journal of Male Feminism*, discussed in the following chapter. The idea that neither women nor queer people were absolved from sexist oppression highlighted an understanding

---

[12] Miqqi Alicia Gilbert (2009), another important trans feminist who was active at the time of the second wave, offers a similar formulation to Schulter's- theorising "bigenderism" as a framework for understanding and challenging cisnormativity.

[13] Schulter returns to this argument in her article for *Gay Community News* the following year where she writes: "In challenging the patriarchal assumption that sex and gender are the simple and unchangeable results of genital anatomy at birth, transsexuals are up against the same sexist oppression which has also kept down women and gay people" (1974, 6).

of sexism that, firstly, doesn't presume a sex assigned at birth and, secondly, doesn't depend on what Janet Halley (2006) critiqued as the m/f logic where gender is binary and males oppress females. Schulter therefore outlines a distinctly trans feminist dimension to sexism—the commitment to a mutually exclusive binary that permits violence on the basis of either sex or gender non-normativity. Sexism in other words, extends to cissexism- and any coherent feminism needs to include a commitment to ending this as an integral part of its vision.

Schulter highlights how both intersex and trans people are negatively affected by this system. She also details how deeply "two-genderism" is infused in mainstream, gay and lesbian, and feminist spaces and offers a great deal of vulnerability in outlining her own experiences as a trans woman. These are rich and wide-reaching, covering first-hand experiences of exclusions in the feminist movement, reflections on passing and ambivalences around hormone tests, and the hypocrisy of a movement committed to "the unity of the personal and the political" (Schulter 1973, 31) yet circumscribing certain personal experiences- intersexuality for example- as being beyond discussion. She recounts being harassed by teenage boys, misgendered on a university campus, excluded from feminist meetings and having her femininity questioned by friends. She describes "finding some genuine beauty and humanness in my own subjectively female sexuality, in spite of all the confusion and ambivalence, but being unable to express a shadow of it to anyone else" (ibid.). The piece, which is "intended neither as a scholarly discussion of transsexual and intersexual states nor as a blueprint for ideal societies" (ibid.) reads as a remarkable combination of auto-theory, social movement praxis and trans feminist epistemology.

At the end of the article, Schulter (1974, 42) urges the feminist movement to move beyond a biologically essentialist understanding of sex and "womanhood"—putting forward the following, as the fourth of five, recommendations to the feminist movement:

> 4. In exclusively female groups, redefine what it means to be female so that male transsexuals may have at least partial membership before surgery. It is just at this transitional point, when the transsexual is beginning to live in her new identity, that communication with her sisters may be important in shaping her life-style and in getting a wider perspective on what it means to be a woman.

Schulter's advice that exclusively female groups redefine what it means to be "female" so that those who were planning to transition but had not yet done so are included, reads as both conciliatory and ambitious. On the one hand, her use of the term "male transsexuals" to describe trans women, whilst reflective of the vernacular of the period, reinforces the centrality of assigned sex/gender to the identity that one inhabits. Likewise, the emphasis on surgery- prevalent at the time- limits the boundaries of female identification, excluding trans women who didn't want or couldn't afford or access surgery, transvestites, cross-dressers or drag queens (to list just some of the prevailing taxonomies). However, challenging cisgender, white women who had defined understandings of "female" on the basis of their experience or anatomy alone, Schulter offers her trans feminist insight into the mutability of "sex" categories, and in turn contributes to the challenges being directed at the category of "woman" from different directions during the second wave. Thus, Schulter's advice to the readers of the *Second Wave* can be read as part of an ongoing effort by those historically outside the contours of normative womanhood, to wrest that category from its essentialist, racialised, hegemonic associations. Insisting that womanhood is not a homogenous category, and that one does not have to be assigned female at birth to *be* female, Schulter contributes to a counter discourse emphasising the diversity of people who operate and deserve protection under the category of "woman".

It is notable that Schulter's argument is not that "exclusively female" groups allow trans people to join, but rather that they (moderately) expand their conception of which trans people are treated as "female". This points to the fact that the parameters of inclusion in second wave feminist spaces were not exclusively along a cis/trans line, but between trans women who had "convincingly" given up their privilege and those who had not.[14] The focus on privilege stemmed from the idea of women as a "sex class" that some radical feminist groups, particularly those who had been involved in the Marxist politics of the New Left, had adopted. According to this view,

---

[14] See Koyama (2020) for a critique of racist and classist logics embedded in the distinction between "pre-op" and "post-op" transsexuals (Koyama 2020). This essentialising distinction overlooks the social, cultural and financial capital required to access gender affirming surgery in the first place. It also reinscribes an essentialist, transphobic equation of the penis with both sex/gender identity, overlooks the priority of self-determination which I have argued is a central component of trans feminism, and attaches gender identification and accomplishment to a clinical temporality. As Koyama also highlights, over-emphasis on genital shape also contributes to the suppression and erasure of intersex people. However "no-penis policies" have been a reoccurring feature of trans-exclusion/inclusion discussions within feminism and trans feminism.

woman "is, a member of a class of something called 'sex'- a thing that is said to be natural, pre-political, an objective material ground on which the world of human culture is built" (Srinivasan 2022, xiii). On this understanding, the best way of determining who occupied this class was, as with classical Marxism, a question of one's relationship to material aspects of privilege. At the end of Schulter's article in *The Second Wave*, she makes clear that a relationship to privilege is central to her own understanding of what it means to be a woman and that this, in turn, shapes her feminist commitments: "I shall always try to be sensitive to the ways in which I have profited by male status, however much I have lost emotionally: for school and job simply being male was an automatic bonus. Of course, I will be renouncing this status, but I cannot renounce the very unjust benefits I have received and which are now unerasable history" (1973, 42). This logic is present too in the 1977 letter penned in response to the transphobia that had erupted over the hiring of Sandy Stone. Olivia Records write in Stone's defence:

> We reasoned that while it requires some material means to undergo the sex reassignment process, a person does not gain privilege by doing it—quite the contrary (a very few well-publicized transsexuals aside). Because Sandy decided to give up completely and permanently her male identity and live as a woman and a lesbian, she is now faced with the same kind of oppression that other women and lesbians face. She must also cope with the ostracism that all of society imposes on a transsexual. In evaluating whom we will trust as a close ally, we take a person's history into consideration but our focus as political lesbians is on what her actions are now. If she is a person who comes from privilege, has she renounced that which is oppressive in her privilege, and is she sharing with other women that which is useful?" (Women of Olivia Records 1977, 6 italics original)

Womanhood for many second wave groups was defined not on the basis of biological factors, but a relational standpoint to masculinity and privilege. Men and women are classified at birth into a sex class: male/female, but this can shift depending on whether the associated privileges are acquired or renounced. Sex and gender are thus entirely relational, political categories (Williams 2020, 719).

There are enormous problems to a focus on privilege as the precondition for participation in feminist spaces. First, it represents the cissexist idea that those assigned male at birth have a monopoly on gender privilege. Second, the idea that surgery constitutes evidence of one's commitment to womanhood is not only essentialist, reinscribing the ana-tomically differentiated body as proof of gender, but highly racialised and classed: it excludes those, disproportionately trans people of colour, with-out the means to pay for often costly operations, from accessing "woman-hood". Moreover, this emphasis on the body also reproduces a highly problematic, phallocentric association of the penis as the source and sym-bol of male power—a perspective that has been weaponised by trans-exclusionary radical feminism which "deploys the penis as a political tool to link societal transphobia with women's fear of male violence" (Phipps 2017, 309). Third, the very concept of a "sex class" illustrates a lack of intersectionality, suggesting that identities can be understood on the basis of sex/gender alone and overlooking the centrality of race, class and sex-ual orientation to one's relationship to privilege. Fourth, and drawing on points one and three, it implies that [white, wealthy] transmasculine peo-ple are privileged vis-à-vis [white, wealthy] cis women. This dichotomises gender according to a m>f logic and overlooks the intersections of gender with other categories of experience. Pointing out what goes unacknowl-edged in such a view, Bobby Noble notes that when we think we see male privilege, "what we're actually seeing is whiteness modifying masculinity to give it power" (2006, 27). Such a focus on male "privilege" without a simultaneous focus on the privileges of whiteness, class and nation, reflects the problematically one-dimensional analyses being advanced by some white women's groups. The idea of a "sex-class" then, reinscribes a binary world view where men and males (including trans men) have power over women and females, power is entirely oppressive, top down and cisgender privilege goes unmarked.

Despite these clear limitations however, the observation in certain femi-nist circles that "post-op" trans women were easily incorporated into the folds of sisterhood remains an important complication to a narrative that elides the existence and complexity of trans and feminist exchanges during the period. What Schulter's essay speaks to is a distinct trans feminist sub-jectivity and the sense that at least some trans people felt that the pages of feminist print publications were spaces where they could inform and edu-cate their cisgender sisters. As Emma Heaney explains, trans women's writing during this period "reinstalls women and the feminine as vital cat-egories for feminist theory and political activity with none of the univer-salising (and thus cis sexist, racist, and bourgeois) baggage that made us turn away from those categories to begin with" (Heaney 2017, 297). In demonstrating that "woman" and "female" are more complex categories than many consciousness-raising groups presumed, Schulter offers a valuable trans feminist contribution to discussions taking place within second wave feminism at the time. Schulter also extends key second wave concepts "patriarchy" and "sexism" to incorporate transphobia, thereby expanding second wave feminist analysis beyond its original referents.

The Second Wave was fairly typical of the community produced feminist publications of the era.[15] Rather than reading as a cohesive entity the pages are full of "multiple voices that sometimes sound like a cacophony, and in other times are in harmony" (Berger Gluck 1998, 54). Given the multiplicity of perspectives expressed, it is not entirely clear how Schulter's article would have been received.[16] This is further complicated by the inclusion of Robin Morgan's transphobic speech at the 1973 West Lesbian Conference where she consistently misgendered Beth Elliot and played into violent, fear-mongering tropes of trans women as predatory. The editorial decision to present these two pieces in the same issue (and to include both as cover stories) represents the all too familiar journalistic strategy of framing and marketising trans lives as subject to "debate". As discussed throughout, it is not my aim to "rescue" the second wave (the journal, or the period) from its problematic dimensions. Rather, I seek to demonstrate the presence of exchanges between trans feminists and the wider feminist movement during this period, which are an overlooked element of second wave feminist history. That perspectives like Morgan's have, over the subsequent decades, become increasingly violent and vocal makes it hard not to grant Morgan's speech more epistemic weight in the development of feminism than Schulter's. Yet, to do so would be to write out the contributions of trans people to the history of feminism, and to naturalise a separation between trans people and other feminists that, as Schulter's essay reveals, is highly contradictory.

Schulter's later article in *Gay Community News* (1975) reflects a more assertive position on what it means to be a "woman" moving from a focus on anatomical attributes (sex) to subjectivity (gender). Joanne Meyerowitz discusses how Schulter in this article challenges to feminists to "accept 'the

[15] *The Second Wave* sought to be a quarterly magazine which would serve nationally as a forum for feminist writings and discussion (Beins 2017, 22).

[16] Later issues indicate that transsexuality continued to be "debated" in the journal—troublingly presented as an issue for cisgender feminists to discuss- and various varieties of TERF arguments are among those expressed. A 1978 issue, for example, nominally opposes "Othering" whilst neglecting to recognise trans individuals' subjectivities (Pilloton et al. 1978).

truly radical' answer to the question of what makes women women" (2004, 261) by calling for self-determined gender. Against a climate of growing backlash towards trans women's participation in feminist spaces that was taking hold in some parts of the country, Schulter uses her platform to explain once again that "male-to-female transsexuals are women" and that "physical sex" does "not necessarily determine gender identity" (1975, 9). Neither "physical sex" nor "gender identity" are absolutely binary and both are subject to change. Addressing widespread ignorance of transsexuality and intersexuality amongst lesbian feminists, Schulter outlines that to be a woman is to experience oneself as aligned with that category on one's own terms. Pointing out the slippery territory that one gets into if either biology or experience is posited as a basis for inclusion within the category "woman" Schulter asks: "What is a woman's body in the first place? Where is the line drawn? Why should it be drawn at all except by patriarchs who are out to defend two-genderism?" (1975, 9). Against such crude, and in her view "patriarchal" definitions of womanhood, Schulter emphasises that what it means to be a woman is to *feel* like a woman: "we are women because we have female gender identities regardless of either our genitals or our adherence or nonadherence to sex roles; in short, we are women because we *feel* ourselves to be women in our own terms" (1975, 9). Schulter articulates an account of gender that derives from subjectivity not substance, such that to feel like a woman is to be a woman and shares her insight as a lesbian trans woman that there is no necessary ordering of sex, gender and desire that needs to align in the production of womanhood. Schulter also discursively positions her trans feminism in the terms of radical feminism's principal convictions around bodily autonomy and resistance to the patriarchal gendering and control of bodies. By maintaining that a resistance to patriarchal and medical control of women's bodies includes challenging hegemonic assumptions about the relationship between bodies and identities, Schulter offers a trans feminist politics of self-determination.

Whilst second wave radical feminism is often represented as seeking to police the borders of womanhood on a biologically essentialist basis, for Schulter there are clear overlaps between a radical feminist interpretation of women's liberation and trans liberation. In her refutation of the heteronormative and cissexist standards of what a body should look like, Schulter's articles put forward for second wave radical feminist consumption that "fundamental to trans feminism is self-determination, the choosing of one's own subjectivity and the expectation that this chosen subjectivity will be the means by which they and those who encounter them engage sociality" (Bey 2022, 55). In consistently clarifying that gender isn't determined by any facts about the body, Schulter demonstrates the alignment between trans liberation and radical feminism on the basis of the right to control the meaning of one's body.[17]

What emerges in both of Schulter's articles is a trans feminist phenomenology of gendered subjectivity that remains valuable for feminist philosophy today. Schulter demonstrates Shanna Carlson's argument that "ostensibly non-transsexual subjects… have no monopoly on the psychic experience of the semblance of 'gender certainty'" (Carlson 2013, 312). To the contrary, "woman" becomes quite simply, as Sara Ahmed writes, a category that groups together "all those who travel under that sign" (2017, 14). Yet, as a collective identity, it offers the possibility for mobilisation and resistance to patriarchally imposed meanings and orders. "Woman" is a category to be self-identified with, rather than imposed from the outside and essentialism is presented not only as a ciscentric construct but a patriarchal one—where "male" definitions are clung to in the face of enormous evidence to the contrary. Sexism emerges in Schulter's

---

[17] The influence of trans men and women on second wave feminist engagements with the medical establishment was not just taking place on the pages of feminist journals. Carol Isaac, who was one of the first creators of the Aradia Women's Health Centre in 1971, recalls the valuable contributions of an unnamed trans woman to the discussions related to sexual identity, lesbianism and gender identity taking place at the women's health clinic (quoted in Nelson 2015, 95). As feminists started organising on overlapping issues around the medical control of bodies, trans people bought their decades long fight with the medical profession to the fore. Point one of the S.T.A.R. manifesto speaks to this priority: "We want the right to self-determination over the use of our bodies; the right to be gay, anytime, anyplace; the right to free physiological change and modification of sex on demand; the right to free dress and adornment" (S.T.A.R. 1970). Whilst S.T.A.R.'s focus remained its queer and trans of colour youth, for some trans activists this focus on bodily autonomy led to involvement with radical feminists in the movement for reproductive rights and independent healthcare provision. As Susan Stryker notes, "in many respects, the transgender movement's politics toward the medical establishment were more like those of the reproductive freedom movement than those of the gay liberation movement" (Stryker 2008a, 98). Similarly, Lou Sullivan writes: "That is exactly why we have a feminist movement- women were seen solely on the basis of reproductive organs" (Sullivan 2006, 162). For many across the anti-violence movement, the reproductive rights movement and the women's health movement of the second wave, what was at stake was not an interrogation into the *being* of bodies, but what was being done to bodies in the name of the "sexist" (read both patriarchal and cisgendered) norm. Rather than being concerned with philosophical questions regarding the ontology of womanhood, trans activists shared with these other radical feminists a commitment to the liberation of bodies from the violence of external interference.

analysis not as the domination of men over women, but as the ideological commitment to two mutually opposed sexes, fixed at birth. This impacts not only women, but people who are gay, trans and intersex equally.[18]

By writing in feminist journals and the underground print culture of the 1970s, trans women such as Schulter were updating readers on the realities of trans lives and forcing the women's liberation movement to expand their conception of who deserved protection under the movement's key sign. Schulter makes clear that a coherent feminist politics requires understanding "women" to include trans women, and "sexism" to include "cissexism". Whilst I don't seek to defend a dynamic where trans folk have to bear the burden of educating others, the pages of print offered—as I discuss in Chap. 3—a place for the working out of ideas in tandem, represented a departure from the more dyadic methods of the New Left and gave trans people an important position in the construction of second wave feminist knowledge. Rather than containing fixed perspectives, the print culture bears witness to what Enke describes as second wave feminism's "grappling"—and, as Enke also points out, "that grappling itself offers useful lessons" (2018, 10). Whilst reifying the dialogical nature of print runs the risk of dismissing the activism of street queens, female impersonators and working-class trans people whose activism, out of necessity, was often more direct, my argument is that these discussions illustrate the heterogeneity of second wave trans feminisms and deserve to be read alongside the more established theoretical texts from the period.

What happens to our understandings of women's liberation then if we don't assume that collective identity required ontological certainty? If the struggle for women's liberation was as much as a struggle over the meaning of "women" as "liberation"? The utopian, coalitional radicalism of the early second wave led many people to identify with the political promise contained in the collective category of "women"—that it could "in fact operate as a resonant framework for political identification and addition" (Wiegman 2012, 63). Focussing on the revolutionary ambitions of women's liberation, which at the turn of the 1970s catalysed vast swathes of the population in the promise of radical social transformation, enables a different reading to one in which participation was overdetermined on the basis of class and racial privilege. In contrast to well-worn accounts of second wave feminism which readily equate the period with a narrow set of white,

---

[18] In *Gay Community News* (1974, 6), Schulter uses the concept "Transsexophobia" to signal the intersection between misogyny, cissexism and homophobia.

middle-class women's interests, when we consider who had the most to gain from the shedding of sex/gender stereotypes and what the promise of an end of domination could deliver, the battle for feminism becomes a necessity not an ideology.

Reconceiving the second wave as a period of redefining what it means to be a woman opens up the period to a trans feminist re-reading. Indeed, as Emma Heaney writes "the right to be a woman was a central concern of 1970s feminist projects and trans feminism clarifies this concern" (Heaney 2017, 274). Trans feminists followed Black feminists and feminists of colour in critiquing the notion that "woman" is an internally homogenous category, a fantasy available neither to women of colour or trans women who "understand these categories to be produced through the differences internal to them" (Heaney 2017, 142). As with Black feminists for whom mobilising around the category of "women" in order to reveal its exclusions, push its boundaries, and fight for protection within its terms (hooks [1981] 2015; Dotson 2014) was a longstanding project, trans feminists, through their claims to self-determination and educating of "cissters" in the movement, participated in productively destabilising and expanding the foundations of feminist activism. The investment of women of colour and trans women in women's liberation is always already marked by a contest over the term's potential; a resignification of its violences and exclusions in the name of collective possibility.

Schulter ends her essay for *Gay Community News* with the following call to arms: "The sisterhood of all transsexuals, and of all Lesbians, does not and must not deter me (or anyone else) from challenging sexist attitudes whenever and wherever they occur in either of the overlapping communities [...] Only by such challenging can lesbians and transsexuals become part of the total movement for human liberation" (1975, 9). Trans liberation, gay liberation and women's liberation are presented not as discrete identity-based movements, but coalitional projects aimed at the pursuit of more liveable lives for all. For Schulter, this work is not easy, and sexist attitudes (patriarchal, heterosexist and cissexist) need to be constantly challenged. However, the gap between a postulation of sisterhood and a reality of sexism is not in itself reason to give up. Schulter's essay speaks to a deeply held belief in the possibility of widescale transformation that coalitional feminism can achieve. By steering liberation away from a rights-based orientation towards a structural challenge, Schulter's vision participates in what Paul Preciado has described as the trans feminist project of rescuing:

"feminism" from its own traps, from being just a humanist and colonial straight-white good-woman task. To move from feminism as identity politics to an extended politics of de-identification. To resist normative identifications instead of fighting to produce identity. If feminism was an answer to 19th-century configurations of power, transfeminism seeks to undo contemporary neoliberal power (Preciado 2015, para 6).

Schulter's trans feminism, likewise, is directed at undoing the ideologies that promote a narrow self-interested identity politics, and at a more radical project of liberation.

The idea that second wave feminism was undone by identity politics not only reinforces a misogynistic lens according to which famous rifts are narrated within the frame of sisterly squabbles—unimportant, yet recurrent and unbridgeable- rather than "instructive mappings of intellectual possibility, as debates to be "worked through"" (Srinivasan 2021, para 12). It also presumes that the collective identity sought by the woman's liberation movement, and the second wave feminism of which it was a part, was to be decided in advance, rather than an aspiration or a horizon to be contested and fought for. These widely rehearsed narratives about the women's liberation movement create a story in which the collective identity that provided the basis for mobilisation, and in whose name political and legislative gains were sought, becomes a question of ontology. In the process, a cisnormative frame is constructed in which to be a woman is to fulfil an immutable set of requirements, either a shared set of biological characteristics or a shared set of experiences; the two pillars of cisnormativity.

Throughout much of the grassroots activism of the 1970s, rather than function as a category that circumscribed the parameters of [cis, white] womanhood, the "women" of women's liberation named a collective identity, a horizon for transformation, and a site of resistance and resignification. Yet feminist historiographies which include a dismissal of pre-poststructuralist frames as indifferent to difference produce "a construction of 'second wave feminism' as a white, middle-class movement rather than a complex and conflicted social and intellectual movement that was struggling over defining the terms of feminism" (Fernandes 2013, 174). Centring the presence of those typically presumed marginal to feminism's development enables an alternative historiography to emerge, one where cis white women no longer have epistemic privilege or a monopoly over feminism's organising terms.

TRANS INCLUSION: FROM DIALOGUE TO DISCORD

In addition to foregrounding the contributions of trans feminists like Schulter to the feminist discussions of the second wave, turning to the print culture from the period also tracks the changing perspectives of individuals and groups over the course of the second wave. Kathryn Thomas Flannery writes that these publications "perform a riot of variations rather than a consistency of positioning" (2005, 41) and this is evident with respect to the development of trans feminist politics over the 1970s. It is interesting, for example, to read the shifting views of Angela Douglas- a prolific journalist in the underground press of the time, and founder of Trans Liberation Group TAO (Transsexual Action Organisation) in 1970.[19] Writing at the beginning of the 1970s Douglas placed a good deal of faith in the prospects of solidarity between trans lib and women's lib.[20] Susan Stryker and Talia Mae Bettcher remind us that Douglas had started TAO "while 'crashing' for a few months at a Women's Centre, where she immersed herself in the feminist literature in the centre's library, attended classes, and participated in the Lesbian Feminist organisation that met in the building—noting (with her characteristic self-aggrandisement), 'To

[19] At its founding in 1970, TAO stood for Transvestite/ Transsexual Action Organization (Meyerowitz 2004, 238).

[20] Whilst trans individuals had been active for a long time in the political organising of the 1960s as well as in resistance to police violence and brutality—notably at Cooper's Donuts in Los Angeles in May 1959 and at Compton's Cafeteria in 1966 (Stryker 2008b), it was in the aftermath of the riots at Stonewall on the 28th June 1969, when an explosion of trans of colour anger and resistance responded to what had begun as just another regular police raid of a gay bar, that trans individuals began to organise collectively in defence of their own gender-specific interests. During this explosive period "new transsexual groups appeared and disappeared in short order" (see Meyerowitz 2004, 237). A few had a more lasting influence: In New York, in 1969, Sylvia Rivera, a Puerto Rican street queen and long term civil rights activist, founded Street Transvestites for Gay Power, later renamed Street Transvestites Action Revolutionaries (S.T.A.R.). S.T.A.R. was a political collective that provided housing and support to "societal outcasts" (Cohen 2008, 90)—homeless LGBT youth, drag queens and sex workers. Along with best friend Marsha P Johnson, Riviera used S.T.A.R. to protect young people who were "rendered economically, socially, and psychologically vulnerable because of gender non-conformity, youth, sexual orientation, race, ethnicity, and poverty" (ibid.). In 1970, drag queen Lee Brewster and heterosexual transvestite Bunny Eisenhower who had met as members of the homophile Mattachine Society founded Queens Liberation Front. The group lobbied New York State legislators for the right to "cross-dress" and aided in organising and financing events such as the LGBT Pride march. They also produced a magazine *DRAG*, which amassed a circulation of over 3500 by 1972 and continued throughout the 1970s and 1980s (Meyerowitz 2004, 235).

some, I was a walking monument to the women's movement, a man who had voluntarily given up male privilege to be a woman—and was now fighting for women's rights'" (Stryker and Bettcher 2016, 9)

During the early years of the second wave, Douglas, a self-identified lesbian transsexual, finds a clear appeal in feminist arguments. Meyerowitz highlights that in a 1970 letter to Harry Benjamin, Douglas wrote "As I progress as a transsexual […] I find myself more attune[d] to women's liberation, in particular the demands and ideas of gay women" and "in a letter to playboy magazine published in 1970 Douglas explained that TAO supported 'both gay liberation and women's liberation: we believe that all victims of prejudice and discrimination must work together to change this society'" (Meyerowitz 2004, 238).[21] However, after Beth Elliot's mistreatment in 1973, Douglas developed the sense that women's liberation didn't care about transsexuals. Writing in the T.A.O newsletter, *Moonshadow*, Douglas cautions that:

> Transexuals involved with women's liberation are warned that many feminists will exploit and use transsexuals for the feminist cause, but will not help transsexuals in return. There are many transsexuals now, associated with women's liberation, and we will help support any transsexual who runs into difficulty, such as the courageous Beth Elliot. We urge transexuals to organize with each other rather than get involved with women's liberation, however.[22] (Douglas 1973)

Douglas became cynical of the women's liberation movement—seeing it as instrumentalising trans people's experiences whilst offering little by way of meaningful protection. She therefore urged trans people to organise independently. Whilst this is indicative of the escalating dynamics of exclusion in (particularly lesbian) feminist spaces, it is important not to reify these over and against the presence, participation and influence of many trans individuals in the women's movement. And if many trans

---

[21] Harry Benjamin was an endocrinologist who was also known as the leading sympathetic doctor on trans issues in the 1950s and 1960s. See Beans Velocci (2021). I also discuss Harry Benjamin in Chap. 5.

[22] Angela Douglas switched between spelling "transsexual" with one or two s's. She explains in her autobiography how in the early 1970s, "a major controversy developed over the word "transsexual," and heated arguments developed whether it should be spelled trans-sexual, trans-sexual or transexual. Some wanted to delete the word completely and use "transgenderist." For a time I used the transexual spelling, but later concluded that transsexual was more correct" (1983, 46).

women wanted protection *as* women, how did this transform the contours of womanhood that were being established in the creation of women's spaces and feminist counter publics in the 1970s?

Whilst Douglas lost her faith in the women's liberation movement, from the origins of TAO she was aware of its appeal to trans women. In a 1970 article in the newspaper *Come Out*, Douglas predicted that as both the openly transgender population and the feminist movement grow, the participation of trans women in women's liberation would increase. "There have been and may be many transvestites and transsexuals active in Women's Liberation, usually unknown to the other females" and Douglas advises feminist organisations to accommodate for this increasing presence: "It would be best if the various feminist groups make clear policies concerning active participation by transvestites and transsexuals, as there will be many thousands more in a few years, and many will want to become active in Women's Lib" (1970, 21). This contention, early in the second wave, that feminist spaces needed to rethink their conceptions of womanhood as the openly trans population was becoming increasingly numerous and politicised, demonstrates a pragmatic sense that feminist contours of inclusion needed to and could be updated.

In many of the lesbian feminist print publications of the 1970s, a gradual increase in hostility towards trans members of the movement becomes apparent. As outlined in the introduction, it was the hiring of Sandy Stone, a trans woman, as a sound engineer for the lesbian feminist recording label, Olivia Records, that launched much of the outward expressions of transphobia across the moment's print culture. A 1977 issue of lesbian feminist journal *DYKE for* instance, in response to the news about Stone's employment, has a six-page spread advancing a particularly violent form of biological essentialism (Penny et al. 1977, 29–35). However, what is also apparent in print is that these perspectives were still only reflective of some of the movement. The "letters" section of *Lesbian Connection*, by contrast, documents many lesbian feminists' anger and disappointment at the printing of the transphobic "Open Letter to Olivia" in a previous issue (Margulies 1977). Of the responses Candace Margulies' open letter generates, there are nine expressing strong disagreement and one in support—perhaps for editorial balance. Readers express their outrage at the transphobic letter: "I felt angry at the writer of the "Open Letter" for being so prejudiced against Sandy Stone"; "To the woman who wrote because she thought Olivia Records was horrible for (1) accepting transsexual Sandy Stone as a woman, and (2) being afraid to admit it [...] I thought we were out to convert the world!"; "In a time when the real oppressors are becoming more powerful, it is unfortunate that the first people we attack are our sisters"; "Assigning sex-roles at birth limits a person from the onset"; "My first question to Candace is 'How many transsexuals do you know, to base your knowledge of transsexualism on?' My guess would be none [...] So, Candace, before you make any more judgements on transsexuals, especially transsexual lesbians, meet one or two and get to know them. Until then, I think you are wrong, wrong, wrong, to put down Olivia for having Sandy on their staff"; "Stone is a woman because [she] had chosen to become one. We are not weakened by the hiring of Stone, as C.M. suggests; we are strengthened" (Penn et al. 1978, 16–17). The authors of the letters articulate distinct reasons for supporting Stone; knowing or loving trans women themselves, opposing discrimination in all its forms, a repudiation of the racist, classist assumption that all lesbian experiences are the same, or simply trust in, and respect for, Olivia's vetting process. What is apparent, however, is that there was a great deal of push back against the transphobia within the movement, and a strong sense among many of its contradictory, anti-feminist basis.[23]

Whilst tail end of the 1970s witnessed the emergence of transsexuality as an "issue" for lesbian feminists, to be debated in community journals such as these by feminists of non-trans experience, in the earlier part of the decade, rather than being the object of debate, trans members of the movement were contributing important, influential articles and advancing the discussions on the meanings of sex, gender and womanhood.

The trans feminist archive is as heterogenous and ambivalent as any, and it has not been my intention to instil a binary with respect to enlightened and ignorant along a trans/cis divide. Not to mention the fact that many ostensibly cisgender feminists at the time did go on to transition, it's important as well to recognise that trans feminists did not have to be perfect to have their contributions recognised. Abram J. Lewis considers that the transgender archive in particular might be "distinguished by materials that seem averse to historical synthesis" (Lewis 2014, 25).

---

[23] The *Lesbian Tide* explores both "sides" noting that: "The conflict between lesbian separatists and lesbian transsexuals is a crucial political dilemma for the lesbian movement, demanding a definition of womanhood so concrete as to be unmistakeable, so cut and dried as to be cold-blooded" (Cordova 1977, 7). Meanwhile Iowa City Women's Liberation Movement, which took a revolutionary, anti-capitalist and pro gay, lesbian and bisexual (but not separatist or identarian) stance in their journal *Ain't I A Woman?*, treats debates over transsexuality as a distraction (Leffler and Williams 1973, 11).

Lewis notes that Douglas' own biography, as well as those of Reed Erickson, who I discuss in Chap. 5, and S.T.A.R. co-founders Marsha P. Johnson and Sylvia Rivera, gesture to the fact that "declension, addiction, paranoia, and delusion appear, in sum, endemic to the transgender archive" (ibid., 23).[24] If the transgender archive is "haunted" then, by the uneven effects of trauma and poverty, Lewis proposes what I would call a vulnerable reading strategy, one which "embraces an epistemic humility" and involves "cultivating openness to irreducible alterity" (ibid., 29). Taking the context and audience into account, and judging contributions not by presentist standards of appropriacy and efficacy, but by the changes that individuals sought to effect at the time and place of writing, provides a means of revisiting trans engagements with second wave feminisms, without the requirement that these can be easily systematised or digested whole.

Conclusion: The Plurality of the Second Wave

Whilst there are occasional acknowledgements of the influence of the women's liberation movement on the development of trans activism in the subsequent decades (1980s and 1990s), and a few stories recounted of the participation of trans activists such as Beth Elliot in the consciousness-raising groups of the women's liberation movement, histories of each are typically told without the other. This chapter has asked what happens if instead we presume that trans people- trans women, trans men, gender non-conforming, genderqueer and non-binary people were central to the movement from the start? Not only does it become impossible to tell the history of the women's liberation movement without highlighting the

[24] Angela Douglas played a leading role in the development of trans liberation as a distinct political movement, argued for the importance of working with Women's Liberation and Gay Liberation groups (Meyerowitz 2004, 238) and left an extensive archive of essays and articles publishes in the underground newsletters of the time and TAO's own journals. However, her political trajectory documented in her autobiographies, as Susana Peña has outlined, "often interprets Latino's and blacks through a racist lens" (2010, 760). Douglas also later underwent "an extreme racist period during 1978–1979 when she actively participated in US Nazi politics" (ibid.). As queer and trans historians have demonstrated, the desire to glorify marginalised ancestors only contributes further to the dehumanisation and unrealistic expectations that already attends queer and trans lives. Angela Douglas' own story is a clear reminder less likeable and reprehensible figures are an inescapable element of any history and that the archive of second wave trans feminism is as ambivalent, unpredictable and often unsavoury as the rest of the second wave feminist archive.

influence of trans people within the movement, but the movement's epistemic legacy and philosophical contributions become markedly more radical than conventionally presumed.

Where dominant dismissals of the women's liberation movement tend to presume that "woman" was a category whose contours were to be delimited in advance, a trans feminist reading illuminates precisely the opposite; that woman was a category to be fought for, a site of contest against overdetermined, patriarchally imposed expectations. And that the fight for the liberation of women, was not just the minimal fight for the rights of cisgender, white, middle-class women. To the contrary, it was the fight for human liberation; a battle for all those defined from the outside, and dominated as a result, to achieve self-determination. This connected women's liberation with anti-colonial movements, black liberation, gay and lesbian liberation, and animal liberation. Rather than authorising those who have historically had access to racialised and classed western ideals of "womanhood" to define "women's liberation", a trans feminist reading of women's liberation positions those fighting to expand that category as the privileged subjects of feminism.

The women's liberation movement, as I have argued is the style of second wave feminism more broadly, was characterised by a real sense of optimism. Whilst the impasses of second wave feminism, and the impossibility of a universal sisterhood, have been taken as reasons to move past it, I propose instead that we think with Lauren Berlant (1994) who writes in defence of attaching oneself to a failed political movement as a political strategy that enables a radical rethinking of failure and time. At the beginning of the 1970s, the sense that real change was on the horizon was as relevant to trans women as the rest of the movement. Returning to the hope and ambition of the second wave in its plurality can inform not the quest for a universal sisterhood, but instead a time where "women" and "sister" are coalitional signs, constantly subject to negotiation and that anyone can adopt on their own terms, under the rubric of a commitment to an end of domination. As Chandra Talpade Mohanty argues, "sisterhood cannot be assumed on the basis of gender; it must be formed in concrete, historical and political practice and analysis" (2003, 24). In forcing the wider movement to recognise their unchecked assumptions, exclusions and elisions, trans feminists- like feminists of colour- were doing the world-building work of second wave feminism.

Whilst I have argued that a trans feminist reading of the second wave understands "woman" as a coalitional category and "liberation" as a horizon, a promise to hold onto as we collectively imagine alternatives to the impoverished and toxic present (Muñoz 2009, 27), this is not a straightforwardly redemptive project. Historicising women's liberation without centring cis white women as the movement's subject enables us to tell a more "mixed-up" story (Enke 2018, 10), and one where trans women and ostensibly cisgender women share genealogies. However, a more "mixed-up" story also recognises that we can return to the women's liberation movement in its messiness. That there was a lot of hostility between lesbian feminists and trans feminists is an important part of this history, and one which may be valuable for understanding the psychic investments in cisnormativity that characterise lesbian feminist transphobia in the present (Worthen 2022).

There is messiness too in the complicated histories of many of my interlocutors. Angela Douglas, for example, was integral to the establishment and success of Transsexual Action Organisation, a movement which went on to have hundreds of members internationally—notably Stephen Whittle in the UK (Stryker 2008a, 88). Yet, over the course of the 1970s her initially anticolonial politics became racist and embattled. Whilst Schulter's biography appears less compromised, her whiteness went unacknowledged in her articles yet likely played a role in how comfortable she felt contributing to the mainstream movement's print culture, as well as her investment in dialogical solutions to transphobia and trans ignorance- in contrast to the direct action of groups such as S.T.A.R. whose temporalities and priorities were very different. Many of the criticisms that have been directed at the white women's movement, that it neglected a *meaningfully* intersectional analysis, are present both in Schulter's essays and in Olivia Records' defence of Sandy Stone—where the concept of a "sex class" overlooks the mediation of sex and gender by race and class.

Woman's liberation retains its mixed record when a trans feminist analysis is applied. However, embracing ambiguities and inconsistencies is an essential ingredient of a trans feminist reading practice. Straightforward rejection and reification are both evidence of reductive readings. I propose that instead we encounter the women's liberation movement vulnerably, allowing ourselves to be moved, affected and most importantly surprised by what we find (Gilson 2014). This will enable us to narrate the history of second wave feminism, not from the perspective of its most privileged or prolific members, but from the vantage point of those whose challenges and labour have the capacity to inspire us today.

BIBLIOGRAPHY

Ahmed, Sara. 1998. *Differences That Matter: Feminist Theory and Postmodernism.* Cambridge: Cambridge University Press.

———. 2017. *Living a Feminist Life.* Durham: Duke University Press.

Angela Lynn Douglas (1983). *Triple Jeopardy: The Autobiography of Angela Lynn Douglas* (self-published), GLBT Historical Society Archives, Francine Logandice collection. Carton 1, Folder 22.

Anon. 1972. A Male-to-Female Transsexual Member of DOB Replies Following. *Sisters* (50, June): 23–24. Gale Archives of Sexuality and Gender. Online. Accessed 6 June 2022.

Beins, Agatha. 2017. *Liberation in Print: Feminist Periodicals and Social Movement Identity.* Athens: University of Georgia Press.

Berger Gluck, Sherna. 1998. Whose Feminism, Whose History. In *Community Activism and Feminist Politics: Organizing across Race, Class, and Gender,* ed. Nancy A. Naples, 31–56. New York; London: Routledge.

Berlant, Lauren. 1994. 68, or Something. *Critical Inquiry* 21 (1): 124–155.

Bettcher, Talia Mae. 2016. Intersexuality, Transgender, and Transsexuality. In *The Oxford Handbook of Feminist Theory,* ed. Lisa Disch and Mary Hawkesworth, 407–427. Oxford University Press.

Bey, Marquis. 2022. *Black Trans Feminism.* Durham: Duke University Press.

Breines, Winifred. 2006. *The Trouble Between Us: An Uneasy History of White and Black Women in the Feminist Movement.* New York: Oxford University Press.

Buechler, S.M. 1990. *Women's Movements in the United States: Woman Suffrage, Equal Rights and Beyond.* New Brunswick; London: Rutgers University.

Carlson, Shanna. 2013. Transgender Subjectivity and the Logic of Sexual Difference. In *The Transgender Studies Reader 2,* ed. Susan Stryker and Aren Z. Aizura, 302–315. New York: Routledge.

Cohen, Stephan L. 2008. *The Gay Liberation Youth Movement in New York: 'An Army of Lovers Cannot Fail'.* New York: Routledge.

Cordova, Jeanne, et al., eds. 1977. *Lesbian Tide* vol. 6, no. 6. (May 1, 1977). https://jstor.org/stable/community.28039278. Accessed 3 July 2023.

Cummings, Laura, and Jo. 1971. Transsexuality. *Mother* 1 (2, July). Gale Archives of Sexuality and Gender. Online. Accessed 9 November 2022.

Curie, Mike. 1973. 'Becoming A Man' in Karen Emden, et al. *Echo of Sappho* 1 (5): 15–17.

Curthoys, Jean. 1997. *Feminist Amnesia: The Wake of Women's Liberation.* London: Routledge.

Davis, Angela Y. 1983. *Women, Race & Class.* 1st Vintage Books ed. New York: Vintage Books.

Dotson, Kristie. 2014. Building on 'the Edge of Each Other's Battles': A Feminist of Color Multidimensional Lens. *Hypatia* 29 (1): 23–40.

Douglas, Angela. 1970. Transvestite & Transsexual Liberation. *Come Out* 1 (5, Sept., Oct.): 21. Gale Archives of Sexuality and Gender. Online. Accessed 5 June 2022.

———. 1971. Letter from A Transsexual. *Everywoman* 2 (8): 12–14.

———. 1973. Transsexual Action Organisation. *Moonshadow*, August. Carton 2 In Francine Logandice Collection. Collection Number: 2002–04. GLBT Historical Society.

———. 1977. Phew!! In *DYKE*, no. 5, Fall 1977: 34. Accessed 30 December 2022. https://jstor.org/stable/community.28035713.

Duberman, Martin B. 1994. *Stonewall*. New York: Plume.

Echols, Alice. 1989. *Daring to Be Bad: Radical Feminism in America: 1967–75*. Minneapolis: University of Minnesota Press.

Elliot, Beth. [1996] 2011. *Mirrors: Portrait of a Lesbian Transsexual*. CreateSpace Publishing. Oakland, California.

Enke, Finn. 2007. *Finding the Movement: Sexuality, Contested Space, and Feminist Activism*. Durham: Duke University Press.

———. 2018. Collective Memory and the Transfeminist 1970s: Toward a Less Plausible History. *TSQ: Transgender Studies Quarterly* 5 (1): 9–29.

Enszer, Julie R., and Agatha Beins. 2018. Inter-and Transnational Feminist Theory and Practice in Triple Jeopardy and Conditions. *Women's Studies* 47 (1): 21–43.

Evans, Sara M. 1979. *Personal Politics: The Roots of Women's Liberation in the Civil Rights Movement and the New Left*. 1st ed. New York: Knopf.

Fernandes, Leela. 2013. *Transnational Feminism in the United States: Knowledge, Ethics, and Power*. New York: New York University Press.

Ferree, Myra Marx and Beth B Hess. 2000. *Controversy and Coalition: The New Feminist Movement across Three Decades of Change*, third edition. New York: Routledge.

Flannery, Kathryn Thomas. 2005. *Feminist Literacies, 1968–1975*. Urbana: University of Illinois Press.

Forster, Laurel. 2016. Spreading the Word: Feminist Print Cultures and the Women's Liberation Movement. *Women's History Review* 25 (8): 812–831.

Freeman, Jo. 1975. *The Politics of Women's Liberation*. New York; London: David McKay.

GCN. 1974. *Gay Community News* 1 (42, 13 April): 4. Gale Archives of Sexuality and Gender. Online. Accessed 6 November 2022.

Gilbert, Miqqi Alicia. 2009. Defeating Bigenderism: Changing Gender Assumptions in the Twenty-First Century. *Hypatia* 24 (3): 93–112.

Gilmore, Stephanie. 2008. *Feminist Coalitions: Historical Perspectives on Second-Wave Feminism in the United States*. Urbana: University of Illinois Press.

Gilson, Erinn. 2014. *The Ethics of Vulnerability: A Feminist Analysis of Social Life and Practice*. New York: Routledge.

Halley, Janet E. 2006. *Split Decisions: How and Why to Take a Break from Feminism.* Princeton, NJ: Princeton University Press.

Heaney, Emma. 2017. *The New Woman: Literary Modernism, Queer Theory, and the Trans Feminine Allegory.* Evanston: Northwestern University Press.

hooks, bell. [1981] 2015. *Ain't I a Woman: Black Women and Feminism.* Boston, MA: South End Press.

Koyama, Emi. 2020. Whose Feminism Is It Anyway? The Unspoken Racism of the Trans Inclusion Debate. *The Sociological Review* 68 (4): 735–744.

Leffler, Anne, and Kathy Williams. 1973. The Following Is An Important Message. In *Ain't I a Woman?* vol. 3 no. 5. (July 20, 1973). https://jstor.org/stable/community.28032145.

Lewis, Abram J. 2014. I Am 64 and Paul McCartney Doesn't Care: The Haunting of the Transgender Archive and the Challenges of Queer History. *Radical History Review* 120 (1. Oct.): 13–34.

Margulies, Candace. 1977. An Open Letter to Olivia. *Lesbian Connection* 3 (5): 3–4. https://jstor.org/stable/community.28039177.

Meyerowitz, Joanne J. 2004. *How Sex Changed: A History of Transsexuality.* Cambridge, MA: Harvard University Press. ProQuest Ebook Central.

Mohanty, Chandra Talpade. 2003. *Feminism Without Borders : Decolonizing Theory, Practicing Solidarity.* Durham: Duke University Press.

Muñoz, José Esteban. 2009. *Cruising Utopia: The Then and There of Queer Futurity.* New York: New York University Press.

Nelson, Jennifer. 2015. *More than Medicine: A History of the Feminist Women's Health Movement.* New York: New York University Press.

Noble, Bobby. 2006. *Sons of the Movement: FtMs Risking Incoherence on a Post-Queer Cultural Landscape.* Toronto: Women's Press.

Peña, Susana. 2010. Gender and Sexuality in Latina/o Miami: Documenting Latina Transsexual Activists. *Gender and History* 22 (3, Nov.): 755–772.

Penn, Kristin. et al. 1978. *Lesbian Connection* 3 (7, Feb.). Accessed 30 December 2022. https://jstor.org/stable/community.28039180.

Penny, D. et al. 1977. *DYKE* (5, Sept.). Accessed 30 December 2022. https://jstor.org/stable/community.28035713.

Phipps, Alison. 2017. Sex Wars Revisited: A Rhetorical Economy of Sex Industry Opposition. *Journal of International Women's Studies* 18 (4): 306–320.

Pilloton, Vivette S. et al. 1978. *Second Wave, The* 5 (2, June). Accessed 31 December 2022. https://jstor.org/stable/community.28044450.

Potter, Claire. 2018. Not in Conflict, But in Coalition: Imagining Lesbians at the Center of the Second Wave. In *The Legacy of Second-Wave Feminism in American Politics*, ed. Angie Maxwell and Todd Shields, 207–232. Cham: Palgrave Macmillan.

Preciado, Paul. 2015. Trans-Fem.i.nism. *Purple Magazine.* 23 October. Accessed 30 December 2022. https://purple.fr/magazine/fw-2015-issue-24/trans-fem-i-nism/.

Rose, Edward Gibbs. 1974. Lesbian Blues Is Powerful! *Gay Community News* 2 (6): 12. Gale Archives of Sexuality and Gender. Online. Accessed 6 November 2022.

Roth, Benita. 2003. *Separate Roads to Feminism: Black, Chicana, and White Feminist Movements in America's Second Wave*. Cambridge: Cambridge University Press.

S.T.A.R. 1970. *Manifesto*. NYPL Digital Collections, The New York Public Library.

Schulter, Margo. 1973. Beyond Two-Genderism: Notes of a Radical Transsexual. *The Second Wave* 2 (4): 40–43.

———. 1974. Transsexophobia: Old Arguments Against New People. *Gay Community News*, March 30: 6.

———. 1975. The Transsexual/ Lesbian Misunderstanding. *Gay Community News*, March 15: 8–9.

———. 2004. Medieval Polyphony. In Blumberg's Musi Theory Cipher for Guitar and Other Stringer Instruments. Accessed 8 November 2022. http://www.thecipher.com/medieval_polyphony_part1.html.

Smith, Barbara. 2020. Where's the Revolution? *The Nation*. August 21. https://www.thenation.com/article/activism/wheres-revolution/.

Snyder, R.C. 2008. What Is Third-Wave Feminism? A New Directions Essay. *Signs* 34 (1): 175–196.

Spelman, Elizabeth V. 1990. *Inessential Woman: Problems of Exclusion in Feminist Thought*. London: Women's Press.

Springer, Kimberly. 2005. *Living for the Revolution: Black Feminist Organizations, 1968–1980*. Durham: Duke University Press.

Srinivasan, Amia. 2021. Who Lost the Sex Wars? *The New Yorker*, 6 September 2021. https://www.newyorker.com/magazine/2021/09/13/who-lost-the-sex-wars.

———. 2022. *The Right to Sex: Feminism in the Twenty-First Century*. London: Bloomsbury Publishing.

Stoljar, Natalie. 1995. Essence, Identity, and the Concept of Woman. *Philosophical Topics* 23 (2): 261–293.

Stryker, Susan. 2008a. *Transgender History: The Roots of Today's Revolution*. New York: Seal Press.

———. 2008b. Transgender History, Homonormativity, and Disciplinarity. *Radical History Review* 100 (1 Jan.): 145–157.

Stryker, Susan, and Talia M. Bettcher. 2016. Introduction: Trans/Feminisms. *TSQ: Transgender Studies Quarterly* 3 (1–2): 5–14.

Sullivan, Lou. 2006. A Transvestite Answers a Feminist. In *The Transgender Studies Reader*, ed. Susan Stryker and Stephen Whittle, 159–165. London: Routledge.

Tholander, Marion E. 1975. Feature Staff. *Gay Community News* 3 (15, 11 Oct.): 4. Gale Archives of Sexuality and Gender. Online. Accessed 6 November 2022.

Thompson, Becky. 2002. Multiracial Feminism: Recasting the Chronology of Second Wave Feminism. *Feminist Studies* 28 (2): 337–360.

Tong, Rosemarie. 2009. *Feminist Thought: A More Comprehensive Introduction.* 3rd ed. Boulder, Colorado: Westview Press.

Valk, Anne M. 2008. *Radical Sisters: Second-Wave Feminism and Black Liberation in Washington, DC.* Urbana: University of Illinois Press.

Velocci, B. 2021. Standards of Care: Uncertainty and Risk in Harry Benjamin's Transsexual Classifications. *TSQ: Transgender Studies Quarterly.* [Online] 8 (4): 462–480.

Wiegman, Robyn. 2012. *Object Lessons.* Durham, NC: Duke University Press.

Williams, Cristan. 2015. The Conversations Project. Trans Advocate. Accessed 6 November 2022. http://radfem.transadvocate.com/.

———. 2020. The Ontological Woman: A History of Deauthentication, Dehumanization, and Violence. *The Sociological Review, University of Keele* 68 (4): 718–734.

Women of Olivia Records. 1977. Olivia Replies. *Sister* 8 (3, June–July): 6–9. Gale Archives of Sexuality and Gender. Online. Accessed 5 June 2022.

Worthen, Meredith G.F. 2022. This Is My TERF! Lesbian Feminists and the Stigmatization of Trans Women. *Sexuality & Culture* 26 (5): 1782–1803.

CHAPTER 3

Trans Feminist Phenomenology and Politics in the Journal of Male Feminism

Journal of Male Feminism
credit: Ms. Bob Davis, founder and director of the Louise Lawrence Transgender Archive and Isaac Fellman, Reference Archivist, GLBT Historical Society Archives for their help and permission for the image to be reproduced. Journal of Male Feminism. 1977. Vol. 77No. 3.

> How we embody gender is how we theorize gender and to suggest other-wise is to misunderstand both theorisation and embodiment
> —Gayle Salamon (2010), Assuming A Body

Encountering the conjunction "male women" from the vantage point of the present, reads as incongruous at best, transphobic and essentialist at worst. Yet in the second half of the 1970s, a community of self-identified "cross-dressers", "transvestites" (TVs), "transsexuals" (TSs), "transgendersists" (TGs) and femmiphiles (FPs)—to list the most common identities expressed- formed a textual community under the umbrella of "male women" and did the work of second wave trans feminism. Assigned male at birth and living some or all of the time as a woman, these male women challenged both the "heterosexual matrix" and the "cisgender matrix" with its assumed alignment of sex, gender and sexuality. By articulating their own experiences and subjectivities, and drawing on discourses of feminism to do so, the journal's contributors theorised gender in new ways at the time of the second wave and reinterpreted both "women" and "liberation" outside of an assumption of cisness.

In this chapter, I turn to the conversations taking place amongst one community that would now fall under the umbrella term "trans" on the pages of the *Journal of Male Feminism* (JMF). The *JMF* was the bimonthly publication of The International Alliance for Male Feminism, which described itself as the "world's largest non-profit social and educational organisation promoting male womanhood and feminism" (Stephens 1977a, 2). The mission of the organisation was to promote self-acceptance and pride in femininity for those assigned male at birth, whether on a part-time basis (TVs, FPs) or a full-time basis (TGs and TSs). It sought to do this on the pages of its journal, through organising regular social events and even through national campaigning.[1] The articulation of identities, solidarities and political visions on the pages of the *JMF* make it a valuable source of trans feminist epistemologies at the time of the second wave.

---

[1] In an issue from 1977, there is a letter from Linda Ann Stephens, the I.A.M.F Chairperson, to the President's wife, Ms. Carter, urging her to extend her "concern for improving the mental health of Americans" to include "those confronting general and sexual minorities". The letter urges the government to "devote significant resources to the fields popularly referred to as 'transvestism' and 'transsexualism'" and to consult "male women practitioners" on the subject rather than just "so-called experts"- enclosing information on male womanhood and the Alliance, and inviting Ms. Carter to a local chapter meeting (Stephens 1977a, 2). Many of the members of the Alliance were well-connected (the board of advisors includes professionals such as the sexologist and gender theorist Vern Bullough, who had close links to individuals in this early trans community) and the sense that public acceptance for gender diversity could be won is apparent. The editor's note in a 1979 issue reiterates that in addition to being a social and support organisation for the community, "the Alliance serves as a centre for educational activities aimed at bringing about a better understanding of this phenomenon to professionals and the public at large" (Jones 1979b, 2).

In many ways the *JMF* can be read as a distinctively "trans" publication, and one with much in common with the trans community print culture of the 1970s. It offered a place for members of the Alliance to share and express their "femme-selves"[2]- either through the inclusion of first-person narratives or via the sharing of photos- to read about updates from local chapters and to make contact with one another. The journal gathered and shared information relevant to its cross-gendered readers seeking to learn more about their "trans" identifications, including clippings of relevant news articles and reading lists for books covering "TV" themes.[3] Like other trans-centric publications, it created a community on its pages that countered the pathologisation and shame that attended trans bodies via the constant reiteration of how "beautiful" and "phenomenal" the community is and reinforcing that Alliance members are at the vanguard of "TV" "TS" knowledges- the scientific community and wider public are playing catch up.

In addition to being a distinctively "trans" resource, the *JMF* also has much in common with the style and substance of feminist periodicals from the period. Its "collaging" style is distinctively second wave- articles written with typewriter print are included alongside magazine and newspaper cuttings. Some of the letters to the editors are handwritten, typos are corrected by hand and pages are decorated with stamps, illustrations and slogans. As a form of "participatory media" the journals function as "spaces in which individuals become creators rather than simply consumers of culture" (Piepmeier 2009, 29–30) and the journal affords a space where the community's values can be identified, discussed and developed.

What is particularly valuable for my discussion is, first, the nuanced articulations of sex and gender that are apparent on the journal's pages, and second, the directness of the Alliance's alignment with the women's

---

[2] "Femme-self" was a term coined by Virginia Prince for a cross-dresser's feminine personality. As Robert Hill elucidates, Prince advanced a philosophy of "dual personality expression" which "held that transvestites possessed both masculine and feminine 'personalities'" (Hill 2007, 66). However, the notion of two selves is also a recurring theme throughout TV print culture and gets formulated in different ways- one alternative is a sibling one- where there is a "brother" and a "sister" personality.

[3] A contributor with the femme name Anita Dawn writes into one issue expressing the desire be given pointers for readings: "I also love to read about TV/TS, female impersonators, etc., but there is not too much information up here (Alberta) to be had on the subjects. If some one (sic) would even tell me or send me some literature on the previous mentioned even if only on loan to read, pleas (sic) send them and I will read them and mail them back" (Stephens 1977b, 34).

liberation movement of the second wave. Whilst complex expressions of sex and gender can be found throughout the trans community periodicals that were circulating from the 1960s onwards, the *JMF* stands out amongst other "TV" and "TS" subcultural publications from the era on account of its mobilising of second wave feminist discourses. It is distinct, for example, among the trans community newsletter's widespread at the time for its interpellation of readers as "feminists", and it extends the meaning of this from simply indexing the "celebration of femininity"—as was more common in the transvestite literature- to being a commitment to and mobilisation of the political goals of feminism. The Alliance's mission statement makes this clear:

> Our major aim is (always has been and continues to be) a strong, united, effective feminist social and educational organization open to feminists of either sex without any sexual orientation restrictions and with promotion of male feminism and femininity as a primary thrust [...] This is truly a "woman's organization". Let's see what concentrated (female & male) womanpower can build. (Journal of Male Feminism 1977, 2)

Readers are addressed first and foremost as "feminists" and feminist political horizons such as the Equal Rights Amendment are identified and pursued. Merissa Sherrill Lynn, who was an active member of the Alliance, confirms that its name was selected in recognition of the political currency of "feminism".[4] In a letter discussing the state of social support for "crossdressing sisters" at the time, Lynn writes that "as the name implies, [the Alliance] placed a heavy emphasis on the politics of male feminism and expected the membership to support these political goals" (Lynn 1978, 2). Whilst the overarching goal of the *JMF* is to promote the acceptance and celebration of feminine expression in subjects assigned male at birth, it is of historiographical and epistemic significance that discourses of women's liberation were engaged as the vehicle through which to pursue these goals.

---

[4] Merissa Sherrill Lynn played a significant role in the emerging trans community in the 1970s and 1980s, founding the International Foundation for Gender Education and *Tapestry* magazine which was started in the late 1970s and became the most widely circulated trans publication on the continent until its final issue in 2008. See her autobiography, *Merissa Sherrill Lynn: Her History As She Wrote It* (2018) which doesn't discuss the International Alliance but gives a good flavour of organising and community amongst trans people in the 1980s.

In the introduction, I drew on Marquis Bey, Finn Enke and Emi Koyama's conceptualisations of trans feminism to argue for the following features of trans feminism as central to my analysis: a rejection of "the genre of the binary" (Bey 2022, 53), a politics of self-determination, a conceptualisation of the category "woman" as multiple and unable to be delineated in advance, and a resistance to the cultural devaluation of the feminine. Here, I argue that editors and readers writing into the JMF advanced these key trans feminist principles and also articulated nuanced reflections on the sensual and embodied dimensions of gender. The *JMF* captures early trans community formation in the 1970s, tracks earnest and often unfiltered expressions of transgendered feelings, and is a textual and visual archive of gender variant embodiment from the end of the 1970s until the beginning of the 1980s. The *JMF* also mobilises second wave feminist rhetoric in pursuit of a trans interpretation of women's liberation. Contributors to the journal employ the movement's key concepts such as "liberation", "sisterhood", "sexism" offering a distinctly trans feminist interpretation of the politics that these entail. Whilst, as I will discuss, the appeal to women's liberation was sometimes strategic, there was also a meaningful identification made by the self-identified cross-dressers of the journal with concepts of "women" and "liberation" that wrested these terms from a cisnormative register.

Focussing on issues published between 1977 and 1979 (the first three years of the journal's publication which span the tail end of the decade associated with the US second wave), this chapter contends that the reader-led reflections on gender and sexuality that infuse the *JMF*, and their placement in a journal which explicitly aligns itself with the women's liberation's movement, demonstrates not only the appeal that the mainstream women's liberation movement had for (some) trans individuals during this period, but also the presence of valuable trans feminist epistemologies circulating alongside and in dialogue with second wave feminism.[5] However, rather than straightforward identification with the feminist movement, the invocation of "women's liberation's" key concepts, this chapter argues, was both utopian and strategic. Whilst many of journal's male women really did believe that they could win widespread support for their bi-gendered or feminine expressions, the mainstream women's liberation movement was also chosen

[5] The issues I have examined are from 1977 and 1979. These are the copies housed in the archives I have had access to: The Transgender Archives at the University of Victoria, the GLBT Historical Society Archives in San Francisco, and the Digital Transgender Archives.

for its domesticating currency. This strategic invocation of liberal feminism by the contributors to the *JMF*, I will argue, is historically significant in that it prefigures the instrumentalisation of liberal feminism by state and subcultural groups seeking to delineate the contours of proper citizenship in the twenty-first century.

EVOLVING TAXONOMIES

Collectively categorising the diverse contributors to the journal as "trans feminist" is a contentious process as it involves the imposition of an identity category from the present onto the past (Rawson 2015). Language used by contributors to articulate their identities is fluid and personal. Whilst some identified in the language of the day as "TV" (transvestite) or "TS" (transsexual) for many, as mentioned in the introduction, terms with the prefix "trans" are rejected for their medical associations and "male women", "femmiphile" (lover of the feminine) and "cross-dresser" are preferred.[6] Therefore, whilst using the umbrella term "trans feminist" to draw attention to the fact that trans feminist epistemologies have been around for as long as feminism has, throughout the chapter I will weave this collective categorisation with a faithfulness to the subjectivities and identities expressed.

Taking the self-authored narratives of contributors to the *JMF* at face value is additionally important given that a more presentist interpretation of the identities constructed might read the largely heterosexual crossdressers of the *JMF* as "tragic figures who could never be their 'true' selves'" (Harsin Drager and Platero 2021, 417). Indeed, from the perspective of the present many of the identities narrated appear outdated or

[6] Virginia Prince, a pharmacologist and revered authority on transvestism by both the medical establishment and the fledgling transvestite community in the mid-twentieth century had invented the term "male woman", along with "femmiphile", as a way to recast transvestism in terms that made it easier both for individuals who experienced dual gender identification, and society, to embrace. For more on Virginia Prince's life and philosophy see: Virginia Prince, "The Life and Times of Virginia," *Transvestia*, 1979, 100: 26; Richard Ekins and David King (2005) *Virginia Prince : pioneer of transgendering* (also published as a special issue of the Oct 2005 issue of the International Journal of Transgenderism), Zagria (2020) "Virginia Prince: A Conflicted Life in Trans Activism" and Robert K. Docter's *From man to woman: the transgender journey of Virginia Prince* (2004). Robert Hill's *As A Man I Exist* (2007) explores the first US Trans community journal: Transvestia. It is well worth a read for its incisive exploration of how identities were co-created through the publications textual community, resisting the medicalisation and pathologisation of cross-dressing, and offering an early instance of trans community formation and expression.

anachronistic. Certainly, in the English-speaking Global North, the identity of "cross-dresser", along with the "transvestite" and "transsexual", has been eclipsed in the public consciousness by the ascendency of "transgender", such that these identities often imagined as "trapped in the wrong time or the wrong place" (Harsin Drager and Platero 2021, 418).[7] Yet not only does such a linear approach to identity formation overlook the felt, material and symbolic distinctions between these positionalities and embodiments but as Emmett Harsin Drager and Lucas Platero remind us, consigning these subject positions to the past, also buries "the fact that there are many living people who still identify with those signs" (2021, 417) and, as I will demonstrate, erases the potential of people who have lived these lives, to contribute meaningfully to knowledge production in the present.

The *JMF* deserves, as I am arguing is necessary for revisiting second wave texts more broadly, to be read reparatively (Sedgwick 2003).[8] Understanding contributors "according to the narratives they meticulously circulated about themselves when they were alive" (Halberstam 2005, 83) presumes that authority and authorial expertise lies with the writer, and reading is an act of listening not translation.[9] One of these narratives is the contributors' femme names. Following Ms. Bob Davis' discussion of the ethics of reproducing information about trans people

---

[7] See *The Lives of Transgender People* (Beemyn and Rankin 2011) for a discussion of the change in (trans)gendered identity categories used by survey respondents in the US of different ages. The authors found that while only 34 of the 3,474 respondents under the age of thirty-two identified as cross-dressers, 222 respondents over the age of thirty-two did.

[8] Eve Kosofsky Sedgwick (2003) proposed "reparative reading" in response to what she termed the "paranoid" critical impulses in queer theory, characterised by negative and defensive affects. "Reparative" reading in contrast allows for a more open and as I read her, vulnerable and affective encounter with the text. See Heather Love (2010) "Truth and Consequences: On Paranoid Reading and Reparative Reading" for a discussion of the distinctions between these approaches, and the value of reparative reading practices.

[9] Marta V. Vicente (2021) discusses the value of combining faithfulness to first-person narratives with contemporary terms like "trans*" to account for the historical variability of cross-gendered experiences. This is an approach also followed by Fernández Romero and Mendieta (2022) in the context of trans masculine identifications in South America. The authors highlight that "the first-person narratives and voices of these men appear in the archive, articulating experiences of their lives and desires that contrast with how they are produced, regulated, and inscribed within discourses of power by dominant institutions such as the tabloid press or historiography" (2022, 526). I agree that foregrounding first-person accounts is a vital way of attending to the variability of gender, remaining open to the multiplicity and mutability of gendered identifications at an individual and social level.

in mid-twentieth-century cross-dressing communities who often led two lives, I will use the femme names given. Davis writes that in contrast to revealing names assigned at birth, given that "these early trans* community members chose to put photos of their femme selves and their femme names in magazines and directories" (2015, 627), reproducing these carefully authored identities is a way of doing justice to the social and intellectual-history that these individuals created.[10] "These acts, risks, and sharing are trans* history" (ibid.) writes Davis, and therefore enabling these authors to speak to trans histories and philosophies under authors' chosen names, is an important way of establishing intergenerational and interdisciplinary dialogues around the lived history of gender.

THE EMERGENCE OF TRANS COMMUNITY PRINT CULTURE

Over the decade prior to the publication of the first issue of the *JMF* in 1977,[11] trans community print culture had exploded. Beginning with transvestite community leader, Virginia Prince's bi-monthly subscription newsletter in 1959, by the mid-1970s print had become for the trans community what it had been for the pre-Stonewall homophile movement; a central site for enabling the formation of community identities (Meeker 2006). Different genres of what can loosely be collected under the banner of "trans print culture" emerged in this period. At one end, there were glossy magazines like *Female Mimics* which were produced commercially, had a wide circulation and were easy to stumble across in pornography shops (Davis and Kleinmaier 1998). Whilst these were not produced by or for trans people, they were many trans individuals' first encounter with "people like me". Still commercial, but community-led and oriented, drag

---

[10] Femme-self is defined by Virginia Prince in a 1968 issue of *Transvestia* as follows: "'Femme-dress, Femme-live, Femme-self': These compound terms (and any others you want to dream up) merely refer to various aspects of ones feminine existence" (1968, 77).

[11] The Alliance had been founded a year earlier, and prior to its relaunch as the *Journal of Male Feminism*, the journal circulated for a year in 1976 as "*Hose and Heel*"—the same name that Prince had given to the first meetings of *Transvestia* subscribers. See Stryker *Transgender History* (2008, 54–55) for a discussion of the Hose and Heels club and *Journal of Male Feminism* Vol. 77, No. 1 (1977a, 1–2) for a discussion of the origins and early development of the Alliance. In its first year, it was for heterosexual male feminists only, and called the "National Alliance for Heterosexual Male Feminism". *Hose and Heel*, issue 5, (1976). In Francine Logandice collection, Carton 1.

queen Lee Brewster's highly successful magazine *DRAG: The International Transvestite Quarterly*, was launched in 1971 and had amassed a circulation of over 3500 within a year. Not dissimilar to the explosion of feminist print discussed in the last chapter, from the end of the 1960s gender diverse individuals were using print publications to make contact with one another and pursue prefigurative, legislative and ideological changes.

Second wave periodicals often served as how-to guides and for the trans community this aspect is particularly important. In the *JMF*, this practical information sharing took multiple forms: the Alliance operated a 24-hour helpline for those seeking "Pride in Female and Male Womanhood and Feminism'" (Stephens eds. 1977a, 2). Issues include the sharing of techniques and survival strategies: there are how-to guides offering cosmetic tips relating to hair, beauty, covering up beards and make up, as well as for legal issues such as how to change your name. There was almost always up-to-date information about electrolysis, and important facts for existence as a transfeminine cross-dresser- such as where to buy clothes or stockings in the right size, and safe public spaces to go when dressed. There are discussions of which hotels, toilets, and shops cater to cross-dressers and through the sharing of experiences and first-hand knowledge, the *JMF* functioned as an important resource for living a non-normatively gendered life in the 1970s.

The *JMF* was one of many underground, community focussed publications which served as a point of contact for those who cross-dressed in private. It didn't have a commercial distribution and, although the Alliance did live up to its international name- with at least one member in Mexico, one in England and a handful in Canada, the journal's readership probably didn't extend much beyond the approximately 250 members of the Alliance. The *JMF* mainly documents the lives of white cross-dressers, and a distinct lack of racial diversity is apparent.[12] The readership of the journal was fairly privileged: many were highly educated, had well paid jobs, and the disposable income to pay for the $20 per year membership of the Alliance—translating as around $80 in 2023 money). As such, many of the subjectivities and perspectives the *JMF*

---

[12] This is in contrast to other TV periodicals such as *Lavender and Lace*, which had a short-lived run in the mid-1960s (see Zagaria 2013). There is also more racial diversity in TV magazines such as *Turnabout, TV Times, TV World Directory* and *Female Impersonator Newsletter*—which focussed on images or classified ads and were often more explicitly sexual than the *Journal of Male Feminism*.

contains reify norms of white, middle-class respectability and domesticity (Skidmore 2011). Cross-dressing, or "male womanhood", is normalised throughout the journal, often through the reiteration of the heterosexuality of the majority of the community (and concomitant stigmatisation of homosexuality). One editorial explains, "As most male women are heterosexually oriented (the best estimates indicate the incidence of homosexuality among male women is approximately what it is for the general public as a whole) we have tended to keep our distance from the Gay Liberation Movement" (Stephens 1977a, 3). Many contributors also appeal to this heterosexual standard of legitimacy "I emphasise, of course, that I am hetero and really love women" (Jones 1979b, 8). Normalisation and acceptability for the community are therefore pursued through a distancing from, and perhaps offloading of, the taint of sexual deviance onto sexual minorities and more financially or racially marginalised gender variant communities.[13]

The publication evidences the appeal of mainstream feminism for a white, professional, socially conservative, middle-to-upper-class cross-dressing community and is not intended to be reflective of the breadth of trans engagements with feminism at the time.[14] It highlights the currency of feminism as a respectable and legitimate discourse of social transformation- in contrast to the more suspect and, at the time, less easily assimilable politics of gay liberation. However, in turning to one community newsletter and exploring the embodied and experiential knowledge documented on its pages, I hope to pave the way for trans community print culture to be consulted as part of and alongside an expanded canon of second wave feminism. In addition, I lay the groundwork for a greater openness to the

---

[13] See Joanne Meyerowitz's *How Sex Changed,* especially Chap. 5 "Sexual Revolutions", for a detailed discussion of these dynamics in the preceding decades. Meyerowitz notes that "Those who identified as homosexual, transvestite, or transsexual sometimes attempted to lift their own group's social standing by foisting the stigma of transgression onto others" (2004, 177).

[14] The Alliance had split from Prince's Tri-Sigma because of her hostility to transsexuals and her "one-person control and decision making" (Journal of Male Feminism 1977, 2). As a result, the readership has many overlaps and much in common with the *Transvestia's* community and the demographics are similar to those of Tri-Sigma. However, the Alliance it is not exclusively for "transvestites". Members also identify as transsexuals and some as transgenderists or bi-gendered. Others are questioning and negotiating their own gendered identities and subjectivities in light of the evolving taxonomies and categories available. The Alliance also operates has a far more open interpretation of who can travel under the banners of "transvestite", "transsexual" or "transgenderist".

intersection of second wave feminism and trans studies, and seek to demonstrate the value of print culture for exploring these epistemic and political overlaps.

AUTOBIOGRAPHY AND COMMUNITY
GENERATED KNOWLEDGE

The *Journal of Male Feminism* was largely user generated. Alongside standard content such as adverts for shops and services relevant to transfeminine cross-dressers, news cuttings and reprints of articles discussing scientific developments either directly or indirectly relevant to the community (one example is an article *Estrogen Therapy: The Dangerous Road To Shangri-La* (Stephens 1977b, 35–38) which links oestrogen to cancer and osteoporosis), the bulk of the content is comprised of submissions from male women or their supportive wives.[15] These submissions include creative work such as poems, fiction writing and cartoons. However, the bulk of the content is autobiographical: true life stories, accounts of "coming out"—to loved ones or at work- discussions of the pleasures of expressing oneself "en-femme" and reflections on Chapter or Alliance social events create an assemblage of first-person narratives about living a cross-gendered life in the 1970s. I will discuss the role of wives in shaping the journal's gender community and politics in the second half of this chapter. Here, I am interested in how the community generated, experiential knowledge facilitated the co-creation and negotiation of gender variant identities, and in the distinctly trans feminist perspectives on "sex", "gender" and "liberation" that these narratives contain.

---

[15] There is a reprint of a news article summarising the findings of the "[John K.] Meyer reports" which argued against surgical operations for transsexuals, concluding that they produced "no objective improvement" for transgender people (Beemyn 2014, 23). Whilst the handwritten editor's note alongside this comments that "I checked with two recognised professionals who are Meyer's peers asking if his views are generally accepted. I was assured they are not and that papers critical of his work can be expected. Your comments on this article are solicited" (Jones 1979a, 28)—the decision to include this article as part of a discussion, rather than downright critique, exemplifies the mixed "scientific" messages circulating via the newspaper cuttings. The Meyer report findings played a role in the closing of the John Hopkins programme for gender confirmation surgery in 1979- and many other clinics across the country followed suit, reducing the number of clinics performing gender surgery in the US from 20 to just two in the mid-1990s.

The space dedicated in the journal to autobiographical writing as a vital source of knowledge was a means for contributors "to give a voice to their self-acknowledged subjectivity" (Whittle 2006, 199) and functions as a counter-discourse to the prevailing "expert" accounts which stigmatised and pathologised cross-gender behaviour. Readers are reminded that "Our Journal is designed to help each of you in the cross-dressing lifestyle. Each of you have a story to tell. We need that story for our Journal" (Jones 1979a, 6). The role of autobiography and self-narrative in the establishment of trans imaginaries is well documented (Prosser 1998; Aizura 2018) and in the journal, the narrating of stories and sharing of experiences is central to the establishment of a collective consciousness.

Throughout issues, a constellation of identities and subject positions emerge as readers negotiate their own subjectivities and embodiments within and against the prevailing medical and subcultural discourses available. For example, "male woman" was a subcultural category created by Virginia Prince to emphasise the cross-*gendered* dimension of cross-dressing.[16] Prince, who was influential both within the white, middle-class

---

[16] Virginia Prince, as I discuss in Chap. 4, had become somewhat of an authority on transvestism by the 1960s and 1970s. She had written numerous books on the topic including: *The Transvestite and His Wife* (1967), *How To Be a Woman Though Male* (1971) *and Understanding Cross-Dressing* (1976). These were recommended readings throughout the transvestite community, and the *JMF*, like other community newsletters, would regularly list *The Transvestite and His Wife* on its recommended "books" pages- spaces where readers could find out where to go for more information about cross-gendered behaviour, experiences and expression. Prince used the pages of *Transvestia* almost like a blog for her evolving philosophy of transvestism and the *JMF* also published an article on masculinity and femininity by her in its first issue (Journal of Male Feminism 1977, 46). Prince travelled internationally, lectured throughout the United States, and was a close advisor to the most influential gender scientists in the United States: Alfred Kinsey, Robert Stoller and Harry Benjamin. Both within the transvestite community, and in the scientific establishment she was a highly influential figure. Her longstanding social organisation Tri-Ess, the name by which it is still known today, bought "a furtive transgender community into the light of day" (Stryker 2005, xv). However, there was a strict vetting policy- including the purchase of multiple issues of *Transvestia*, and an interview with an area counsellor. As Prince's philosophy developed, and she began to publish and lecture on transvestism, sex and gender, she distinguished the "true transvestite" (or male woman) from the transsexual noting that transvestism is purely about *gender* not sex or sexuality. True transvestites are "exclusively heterosexual... Frequently they are married and often fathers." She continues, "The transvestite values his male organs, enjoys them and does not desire them removed" (quoted in Ekins and King 2005, 9). Tri-Ess had begun as the Hose and Heels Club in 1961, before being renamed the Foundation for Personality Expression (FPE or Phi Pi Epsilon). In the mid-1970s it become the Society for the Second Self (Tri Sigma) (Ekins and King, 2005; Stryker, 2008, Beemyn 2014).

cross-dressing community and in the North American scientific world, had initially established the category of "male woman" to describe someone who understood themselves to be male in anatomy, male in desire (hetero-sexual), and who had a feminine personality. Within the shifting rhetorical landscape of the journal, however, "male woman" takes on a number of different meanings: "bi-gendered", "20% feminine", "womanly all the way" (Margot C 1979, 28).[17] The Alliance had been started as a splinter group from Prince's own longstanding cross-dressing organisation, Tri-Sigma, by members who wanted a break from her "one person control and decision making" and an end to "sexual orientation restrictions" (Journal of Male Feminism 1977, 2). As such it is not surprising that much of Prince's philosophy of transvestism occupies the pages.[18] However, rather than being deployed deferentially, Prince's terminology enters the journal as part of an ongoing process of identity construction and negotiation.

The understanding of sex and gender presumed by the category "male woman" that emerges in the *JMF* is more fluid than it had been for Prince for whom there was a clear distinction between sex ("between the legs") and gender ("between the ears") (Jones 1979a, 29), and a heteronormative presumption of sexuality as opposite sex attraction. Whilst there are many heteronormative elements to the journal, the membership are not exclu-sively heterosexual. Cathy Roberts, who describes herself as a "bisexually oriented" "male woman", for example, explains that "as a male woman" she prefers "male lesbians" to "homosexuality from a man who loves me as a woman" (Canon 1979, 48).[19] Roberts therefore confounds the initial delineation of male womanhood within a heterosexual framework, and in the process redefines maleness outside of the heterosexual matrix, wresting the category from any necessary relationship to desire. Roberts' identifica-tion is not only significant historiographically, challenging the "predomi-nant narrative of how *lesbian* and *trans* supposedly fell out of step" (Gill-Peterson 2022, 143) in the 1970s, but epistemically. Although con-temporary taxonomies avoid fixing subjects to the sex they were assigned

---

[17] I take the term rhetorical landscape from K.J. Rawson and Cristan Williams who apply Gregory Clark's concept as a "framework and method for analysing transgender" (Williams and Rawson 2014, italics in original).
[18] For Prince's philosophy of transvestism see Prince et al. ([1973] 2005), Hill (2007) and Ekins and King (2005)).
[19] The terms "male-feminism" and "male lesbianism" are attributed in the journal to Cathy Douglas, an Alliance member and contributor to many of the TV/ TS publications (Stephens 1977b, 61).

at birth, and therefore have no space for "male lesbians" (subjects assigned male at birth who express themselves in the feminine mode some or all of the time, and who desire women), their presence in the archive points to a complex understanding of the relationship between sex, gender and desire that both queers and trans' the heterosexual matrix. "Male woman" therefore appears in the journal as an umbrella term for a spectrum of transfeminine genders and sexualities including, but not limited to, periodic cross-dressers, bi-gendered men who are in the closet, those that are out to their families, and those that identify as transgenderist or transsexual and lived full-time in the opposite gender role. In refusing the coercive character of the binary, and challenging the cultural devaluation of the feminine by elevating typically feminine characteristics such as "a much greater capacity to give and receive love and affection" (Canon 1979, 48), Roberts' letter reads as an example of trans feminism circulating at the time of the second wave.

As a platform where contributors are able to narrate their own unique embodiments, subjectivities and desires, prevailing medical and subcultural vernaculars are destabilised throughout the journal. There is no one authority on the meaning of male womanhood and the pages are a space where both individual and collective identities can be expressed, negotiated and contested. The open listings where members wanting to make contact with one another can post their contact details create a place for additional categories and identifications to be voiced: "dresses at home", "dearly love to dress, and do so every day", "in closet" (e.g. Stephens 1977b, 5). These listings enabled members to meet others who would only know them as their femme selves, therefore offering an important space for both contact with others and the crafting of one's femme identity. By writing in as themselves, the readership of the *JMF* are crafting and sharing identities that resist cisnormative alignments of sex and gender, and creating spaces for self-determination and the externalisation of interior subjectivities.

Despite the contradictory inclusion of questionable scientific news articles, contributors and editors are clear that the membership is the best authority on gender related issues. "So-called experts" are regularly taken to task for their ignorance on gender issues. Linda B for example writes, "For what my judgement is worth, I will say that all reputable books and articles I have read on such matters are in error to the point that one wonders if sociologists and psychologists falsify deliberately. The answer is no they don't, but the results are as if they did" (Linda B, in Canon 1979,

32). By contrast, there is a strong faith in the ability of the membership to inform one another, and to generate the shared knowledge that would lead to public acceptance of femininity in subjects assigned male at birth. As an editorial by Susan Canon makes clear,

> Our Journal, then, is in a position to be the leading journal of opinion on our subjects [...] One thing is clear: we must have input, a direct input of experiences, from the membership. We cannot be factual, authoritative, believable, on the basis of what poorly briefed reporters and psychologists say about us. We must go back to the sources again and again; and on most of our subjects, our sources are not Freud or Kinsey or Johns Hopkins or the nearby Gender Orientation enthusiast. The sources of knowledge about ourselves are ourselves. (Canon 1979, 4–5)

Canon proposes that the journal, and individuals' experiences, can combine to create a community-generated sociology of the self, offering readers the necessary reassurance that "your experience will be taken seriously as primary data about ourselves" (ibid., 5). This is reflected in a letter to the editor in an earlier issue by Micheline Johnson, which ends: "Please excuse this outpouring of personal thoughts, but I think it would be healthy for our community if more of us did, so that we can compare our thinking with that of others, and see how we differ or are similar" (Stephens 1977a, 27). Contributors partake in "an active, iterative process of forging new conceptual understandings of gender and the possibilities for gendered subjectivity" (Meadow 2016, 322) and by sharing experiences of their femme selves and femme subjectivities, both individual and communal identities are negotiated and established.

In the context of the Chicana feminist print culture of the period, Maylei Blackwell has discussed the translocal strategy where "regional updates and differences would be shared, as part of the formulation of a larger imagined community, enabling the "multiple political and regional meanings of Chicana identities" to generativity co-exist (Blackwell 2003, 73). A similar translocalism is present in the JMF too, which includes member's reflections on local Chapter events, or larger national TV gatherings. These offer a space for processing the experience of being able to go out of the house as one's femme self, including the expressions of exhilaration and self-acceptance that this gave rise to. After one dinner, Gypsy, a subscriber to the Journal and member of the Alliance, wrote in to the editor, thanking the organisers of the Baltimore DC Alliance Dinner Party and sharing her experience:

> The dinner Saturday night was my first public appearance [...] It also left me with a real sense of acceptance, for probably the first time in my life and as I write this I wonder how many male women have yet to venture outside and be able to feel all these beautiful and wonderful feelings that I felt Saturday night. (Stephens 1977a, 28)

Gypsy's encouragement of other readers to participate in the next Chapter event so that they too can step out of the "locked room" stage and "experience the happiness and reassurance that came with greater degrees of sociality and interaction" was a common feature of this reflective form of submission (Hill 2007, 109). Documenting the joys that going out "en-femme" gave rise to becomes central both for self-affirmation and the creation of "care webs" (Malatino 2022). Through the detailed reflections on the pleasures of navigating the world in feminine dress, contributions to the *JMF* not only normalise and celebrate feminine expression in subjects assigned male at birth, but contribute to a second wave trans feminist standpoint theory, where the particular challenges the universal, and the authority of experts is collectively refused.

The affect of the journal is therefore demonstrably positive. Editorials and submissions regularly address the readership in fond, loving terms: "You people are neat. I really love all of you very much" (Jones eds. 1979a, 9) writes chairperson Glenda Rene Jones, and "The Alliance is by far and away the most interesting and beautiful group of people I have ever met anywhere [...] I love you from the bottom of my heart" (Jones eds. 1979b, 30). Reflecting on a social event, Alice and Corrine end "Y'all stay as sweet and lovely as you are: We luvs y'all" (Stephens eds. 1977a, 8). By celebrating their own and one another's femme selves, prevailing associations of cross-dressing with shame and secrecy are contested. This valorisation of joyful experience as relevant epistemology was distinctly important for the consolidation of an early trans community who would, until recently, have encountered one another chiefly, if at all, through police and psychiatric stories, and sensationalised media coverage.

Photography, Autobiography, Epistemology

Chase Joynt and Harsin Drager write that in the establishment and communication of trans epistemologies there is a "dialectical relationship between autobiography and photography" (2019, 3; see also Lehner 2022), and in the *JMF* the visual register enables Alliance members to experience themselves within a broader cross-dressing community. Photos are highly valued, cultivating visibility among a community that was otherwise hidden, and readers are constantly enlisted to send in more pictures: "One picture is worth a thousand words" (Stephens 1977a, 18) an editorial writes, soliciting more photos from members. Internal realities are externalised through dress, and then submitted for recognition by the rest of the readership. The dedication of space for photos of members creates a "visual archive of photographic presentations of self" (Hill 2007, 42). The images affirm members' femininity and allow for the externalisation of subjectivity and the visual transmission of felt knowledges. Submitting a photo of oneself "en-femme" is also central to the claiming of one's own subjectivity and agency. As home snapshots take the place of medical mugshots (see Joynt and Drager 2019), contributors are able to reverse the clinical gaze, taking control of one's own image and the meanings it transmits.

Alongside an editorial discussing Anita Bryant's assault on lesbian and gay rights, is a photograph of "Canadian Alliance gal" Micheline Johnson perched on the side of an armchair, wearing a knee-length black skirt and a white shirt with a sleeveless cardigan on top. In keeping with the Alliance's aesthetic which mandated a no '"swinger" or "drag queen" type of image', her sandals have a small heel, her make up is minimal and the background is a simple white wall with a bookshelf on one side. The accompanying caption: 'A penny for your thoughts. They seem serious', addresses Micheline's formal style and concentrated expression.[20] On the following page, alongside newspaper cuttings, is a slightly more party-ready Cathy P, in a white blouse and a bouffant skirt just grazing her knees. Exemplifying a trans feminist version of what Kathryn Thomas Flannery describes as the "darkly comic" (2005, 39) character of many feminist periodicals from the period

---

[20] There were a wide variety of transvestite community publications circulating throughout the 1970s. Many of those produced by and for "the community" had a much more open policy on nudity and sexual expression. These include *TV Times, TV World Directory, Transvestite Photo club Magazine, Image, New Trenns, Empathy, The Transvestite.* (In Francine Logandice collection, Carton 1 and Carton 2).

the caption this time reads: "All dressed up and nowhere to go" (Stephens 1977a, 4). The interspersion of these loving photographs of members, regularly accompanied by tongue-in-cheek captions, highlights the central-ity of photographic contributions in community formation. As one Alliance member Sherri emphatically explains, the photos have a transformative effect on her own sense of self: "relieve tension is not the word for what those pictures have done for me. More like released me from my closet of torture, dark dungeon of invisibility" (Journal of Male Feminism 1977, 28). Autobiography and photography are thus thoroughly entangled in the publication's principal ambition to "be the leading journal of opinion on our subjects" (Canon 1979, 32).[21]

As a site where narratives of belonging are produced, the images also function to communicate standards regarding the respectable cross-dresser style, thereby circumscribing the borders of the community. Editors publish a clear set of decency standards: "What we do not want to publish are: (1) Only pictures of people standing by a motel door, (2) pornography, and (3) gaudy cheesecake and flashy drag-queen crap. We simply wish to document our female and male women in everyday situa-tions having a good time in a proud and unashamed manner" (Stephens 1977a, 18). Whilst pride and avoiding shame are central to the transmis-sion of images, more sexualised styles of cross-dressing remain stigma-tised. Robert Hill has outlined how the cross-dressing community of Prince's publication *Transvestia* were bound by post war norms of bour-geois respectability, cultivating "tasteful and respectable" (2007, 8) clothing styles and likewise the femme attire of *JMF* contributors is rela-tively conservative. The majority of Alliance members were professional white, heterosexual men with families and secure employment and the fashion is imbued with signifiers of white, middle-class, respectability: most members' fashion reflecting that of "the suburban housewife" (Hill 2007, 9) of 1950s America. Given the social standing that contributors had access to, they had "a lot to lose" in their male lives, and therefore negotiating "appropriateness" was a means of holding onto well paid,

---

[21] For more on the significance of images and the visual for queer and trans politics see: Lewin and Jenzen (2023) and Olu Jenzen and Tessa Lewin's special issue of *The Journal of Cultural Analysis and Social Change* (2022), especially Ace Lehner's "The Transgender Flipping Point".

professional jobs and nuclear families.[22] Alongside these pragmatic considerations, a racialised, homophobic and class bias led the male women of the *JMF* to regard "camp" or sexualised expressions of femininity as tacky and inauthentic. This community sought to present themselves as simply "plan, ordinary, basic, dull, hetero TVs" (DiCesare 2020) and therefore as no threat to racial capitalism or the status quo. The community imagined and established on the pages of the *JMF*, is one of "normal" (read white, middle-class, professional) men, seeking to be free from the arbitrary social restrictions that prevent the wearing of feminine dress and expression in subjects assigned male at birth.

By writing in and sharing experiences, descriptions and photographs, these male women and their wives created an archive of trans embodiment at the time of the feminist second wave. Historians and archivists who have studied similar cross-dressing communities in the US in the 1950s, 1960s and 1970s agree that whilst they may not have used the term "trans" for themselves, these individuals- their "acts, risks and sharing" (Davis 2015, 627) are an important part of trans* history (e.g., Hill 2007; Davis 2015; Beemyn and Fairfax 2021). In resisting the authority of experts, and deferring to one another, contributors to the *JMF* created a lexicon and community outside of the dominant patriarchal, cisnormative and medical categories available. By becoming themselves and supporting each other in the process of doing so, readers are collectively, caringly creating the conditions for trans embodiments to be explored, expressed and celebrated.

FEELING LIKE A WOMAN: A TRANSFEMININE PHENOMENOLOGY OF WOMANHOOD

The male women of the *JMF* can also be read as contributing to second wave feminist perspectives on sex, gender and womanhood. Contributors share lived experiences of gender fluidity, are clear that womanhood is attainable to anyone who desires it, and that there is no necessary relation between sex and gender. Lorean Lee St. Grace, in an article discussing her experience of coming out of the closet, for example, writes, "I am a woman now, though the clothes I wear don't necessarily dictate my sex, it has

---

[22] I take the notion of "a lot to lose in their male lives" from Ms. Bob Davis' discussion of the Trans* Women of Casa Susanna (2015, 526), a hide-away resort for a community of cross-dressers who also had similar professional and family lives to maintain as many readers of the *JMF*.

helped me to feel more apart of the world. Regardless of my physical body may tell me, I am a woman" (Jones 1979a, 26). Here St Grace articulates the trans feminist insight that anatomy implies nothing about sex/gender and that womanhood is a category to be assumed rather than assigned. Merissa Sherrill Lynn, in a submission titled "A Reason to Cross Dress", articulates the feelings of self-acceptance that come through transcending the gender binary: "There is really no describing the sense of satisfaction the sense of completeness, of wholeness, and of a unique sense of wisdom that being able to transcend gender distinctions affords me. I am at peace with my masculinity because I am finally at peace with my femininity" (Jones 1979a, 11). In contrast to associations of second wave feminism with essentialist perspectives on sex and gender, the *JMF* reflects an alternative phenomenological account of womanhood, where what constitutes *being* a woman is *feeling* like a woman. You can be a woman on a full-time basis, a part-time basis or not at all.[23]

One part-time woman, Patricia Louise, explains her sensual investment in being a woman "It's so delightful. So much fun in being, becoming- a woman. It's a feeling- a state of being- a condition which a non-caring, non-understanding person (male or female; family or stranger) can't comprehend" (Canon 1979, 49). Patricia Louise draws on Prince's transvestite philosophy of "dual personality expression", wherein transvestites navigate two differently gendered words, and maintained two distinct personalities: "a feminine persona or personality with hobbies, interests and personality quirks distinct from those belonging to their "masculine selves"" (Hill 2007, 9). "To me there is no incongruity-Patricia and Paul are part of a single entity- and that is why (I believe) I have been so successful as a Personal Relations Manager" (Canon 1979, 49). Here gender is presented as both an achievement, a successful performance, but also something innately and deeply sensed. Whilst not essentialist then, there is a materialism of sorts in the contention that this feeling, which constitutes Patricia's womanhood, is not available to "non-caring, non-understanding" people. Patricia's womanhood runs deeper than discourse and speaks to a

---

[23] Emma Heaney elaborates on the centrality of self-knowledge for a materialist trans feminist epistemology noting that "being a woman is, in part, a matter of self-knowledge, a self-knowledge about which there is very little to be said, and a question of being seen as or treated as a woman, an experience that is indissociable from the operation of "harsh" and stupid misogyny."

second wave materialism that resists ontology; it can, after all, be something that can be shed in place of business executive Paul James.

Offering accounts of "womanhood" such as these that challenge essentialism is one of the key contributions of the *JMF*. Moreover, the contradictions of a feminism which seeks to police the boundaries of "womanhood", that was gaining traction within currents of the feminist movement as explored in the last chapter, are explicitly tackled head-on. In a three-page double spread: "Feminism: An Editorial", the editor, Susan Canon, challenges the cisnormative idea that "womanhood" can be determined on either an anatomical or binary basis: "A woman is a woman is a woman [...] A woman with male sexual organs is conditioned in some ways in her womanliness; but so too is a woman 4ft. 0 in height. And both can be more womanly than a handsome female 5ft. 10 in. who has a dull face and no energy or enthusiasm" (Canon 1979, 4). Canon goes beyond simply reproducing second wave feminist discourses here and advances a distinctly trans feminist engagement with the philosophy and phenomenology of womanhood, offering a series of definitions of women that don't presume specific body parts. Canon also directly contests prevailing biomedical orthodoxies instead advancing a straightforward understanding of "woman" as a sign under which anyone who chooses to, can operate:

> We are what we are, and attempts to fit us into medical categories or even biological ones are so misleading that even the Federal Courts have wisely given up on it [...] The power to define is the power to abolish your existence by fiat [...] So I am not a trans-woman, or an off-brand woman, or anything but a woman; and I am fairly sure that my most basic conduct forming biological feature is the fact that I am over six feet tall and have been since I was 14. People this large live, I am convinced, in a different physical and emotional world from those who are five feet and under. (ibid.)

This combination of dry wit and direct engagement with the medical and juridical frameworks, is intended to expose the absurdity of a bi-gender system which proposes that two categories have the power to neatly divide and contain complex, heterogenous human beings. Moreover, Canon's elucidation of the "power to define" being the power to define out of existence, speaks to the enduring priority of self-determination for all non-normatively gendered people, and sadly prefigures contemporary battle lines over the parameters of "womanhood". Feeling like a woman becomes central to the meaning of womanhood in the journal, and this itself is a radical challenge to the hegemony of western bioessentialism.

In addition to contesting biological essentialism, contributions directly engage second wave feminist principles as important for dismantling not only cisgendered patriarchal inequalities, but the gender binary altogether. Second wave feminist slogans are reinterpreted in the stamps which decorate the pages. A recurrent stamp, "Liberated MEN are better" (e.g. Stephens 1977a, 9), derives from Prince's interpretation of women's liberation as the liberation of the inner woman in every man. Meanwhile, the playful yet sincere stamps "Stereotypes are a BORE" (ibid, 7), and "Biology is Not Destiny" (ibid., inner cover) both echo the mainstream women's movement's rhetoric whilst challenging its presumption of binary gender through the contention that shedding oppressive stereotypes is not only important for "genetic women" in their subordination to the male role, but also for those assigned male at birth—who are unable to access conventionally feminine attributes, styles and characteristics.[24] In highlighting the coercive character of the sex/gender system for all subjects who find their gender role restrictive, contributors advance a distinctly trans feminist interpretation of second wave feminist principles.

One anonymous reader writes in offering her own understanding of what liberation would look like: "the issue is freedom from sex role stereotypes" (Jones 1979b, 22). Whereas the mainstream, white feminist movement had focussed on sex role stereotypes as damaging to [cisgender] women, readers of the *JMF* extend a critique of the arbitrary division of human characteristics to half of the population to those assigned male at birth and also revalue feminine traits that certain parts of the women's movement had accepted as inferior. Embracing femininity and womanhood in bodies assigned male at birth, readers are refusing the hierarchical and structural imposition of the gender binary and challenging the violent social structures of cisnormativity which compel people to assume a gender at birth and stay that way.

Moreover, in challenging the widespread societal devaluation of feminine characteristics and celebrating its flourishing in subjects assigned male at birth, the journal's cross-dressers critique and resist not only "traditional sexism" i.e. "the belief that maleness and masculinity are superior to

---

[24] "Genetic women" is the language used in the *Journal of Male Feminism* to distinguish between women who were assigned womanhood at birth, and "male women"—who were assigned male at birth.

femaleness and femininity" (Serano 2007, 14) but also what Julia Serano terms oppositional sexism: "the belief that female and male are rigid, mutually exclusive categories, each possessing a unique and nonoverlapping set of attributes, aptitudes, abilities and desires" (2007, 13). Stamps such as "sexism is a social disease" (Stephens 1977a, 22) are repurposed to emphasise the structural character of sexism, not something that individuals or half the population do to one another but rather a set of processes that envelop all those living within the coercive sex/gender system. Like Margo Schulter's contributions to the feminist and gay presses discussed in Chap. 2, the *JMF* expands the meaning of sexism to include cissexism and clarifies that trans misogyny is an inseparable dimension of misogyny. Not only are second wave feminist principles engaged in the journal, but by framing sexism as a problem of the sex/gender binary, a distinctively trans interpretation of second wave feminism's key concepts is developed.

FEMONORMATIVITY

Whilst the cross-dressers of the *JMF* "transed" the meanings of "woman" in the second wave by clarifying that there is no one way of being a woman, the investment in the mainstream women's liberation movement as the vehicle for liberation from the coercive sex/gender system more broadly reads as highly utopian. Certainly, from the vantage point of the present, as Hil Malatino writes, the optimism expressed in these journals by transfeminine individuals' identification with feminism is simultaneously moving and saddening in light of the neglect and oppression of trans women by feminists that subsequent decades would bring (2021, 828). However, Malatino also writes that the "phrase male feminism indicated a *strategic* alignment of trans subjects assigned male at birth with the feminist movement" (ibid., italics mine), suggesting that rather than an expression of naïve optimism, the identification with mainstream feminism was politically pragmatic.

In the rest of this chapter, I will interrogate this idea that the decision to align with the mainstream women's liberation movement may have been as much of a tactical decision as an ideological one. Combining Sara Farris' (2017) concept of femonationalism (the discursive formation that co-opts feminist ideals into nationalist, anti-immigrant politics) and queer theory's critiques of normativity (e.g. Warner 1999), I propose that the explicit alignment with the liberal feminist movement can be read through the lens of "femonormativity": an appeal to feminism as a strategy of normalisation.

For Farris, the prefix "femo" names the mobilisation of feminist ideas for- in her analysis- nationalist policies. Nationalism is relevant to my discussion too. For example, there are patriotic appeals to the Equal Rights Amendment being "The American Way" and what is sought in the crafting of liberal feminist subject positions is a form of citizenship not available to other minorities. At a time when the legacy of "mutual aversion" (Meyerowitz 2004, 184) that had characterised relations between groups on the sex/gender margins during the 1950s and 1960s still lingered, I propose that the mainstream feminism held a legitimising and normalising currency. This is not to argue that the trans feminist epistemologies discussed thus far are also illustrations of femonormativity. As I have discussed, the anti-essentialism, revaluation of femininity, and reconfiguration of the terms "woman", "liberation" and "sexism" beyond a binary frame point towards a radical trans feminist horizon. It is here, however, in the disconnect between the radical trans feminist vision contained in contributions such as Susan Canon's editorial, and the relatively conservative version of feminism directly aligned with, via the inclusion of adverts for the National Organisation for Women, for example, that my question of strategy arises. After all, this was a moment when some of the transformations that contributors sought- the loosening of post-war ideals of normative masculinities and femininities- had been, to some degree at least, achieved. From sixties hippy culture to the masculine aesthetic styles of some second wave radical feminists and lesbian feminists, the direct correlation between the sex one is assigned at birth and the gender that one presents had been softened (Hill 2007, 102). Therefore, the decision to align with the white liberal feminist movement, which remained attached to more institutional routes for change and binary understandings of gender appears to be inconsistent with the more transformative impulses of many of the contributions.

When read through the lens of Virginia Prince's politics and philosophy of transvestism, the impulse to politically attach to liberal feminism makes more sense. Richard Ekins and Dave King discusses how Prince's goal was the normalisation of transvestism (2005, 13). She deployed the sex/gender distinction to argue that gender fluidity was normal, just an expression of the "full personalities" available to those who didn't restrict themselves to arbitrary clusters of masculine or feminine character traits. By contrast, sex was fixed. Despite taking hormones, she maintained a clear line between transvestites and transsexuals, on the basis of whether one pursued surgery for one's gender expression- and believed that transvestism was a superior subject position. The line between these identities is a lot less clear in the *JMF*, yet Prince's distinction between the "normalisation" of cross gender expression as compares with the more deviant or pathological identities of gay and transsexual individuals remains. Prince therefore viewed opposite sex attraction and external sex characteristics as the bestowers of sexual "normalcy", and distanced her campaign for transvestite inclusion from associations with the gay liberation movement (Hill 2007, 55–75). Reading the journal's feminism through an allegiance to Prince's understanding that normalising transvestism required forging gender identities in relation to white heteropatriarchy, it becomes apparent the mainstream women's liberation movement offered a vehicle for social change, without threatening many of the race, class and sexuality-based norms that an increasingly right-wing political climate sought to uphold.[25]

Femonormalisation interprets the appeal of the liberal feminist movement as the socially acceptable route to transvestism.[26] That the movement had achieved a mainstream status is flagged for readers by the inclusion of a cutting from the New York Times which announces approvingly: "NOW's new president, Eleanor C. Smeal, bills herself as a housewife, a description any good feminist would have disdained seven years ago". The article continues to reference the movement's deradicalisation, and increasingly mainstream, unthreatening status, as a positive development: "The women's movement is learning, as the civil rights movement did before it, that beyond the heady early victories lies the hard scrabble of institutional reality. The contributions of the women's movement have already been enormous, and it appears that NOW is prepared to lead the movement down the harder roads ahead" (Stephens 1977a, 37). The editorial decision to present this seal of approval from a mainstream

---

[25] By contrast, groups such as Queens Liberation Front worked alongside gay liberation. Formed in the aftermath of the Stonewall riots, Queens Liberation Front fought for and achieved important legislative changes. It overturned a New York City ordinance against cross-dressing and won the right to congregate in 1969- essentially legalising drag balls which previously permitted "men" dressed in female attire from taking part. It also fought for anti-discrimination against queer people in employment, housing and public accommodation. (see Zagria (2020), Stryker (2008, 96), Matte (2014) Meyerowitz (2004, 235–6)).

[26] Susan Stryker notes how the appeal to feminist rights-based arguments is present in the early editions of *Transvestia* in the early 1950s, which launched with the name *Transvestia: Journal of the American Society for Equality in Dress*. Stryker observes that this group "had embraced the rhetoric of first wave feminism and applied the concept of gender equality to the marginalised topic of cross-dressing" (2007, 60).

newspaper for Alliance members to consume, suggests that Malatino is correct that there is a strategic element to the feminist identifications voiced. Whilst C. Riley Snorton and Jin Haritaworn have highlighted that " "women's liberation" and "gay liberation" became respectable and assimilable through the abjection of gender non-conformity (2013, 67), the JMF indicates that this relation can be reversed, that gender non-conformity at the end of the 1970s looked to become assimilable through the women's liberation movement.

The discursive alignment of white professional cross-dressers with the liberal discourse of "women's liberation" (equal rights and inclusion rather than structural transformation), reflects the *JMF's* transnormativity "shaped by adherence to respectability politics, heteronormative standards, and class privilege" (Glover 2016, 340).[27] The relatively privileged preoccupations of the membership are also reflected in the topics that do and don't get covered. For instance, whilst workspace discrimination was an issue affecting all trans people, it is notable that the *JMF* includes multiple articles about discrimination in the army whilst sex work is never explicitly touched upon. Similarly, whilst there are discussions of border harassment, key issues facing trans women of colour and poor trans women were police scrutiny, surveillance, criminalisation and incarceration. Yet the intersections of transgender discrimination with the policing of other "problem bodies", such as sex workers and immigrants, is not explored.

The journal's aspirations towards normativity are most marked in discussions of the role of wives which occupy a significant proportion of the *JMF's* content. Robert Hill, in the context of *Transvestia*, explains how wives were central to the normalising mission of heterosexual, professional transvestites. Standing as markers of a cross-dresser's manhood and heterosexuality, "they served as conduits for the politics of respectability that infused every aspect of the magazine" (Hill 2007, 746). Alliance membership dues "cover two women, provided at least one is female" meaning that wives and girlfriends get free membership and are encouraged to join, to learn about their husband's femininity, and to relieve other wives of any

---

[27] Professionalism, understood as productivity, was also a clinical requirement for transition. Like heterosexual success (intercourse), employment was a standard by which the success of gender confirmation surgery could be measured (and the likelihood of employment prospects afterwards, a pre-condition condition for transition in the first place, discerned). This clearly exacerbated the class and racial bias of trans affirmative healthcare. See Dan Irving, *Normalised Transgressions* (2013) for a discussion of the intersection between gender normativity and productivity.

concerns- especially around gender and (hetero)sexuality. Wives put a big emphasis on their man's manliness when reassuring other wives about the benefits of having a "TV" husband, often through the appeal to hetero-sexual prowess. "Who is going to argue about the masculinity of the best guy you have ever slept with?" (Jones 1979a, 17). Their partners' cross-dressing becomes incorporated into the domestic scene, either as irrele-vant; "a harmless pastime", or an added bonus to an already ideal heteronormative coupling: building trust, communication and occasion-ally a more equal share of the domestic labour.

Given the white, middle-class norms of femininity that are present throughout the journal, the valorisation of wives is perhaps unsurprising. For the successful accomplishment of post-war, white, middle-class gen-der ideals, participation in the nuclear family structure is presented as an important ingredient. For the contributors to the *JMF*, seeking to affirm their masculine selves, whilst also enabling the fulfilment of their femi-nine selves, the nuclear family was an important goal. As such, there are repeated discussions about when and how to disclose one's cross-dressing status to your wife, and wives are described as 'class A' if they are fully accepting of their husbands' femme side, will support them, help them with their hair, and introduce them to make up. (They are class C or below if they are hostile). One lengthy article by editor, Glenda Rene Jones, titled "How To Catch a Class A Wife" offers advice to the "single TV who is looking for a relationship". Readers are reassured that "A TV who has his head together is a damn good catch. A TV husband is above average in intelligence, usually well educated and good looking". However, given that 'the "cross-dressing hurdle" must be surmounted', "the TV needs everything going in his favor" which means he can't afford to overlook "the old rule of brushing three times a day and flossing twice, seeing the dentist twice a year, and by all means the daily bath is essen-tially important". Where to find single people? Churches and special interest groups with a single's component—as an example "single back-packers" are good places to start—but beware, however, "single's bars can be very good or very very [sic] bad. Exercise due caution" (Jones 1979b, 15, 31). Finally, whilst it's not recommended to bring up cross-dressing status early on, later, and certainly before marriage, "the lady must be told" (ibid., 31) and strategies of how to ease her into this infor-mation are suggested. The centrality given to the role of accepting wives indicates a distinctly transnormative and heteronormative agenda to the *JMF*. The feminist subjectivity that emerges is one where equal rights and respectability for women and male women on a par with what white middle-class men are entitled to, is sought.

Femonormativity becomes a discourse through which the cross-dressers of the *JMF* could seek mainstream recognition and protection for their diversely gendered lives. Whilst some who were exploring their gendered identities on the pages of the journal did go on to transition and live full-time as women, many split their time between their male and female personalities, maintaining comfortable heterosexual relationships, often within a nuclear family structure, in their male lives. Returning to Andrea Long Chu's assertion that "transness requires that we understand, as we never have before, what it means to be attached to a norm—by desire, by habit, by survival" (Chu and Drager 2019, 108), the pull of heteronormativity and domesticity in the *JMF* is apparent.

CONCLUSION: TOWARDS AN ARCHIVE OF TRANSFEMININE EMBODIMENT

The *JMF* is one example of what Susan Stryker and Aren Aizura describe as the way that intra-community conversation functioned to enable the development of trans identities outside of "diagnostic categories". Through photography and autobiography, the trans individuals writing into the *JMF* "found new ways to enter into conversation with others about the objective and subjective conditions of gendered embodiment, rather than remaining mere objects in the discourses of others about them" (Stryker and Aizura 2013, 1–2). Embodiment and theory is entirely intertwined and external performances of femininity come to express the felt dimensions of womanhood that members acutely possess. In creating liveable lives in their chosen identities, sharing their stories, and refusing the authority of experts, the male women of the *JMF* transed and transformed the meanings of "womanhood" and "feminism", and imagined a future where gender would be fully self-determined and fluid, and femininity revalued as a source of strength.

Exploring how editors and readers of the *JMF* crafted identities at the intersection of feminism and white heterosexual transvestism, and how they resignified liberal feminist commitments in the process, offers an insight into an overlooked dimension of second wave feminism's appeal. Second wave feminist discourses bolstered the sense of community fostered on the page by offering a pre-existing script for the promise of liberation. Moreover, aligning with the discourses of liberal feminism was strategically advantageous as it allowed a socially suspect community of "gender outlaws" to distance themselves from the more stigmatised "sexual deviants" and to discursively operationalise an already successful and acceptable narrative of liberation. Yet in creating the space for a community of (white, middle-class, professional) male women to be established and claiming the labels of "feminist" and "woman" in the process, the *JMF* and its readership challenge the naturalisation of a separation between women and trans people in the prevailing medical and political culture. Throughout issues, via the *JMF's* invocation of male women *as* women, the category of womanhood is destabilised and de-essentialised.

Contributions to the *JMF* speak to a prefigurative politics, characteristic of the second wave, which put into motion the seemingly straightforward argument that what constitutes womanhood is feeling like a woman. That to *feel* like a woman is enough to *be* a woman in this journal, there is a phenomenological ontology and radical politics to be derived from what on the surface could be a largely liberal set of investments. Simultaneously straightforward and radical- what remains valuable in the *JMF* is a philosophy of gender where male womanhood didn't stand as a contradiction in terms, merely one of the many modifiers available to an ever expanding and increasingly differentiated constituency of politicised feminists. Following in the revolutionary upheaval of the first half of the 1970s, the struggle *for* women's liberation that was central to US feminism's second wave, was also the struggle over the meaning of "women" and the meaning of "liberation". The male women of the *JMF* played an important, largely overlooked, role in this moment of historical rupture.

That there are nuanced engagements with philosophies of sex and gender in 1970s community produced print culture, and that the experientially derived knowledges that are shared on the pages remain theoretically valuable presently, are not tangential to the medium. Adding the *JMF* to the long list of feminist print publications produced during the US second wave, complicates the idea that we can tell the history of feminism without centring the presence of trans people. The conversations in print clearly demonstrate how trans folk were working together to be at the forefront of sex and gender knowledges in this period and sought to update and inform the medical and political orthodoxies of the day.

The *JMF* also offers important insights into how subcultures can become scenes of exclusions themselves, and present cautionary tales about how border skirmishes and logics of disavowal ultimately reinforce hegemonic and oppressive norms. Pursuing a strategy of femonormativity and practising a respectability politics made possible on the basis of the whiteness and wealth of the readership, the *JMF* reflects a largely white, heteronormative and transnormative set of trans feminist interests. Moreover, what is clear is that rather than gender variance being the primary predictor of identification with second wave feminism, race, class, and style of femininity played an equally significant role in whether trans people saw themselves or invested in the utopian aspirations of the women's liberation movement: a future free of compulsory gender roles and the misogynistic devaluation of femininity, but which paid insufficient attention to the way that these experiences are always traversed by race and class. Whilst complicating a narrative of second wave feminism as trans-exclusionary, and pointing to a longer genealogy of trans feminisms, the *JMF* also demonstrates how the era's exclusionary dynamics were not just a feature of the mainstream, white middle-class movement and cannot be tidily mapped onto a mainstream/grassroots, cis/trans binary.

In turning to the physical archive of second wave feminism, I have asked questions about the metaphorical archive; the politics of knowledge production whereby certain lives are incorporated in the stories of second wave feminism and others presumed in advance to be other to, and outside of, this past. The material dimensions and the theoretical dimensions of the transgender archive are inseparable and in mining recent historical materials, I have sought to make an epistemological challenge. The *JMF* disrupts chronologies of trans feminism as a distant horizon, the transgender body as "futurity itself, a kind of heroic fulfilment of postmodern promises of gender flexibility" (Halberstam 2005, 18) and refutes prevailing narratives of second wave trans feminism as a contradiction in terms. Exploring the *JMF* has also enabled subjectivities and experiences that had previously gone unacknowledged-here trans women's liberationists- to emerge as part of various utopian investments in second wave feminism. That the contributors to the *JMF* drew on feminist perspectives to construct their arguments, complicates notions of a necessary antagonism between feminists and trans people during this era. By turning to one journal, produced by a community that would now fall under the umbrella term "trans" during American feminism's second wave, I hope to have laid the groundwork for a more plural understanding of second wave feminism: its actors and aspirations, and in so doing, to re-assess its more enduring political and theoretical contributions.

BIBLIOGRAPHY

Aizura, Aren Z. 2018. *Mobile Subjects: Transnational Imaginaries of Gender Reassignment*. Durham: Duke University Press.

Beemyn, Genny. 2014. Transgender History in the United States. In *Trans Bodies, Trans Selves: A Resource for the Transgender Community*, ed. Laura Erickson-Schroth and Jennifer Finney Boylan. Oxford; New York: OUP US.

Beemyn, Genny, and Jane Ellen Fairfax. 2021. Tri-Ess. In *The SAGE Encyclopedia of Trans Studies, SAGE Publications, Inc*, ed. Abbie E. Goldberg and Geeny Beemyn, 886–887. Thousand Oaks.

Beemyn, Genny, and Sue Rankin. 2011. *The Lives of Transgender People*. New York: Columbia University Press.

Bey, Marquis. 2022. *Black Trans Feminism*. Durham: Duke University Press.

Blackwell, Maylei. 2003. Contested Histories: Las Hijas de Cuauhtemoc, Chicana Feminisms, and Print Culture in the Chicano Movement, 1968–1973. In *Chicana Feminisms: A Critical Reader. Post-contemporary Interventions*, ed. G.F. Arredondo, 59–90. Durham, NC: Duke University Press.

Canon, Susan (eds.). 1979. *Journal of Male Feminism* Nos. 1–2. *Digital Transgender Archive*. Accessed 2 January 2023. https://www.digitaltransgenderarchive.net/files/7p88cg698.

Chu, Andrea Long, and Emmett Harsin Drager. 2019. After Trans Studies. *TSQ: Transgender Studies Quarterly* 6 (1): 103–116.

Davis, Bob. 2015. Using Archives to Identify the Trans Women of Casa Susanna. *TSQ: Transgender Studies Quarterly* 2 (4): 621–634.

Davis, Bob, and Carol Kleinmaier. 1998. The History and Significance of Female MIMICS Magazine. *AEGIS News* 2 (1): 2–3.

DiCesare, Morgan. 2020. Revisiting Transvestite Sexualities through Anita Bryant in the Late 1970s. *Peitho: Journal of the Coalition of Feminist Scholars in the History of Rhetoric & Composition* 22 (4). Available online. https://cfshrc.org/article/revisiting-transvestite-sexualities-through-anita-bryant-in-the-late-1970s/. Accessed 3rd June 2023.

Docter, Richard F. 2004. *From Man to Woman: The Transgender Journey of Virginia Prince*. Northridge, Calif: Docter Press.

Ekins, Richard, and Dave King. 2005. Virginia Prince: Transgender Pioneer. *The International Journal of Transgenderism* 8 (4): 5–15.

Farris, Sara R. 2017. *In the Name of Women's Rights: The Rise of Femonationalism*. Durham: Duke University Press.

Fernández Romero, Francisco, and Andrés Mendieta. 2022. Toward a Trans* Masculine Genealogy in South America. *TSQ: Transgender Studies Quarterly* 9 (3): 524–534.

Gill-Peterson, Jules. 2022. Toward a Historiography of the Lesbian Transsexual, or the TERF's Nightmare. *Journal of Lesbian Studies* 26 (2): 133–147.

Flannery, Kathryn Thomas. 2005. *Feminist Literacies, 1968–75.* Urbana: University of Illinois Press.

Glover, Julian Kevon. 2016. Redefining Realness?: On Janet Mock, Laverne Cox, TS Madison, and the Representation of Transgender Women of Color in Media. *Souls* 18 (2–4): 338–357.

Halberstam, Judith. 2005. *In a Queer Time and Place: Transgender Bodies, Subcultural Lives.* New York: New York University Press.

Haritaworn, Jin, and C. Riley Snorton. 2013. Transsexual Necropolitics. In *The Transgender Studies Reader 2*, ed. Susan Stryker and Aren Z. Aizura. New York: Routledge.

Harsin Drager, Emmett, and Lucas Platero. 2021. At the Margins of Time and Place. *TSQ: Transgender Studies Quarterly* 8 (4): 417–425.

Hill, Robert S. 2007. 'As a Man I Exist; as a Woman I Live': Heterosexual Transvestism and the Contours of Gender and Sexuality in Postwar America. PhD dissertation. University of Michigan.

Hose and Heel. 1976. Issue 5. In Francine Logandice collection, Carton 1 Collection Number 2002–04. *The Gay and Lesbian Historical Society Archives*, San Francisco, CA.

Irving, Dan. 2013. Normalized Transgressions. In *The Transgender Studies Reader*, ed. Susan Stryker and Aren Z. Aizura. New York: Routledge.

Jones, Glenda Rene. (eds.) 1979a. *Journal of Male Feminism* No. 3 *Digital Transgender Archive.* Accessed 6 January 2023. https://www.digitaltransgenderarchive.net/files/np193931r.

———. (eds.) 1979b. *Journal of Male Feminism* No. 4 *Digital Transgender Archive.* Accessed 6 January 2023. https://www.digitaltransgenderarchive.net/files/h702q6560.

Journal of Male Feminism. 1977. Vol. 77, No. 1. *Digital Transgender Archive.* Accessed 6 January 2023. https://www.digitaltransgenderarchive.net/files/z316q178t.

Joynt, Chase, and Emmett Harsin Drager. 2019. Condition Verified: On Photography, Trans Visibility, and Legacies of the Clinic. *Arts* 8 (4): 150.

Lehner, Ace. 2022. The Transgender Flipping Point: How Trans Instagrammers Flip the Script on Identity. *Journal of Cultural Analysis and Social Change* 7 (2): 18.

Lewin, Tessa, and Olu Jenzen. 2023. Chapter 21: LGBTQ+ Visual Activism. In *Research Handbook on Visual Politics.* Cheltenham, UK: Edward Elgar Publishing.

Logandice, Francine. 13. 12. 2002. Francine Logandice Collection. Carton 1 and Carton 2, Collection Number 2002–04, *The Gay and Lesbian Historical Society Archives*, San Francisco, CA.

Love, Heather. 2010. Truth and Consequences: On Paranoid Reading and Reparative Reading. *Criticism* 52 (2): 235–241.

Lynn, Merissa Sherrill. 1978. Letter by Merissa Sherrill Lynn. *Newsletter.* Digital Transgender Archive. Accessed 31 December 2022. https://www.digitaltrans-genderarchive.net/files/dn39x152w.

———. 2018. *Merissa Sherrill Lynn: Her History As She Wrote It.* Independently Published.

Malatino, Hil. 2021. The Promise of Repair: Trans Rage and the Limits of Feminist Coalition. *Signs: Journal of Women in Culture and Society* 46 (4): 827–851.

———. 2022. *Trans Care.* University of Minnesota Press.

Margot, C. 1979. Is There a Cause of Being Normal? *The Journal of Male Feminism.* In Canon, Susan (eds.) *Journal of Male Feminism* (1–2). *Digital Transgender Archive.* Accessed 2 January 2023. https://www.digitaltransgen-derarchive.net/files/7p88cg698.

Matte, Nicholas. 2014. *Historicizing Liberal American Transnormativities: Medicine, Media, Activism, 1960–1990.* ProQuest Dissertations Publishing.

Meadow, Tey. 2016. Toward Trans* Epistemology: Imagining the Lives of Transgender People. *WSQ: Women's Studies Quarterly* 44 (3–4): 319–323.

Meeker, Martin. 2006. *Contacts Desired: Gay and Lesbian Communications and Community, 1940s–1970s.* Chicago: University of Chicago Press.

Meyerowitz, Joanne J. 2004. *How Sex Changed: A History of Transsexuality.* Cambridge, MA: Harvard University Press. ProQuest Ebook Central.

Piepmeier, Alison. 2009. *Girl Zines: Making Media, Doing Feminism.* New York: New York University Press.

Prince, Virginia Charles. 1967. *The Transvestite and His Wife.* Los Angeles: Chevalier Publications.

———. 1968. Observations by Virginia. *Transvestia* 9 (54).

———. 1971. *How to Be a Woman, Though Male.* Los Angeles: Chevalier Publications.

———. 1976. *Understanding Cross Dressing.* Tulare: Chevalier.

———. 1979. The Life and Times of Virginia. *Transvestia* 100: 26.

Prince, Virginia Charles, Richard Ekins, and Dave King. 2005. *Virginia Prince: Pioneer of Transgendering.* Binghamton, NY: Haworth Medical Press.

Prosser, Jay. 1998. *Second Skins: The Body Narratives of Transsexuality, Gender and Culture Series.* New York: Columbia University Press.

Rawson, K.J. 2015. Introduction. *Transgender Studies Quarterly* 2 (4): 544–552.

Rawson, K.J., and Cristan Williams. 2014. Transgender*: The Rhetorical Landscape of a Term. *Present Tense: A Journal of Rhetoric in Society*, 3 (2). Accessed 24 December 2022. online: http://www.presenttensejournal.org/volume-3/transgender-the-rhetorical-landscape-of-a-term/.

Salamon, Gayle. 2010. *Assuming a Body Transgender and Rhetorics of Materiality.* New York: Columbia University Press.

Sedgwick, Eve Kosofsky. 2003. Paranoid Reading and Reparative Reading, or, You're So Paranoid, You Probably Think This Essay Is About You. Essay. In

Touching Feeling: Affect, Pedagogy, Performativity, 123–152. Durham: Duke University Press.

Serano, Julia. 2007. *Whipping Girl: A Transsexual Woman on Sexism and the Scapegoating of Femininity*. Emeryville, CA: Seal Press.

Skidmore, Emily. 2011. Constructing the 'Good Transsexual': Christine Jorgensen, Whiteness, and Heteronormativity in the Mid-Twentieth-Century Press. *Feminist Studies* 37 (2): 270–300.

Stephens, Linda Ann (eds.). 1977a. *Journal of Male Feminism*. Vol. 77, no. 3. *Digital Transgender Archive*. Accessed 2 January 2023. https://www.digitaltransgenderarchive.net/files/9c67wm95d.

⸻ (eds.). 1977b. *Journal of Male Feminism* Vol. 77, Nos. 4 & 5 *Digital Transgender Archive*. Accessed 6 January 2023. https://www.digitaltransgenderarchive.net/files/05741r89r.

Stryker, Susan. 2005. Foreword. *The International Journal of Transgenderism*. [Online] 8 (4), xv–xvi.

⸻. 2007. Transgender Feminism: Queering the Woman Question. In *Third Wave Feminism: a Critical Exploration*, expanded second edition, ed. Stacey Gillis et al.: 59–70. Basingstoke: Palgrave Macmillan.

⸻. 2008. *Transgender History : The Roots of Today's Revolution*. 1st ed. New York: Seal Press.

Stryker, Susan, and Aren Aizura. 2013. *Introduction*. In *the Transgender Studies Reader 2*, ed. Susan Stryker and Aren Z. Aizura, 1–12. New York: Routledge.

Vicente, Marta V. 2021. Transgender: A Useful Category? *TSQ. Transgender Studies Quarterly* 8 (4): 426–442.

Warner, Michael. 1999. *The Trouble with Normal : Sex, Politics, and the Ethics of Queer Life*. New York: Free Press.

Whittle, Stephen. 2006. Foreword. In *The Transgender Studies Reader*, ed. Susan Stryker and Stephen Whittle, xi–xvi. New York: Routledge.

Zagria. 2013. Virginia Prince: Part II—Second Marriage. *Gender Variance Who's Who*, 15 March 2013. https://zagria.blogspot.com/2013/03/virginia-prince-part-ii-second-marriage.html#.Y6KPqezMI-R.

⸻. 2020. Virginia Prince: A Conflicted Life in Trans Activism. *Gender Variance Who's Who*. 31 July 2020. https://www.academia.edu/43755193/Virginia_Prince_A_conflicted_life_in_trans_activism.

CHAPTER 4

Andrea Dworkin and the Social Construction of Sex

The assault here, however modest and incomplete, is to discern another ontology, one which discards the fiction that there are two polar sexes
—Andrea Dworkin, *Woman Hating*

"Andrea Dworkin made people angry. In fact, Dworkin made me angry" (Grant 2006, 967) writes Judith Grant, in one of the few academic feminist retrospectives of Dworkin's work to emerge in the aftermath of her death in 2005, aged 59. During her lifetime, both within feminist circles, and in the mind of the general public, Andrea Dworkin was an incendiary figure. Anti-pornography and anti-sex, to many she was the quintessential man-hating feminist. Her uniform: dungarees. Her [caricatured] belief: all men are rapists. Fat and unapologetic, to the American press she was "the horror of women's lib personified, the angriest woman in America" and throughout her life, "Dworkin, the persona—the mythical figure, the inverted sex symbol—eclipsed Dworkin the writer" (Levy [1987] 2007, xi). She wrote in a lyrical yet uncompromising manner and her penetrating, unsettling writing style was intended to dislodge readers from the haze of complicity with the normalisation of women's subordination. Sentences such as "seduction is often difficult to distinguish from rape. In seduction, the rapist often bothers to buy a bottle of wine" (1988, 119) and "rape is in fact, simple, straightforward heterosexual behaviour in a male dominated society. It offends us when it does, which is rarely, only because it is a male-female relation without sham—without the mystifying romance of the couple, without the civility of the money exchange" (1974, 83–4) incited inflammatory and defensive responses from readers (Cameron 2017).

In feminist classrooms today, her reputation continues to precede engagement with her writing. Her work comes in for "derision" among students and educators (Walters 2016), and when her spectre is conjured, it is typically as the "censorial demagogue to shoot down" (Fateman 2019, 12). As Grant summarises, she is most commonly depicted as an "unreconstructed radical feminist whose rhetoric was an embarrassment to a movement now established in universities, with members who wrote for prestigious journals and were courted to publish with top university presses" (2006, 967). On the "losing" side of intellectual feminist history, her arguments are usually presented as exemplary of second wave feminism's worst excesses and "at worst, Dworkin is discounted as a ranting fanatic or irrelevant ideologue who does not contribute to real scholarship" (Cameron 2018, 22). More sympathetic engagements with her writing tend to begin with the caveat that she was writing from a place of pain—an assertion that contextualises her contribution whilst also discrediting her epistemic credibility. Her rage and her experiences of sexual violence are frequently evoked with the aim of discounting the objectivity and impartiality of her writing. Passionate and principled? Perhaps. Intelligent and theoretically respectable? Certainly not. Defences of Dworkin's work rarely extend further than acknowledging her own autobiographical investment in her subject matter.

Slowly, however, there is an emerging sense that it might be time to reassess Dworkin's philosophical and political contributions.[1] For

---

[1] Offering a vision of a world where sexual violence was omnipresent, and an analysis of the socially-sanctioned misogyny that underscores it, Dworkin's views on the politics and philosophy of hetero-sex have received something of a post-#MeToo revival. When millions of women across the world took to social media to name their less positive and decidedly non-agentic experiences of [hetero]sexual encounters, Dworkin's world, in which rape "is the logical consequence of a system of definitions of what is normative [...] it embodies sexuality as culture defines it" ([1976] 1981, 45–46) started to look a little less "hyperbolic and deluded" (Glaser 2021, para 2) than it had been received as being during the post-feminist, sex-positive climate of the nineties and noughties. The pertinence of observations such as the "a woman is only believed if and when other women come forward to say the men or men raped them too" (2006, 117) instilled a sense that revisiting Dworkin's radical feminism might have something to offer a diagnosis of heterosexuality. As critic Dana Glaser remarks, "there's a growing sense among some critics and feminists that this may be the moment we're ready for Dworkin; or actually, that it's been Dworkin's world all along and the rest of us are only just realising it" (Glaser 2021, para 2).

Katharine Jenkins, Andrea Dworkin "is one of the most distinctive and prominent feminist philosophers to have written about sex" on account of her arguments about the social construction of "sex in the sense of 'sexual activity'" (2018, 144). In this chapter, it is Dworkin's philosophy of sex assignment, rather than her better-known arguments about sexual activity—particularly heterosexual intercourse—that I focus on. I intend to demonstrate that when read outside of a presumption of cisness, Dworkin does not only have valuable arguments on the politics of sex (the act), but that these are inseparable from her remarkably trans positive philosophy of sex (the assignment). I will argue that reading Dworkin through a trans feminist lens according to which neither sex, nor gender, are binary, and womanhood is a category to be assumed, rather than assigned, demonstrates the overlap between [some] second wave radical feminist and trans feminist priorities. I will argue that existing engagements with Dworkin's work from both feminist and queer perspectives have overlooked the centrality of binary division to her critique of sex and gender, and therefore reproduced a cisnormative interpretation of male and female as foundational categories in her analysis—when in fact, they are the foundation of critique. Reading Dworkin through Emma Heaney (2017) and Hil Malatino's (2019) materialist trans feminisms illuminates a critique of "cisgender ideology" running through Dworkin's work. Patriarchy emerges not simply as a culture of male superiority and supremacy (although it is that), but also a "culture of male-female discreteness" (1974, 186)—which I will argue can be translated as cisnormativity. Bringing Dworkin's trans positive understanding of gendered embodiment in line with her critique of sexual violence demonstrates an important affinity between trans people and cisgender women, in resisting the violence of compulsory and coercive gender.

Considering Dworkin in the context of trans feminism is a fraught endeavour. She has been championed in recent years by people trying to bridge radical feminism and trans feminism (Mackay 2021; Stoltenberg 2020; Williams 2016; Duberman 2020) as well as by trans-exclusionary radical feminists who weaponise her analysis of phallic dominance to present trans women as "predatory, dangerous and essentially male" (Phipps 2016, 311) or to claim cis women as the only subjects of radical feminism, with a monopoly on the experience of vulnerability to violence. As a white, queer, non-binary scholar whose early encounters with Dworkin were formative in my own understandings of the complex enmeshment of gendering processes with sexuality, I have, like Sara Ahmed, wanted to "pass [TERFs] a copy of Andrea Dworkin's *Woman Hating,* a radical feminist text that supports transsexuals having access to surgery and hormones" (2017, 269–27, note 7). However, this chapter is not intended to be a straightforwardly redemptive project and there is much that Dworkin did and said in her own life, as well as in the way her arguments circulate, that makes me angry. She wrote a positive endorsement of Raymond's *The Transsexual Empire* (1979) the text which established the rhetorical counters of trans exclusionary radical feminism, and there is evidence of a friendship between the two that extended to intellectual respect.[2] Furthermore, whilst I did not live through the sex wars, I imagine that if I had it would be hard to separate the arguments about sex that Dworkin penned, from the attacks that she levied on fellow feminists' sexual practices.[3]

As with much of the second wave, I receive Dworkin's output as an ambivalent archive. Negotiating this ambivalence, particularly in light of the polarising interpretations of her arguments for trans positive feminism, I am grateful to Blase A. Provitola's recent grappling with Monique Wittig's similarly complex legacy (2022). Provitola notes that Wittig oscillates between being claimed by trans-exclusionary radical feminists as well as by queer and materialist trans feminists and makes clear that the goal of their contribution is not "establishing whether she [Wittig] was either of those things but, rather, reflecting on what we can and cannot do with the tools that she provides" (2022, 401). Likewise, the genre of my

[2] Whilst Raymond's book is a classic example of TERFism, as a surprising number of scholars in trans studies have noted, there are elements of her critique of the medical profession that, in different ways, are shared concerns for trans politics. Kate Bornstein for instance writes: "Despite her vicious attack on transsexuals, Raymond's book is a worthwhile read, chiefly for its intelligent highlighting of the male-dominated medical profession, and that profession's control of transsexual surgery (1994, 47). Likewise, Finn Mackay notes that "it could be argued that Raymond's main argument in this most famous book at least was not so much with trans people themselves though, but with the medical industry; indeed, this is the toxic empire that she refers to" (2021, 57). I don't want to reproduce, let alone defend, Raymond's dehumanising arguments, but merely point out that when Dworkin describes *The Transsexual Empire* as "challenging, rigorous, and pioneering. Raymond scrutinises the connections between science, morality, and gender" (quoted in Chesler 2021, 8) it was to Raymond's critique of the role of the medical profession in the regulation and control of gender and sexuality that she was referring. This is also, it must be noted, not exactly a resounding endorsement from Dworkin who made a point of choosing her words carefully.

[3] Gayle Rubin, Joan Nestle, Ellen Willis, Patrick Califia, Deb Edel and Amber Hollibaugh are among those whose sex-positivity Dworkin vehemently condemned, and whose intellectual and activist work I am deeply indebted to. See Fateman and Scholder (2019, 213–217) for a reprint of Dworkin's previously unpublished essay: "Goodbye to All This" (1983) which contains particularly hostile, demeaning and highly personal take-downs of pro-sex feminists.

engagement is not to propose that Dworkin has been misread or misunderstood, that the charges against her are misplaced or somehow overlook a context that would permit a more forgiving reading. I submit, more minimally, and more modestly, that she deserves to be read and that a trans feminist lens offers a valuable framework for doing so.

Rather than trying to smooth over the less palatable aspects of her work, this chapter focusses on Dworkin's arguments about the social construction of sex. In doing so, I seek to highlight both the presence of trans feminist epistemologies circulating in more well-known second wave feminist arguments, and the insight that these contain: that sexual violence and normative violence are both the product of cisgender ideology. The presence in Dworkin's work of an anti-violence politics that extends beyond a critique of violence against women, to argue against the violence of *all* coercive categorisation and gendering practices, is an important challenge to contemporary TERF arguments which naturalise a separation between the bodies of trans people and cisgender women on account of Dworkinesque priorities of taking violence against women seriously.[4] As Joanna Fateman (2019, 12) writes:

> In the feminist insistence that women have the right to make and use pornography, to choose sex work, to engage in every kind of censorial act without shame, and to do so as revolutionaries, Dworkin is the censorial demagogue to shoot down. But nearly four decades after the historic Barnard Conference on Sexuality, which drew the battle lines of the feminist sex wars […] and nearly three decades since the ascendance of the third wave signalled her definitive defeat, we hope it's possible to consider what was lost in the fray.

It is here, with the benefit of time and distance, and in the wayside of the sex wars, that my own reconsideration of Dworkin also resides.

EMOTION, EXPERIENCE AND EPISTEMIC (IN)CREDIBILITY

Dworkin's "unruly emotions" (Palmer-Mehta 2016) have regularly been invoked in order to discredit her arguments. She refused the detached, masculinist style of academic convention and frequently wrote herself into

---

[4] See Schotten (2022) for a discussion of two different varieties of TERFism: predation TERFism which argues that "trans women are agents of (cis) women's oppression and constitute active threats to (cis) women by their very existence and Extinction Phobia TERFism which presents trans people as a threat to (cis) women's survival (2022, 334–7).

her work, firmly believing in "the radical feminist maxim that politics should be based on experience" (Serisier 2013, 29). Dworkin wrote in *Right-Wing Women*, that "in addition to being too emotional, women can be too fat" (1983, 159). Dworkin was both. Frequently represented by the press as "the quintessential emotional woman […] angry, bewildered, hysterical, pitiably, and crazy" and misogynistically tied to her body, "the feminist as fat, hairy, makeup-scorning, unkempt lesbian" (Pollitt 2015, para 5), her contributions as a writer were drowned out. Throughout her life, her reputation preceded intellectual engagement with her arguments.

Dworkin was one of the first feminists "to use her own experiences of rape and battery in a revolutionary analysis of male supremacy" (Fateman 2019, 12) and like contributors to the *Journal of Male Feminism*, her experiences were her own data. After escaping an abusive marriage, Dworkin recalls that she "made the vow, which I have kept, that I would use everything I know on behalf of women's liberation" […] "I felt the need to try to make people understand how destructive and cruel battery is—and how accepted, how normal, how supported by society" (1997, 17). I receive Dworkin's auto-theoretical style and mining of her own experience as a valuable element of her second wave feminist style and indicative of the parallels between some second wave feminist and trans feminist approaches. As discussed in Chap. 3, autobiography and narrative has played a central role the development of trans epistemologies, resisting externally imposed expectations for what embodied experience consists of, and thus for the development of counter narratives and new taxonomies. Whilst starting from a very different positionality, there are methodological overlaps in as far as Dworkin documented her experiences of male brutality at a time when there was very little language available to make sense of what she had lived through. Her approach was phenomenological and structuralist, beginning with the lived body and extrapolating out to otherwise naturalised systems of oppression. Sara Ahmed highlights the relationship between the individual and the institutional (2017, 30)

> The personal is structural. I learned that you can be hit by a structure; you can be bruised by a structure. An individual man who violates you is given permission: that is a structure. His violence is justified as natural and inevitable: that is a structure. A girl is made responsible for his violence: that is a structure. A judge who talks about what she was wearing: that is a structure. A structure is an arrangement, an order, a building; an assembly.

Dworkin likewise pieces together her own experiences, and the testimonies of others who reached out to her, to theorise violence against women as structural. Not exceptional, but invisible—the product of the social meaning of women's bodies. Giving voice to her own experiences was a necessary first step to challenging an epistemology in which women's inferiority is so naturalised, where "one's body is always already under siege, in violation" (Doyle 2015, 50), that violence against women is invisible, even to its victims. Beginning with the embodied self, in order to illuminate the structure, aligns Dworkin's autotheoretical elements with trans feminism's focus on questions of embodiment and identity. For both, the aim is an alternate ontology—and this can be accessed somatically.

After publishing her first work of non-fiction, *Woman Hating*, in 1974, Dworkin began to tour the country giving talks and lectures. For many of the women who attended, her frankness, lack of shame, openness and commitment to turning victimisation into resistance, was transformative: "Dworkin would stand before her followers onstage, huge and hollering, an evangelical, untouchable preacher for the oppressed" (Levy 2007, xix). For her audiences, "Dworkin was a savior goddess, a knight in shining armor" (Levy 2007, xix) and throughout her career, it was these women, and those who, like her, had been subject to male violence, that Dworkin wrote for. Dworkin was uninterested in the emerging academic feminist climate and had no time for "cerebral wisdom or academic horseshit" (1974, 17). She styled herself as a visionary, a revolutionary and "a feminist militant" (Serisier 2013). Her goal was transformation.

Dworkin's political consciousness was also profoundly shaped by her Jewishness, a background she shared with other radical feminists at the time (see Antler 2018).[5] She writes that "being a Jew, one learns to believe in the reality of cruelty and one learns to recognise indifference to human suffering as a fact" (1988, 97). Her parents were refugees of Hungarian Jewish and Russian Jewish descent and, as for many second wave radical feminists, World War Two was an important background to Dworkin's

---

[5] Joyce Antler (2018) has highlighted how Jewishness is an overlooked aspect of many influential radical feminist's backgrounds and was central to "the revolutionary potential of radical feminism" which "lay in the way it channelled women's feelings of otherness into a protest against the social structures and prejudices that marginalised and excluded them" (2018, 16). Antler points out that Dworkin describes her Jewishness as "the background that most influenced my values". Indeed, her Jewishness is an overlooked influence on her politics and philosophy: "everything" Dworkin writes, that "I know about human rights goes back in one way or another to what I learned about being a Jew" (quoted in Antler 2018, 20).

thinking about violence and oppression. Dworkin describes being ten years old and watching her cousin break down during a flashback as she recalled her sister being killed in front of her at Nazi concentration camp as one of the most formative experiences of her life ([1976] 1981, 5). This was one of the first of three experiences that would go on to shape her vision of the world; one with untold cruelty, particularly towards women and racialised groups, but one in which she fundamentally believed change was really possible.

In her final book *Scapegoat* (2000), Dworkin explored, with varying degrees of success and sensitivity, the overlaps between misogyny and anti-Semitism. She argued that there were meaningful similarities between the treatment of Jewish people and the treatment of women; both feminised, demonised, violated and expendable. Sentences such as: "contempt for Jews is warranted because contempt for women is normative" (ibid., 102) and "if the Holocaust can be denied—how can a woman raped or tortured or beaten be believed?" (ibid., 274) demonstrate both her capacity for attending to the *dynamics* of oppression, as well as her flattening out of the distinctive characters of racism and sexism.[6] However, I take her Jewishness to be an important epistemological undercurrent to her writing, and one that illuminates Dworkin's commitment to an anti-violence politics that extends beyond an opposition to violence against women.

Dworkin's humanism, which I have argued is also a central element to second wave feminism more broadly, is apparent when she says, only half ironically, whilst addressing an audience of men in a speech calling for a 24-hour truce from rape: "Have you ever wondered why we are not just in armed combat against you? It's not because there's a shortage of kitchen knives in this country. It is because we believe in your humanity, against all the evidence" (1988, 169–170). Dworkin regards women and Jewish people to both be among society's devalued, socially expendable others. Like Margo Schulter discussed in Chap. 2, Dworkin is motivated by a

---

[6]An inattention to the specificities of oppression recurs in Dworkin's approach which, whilst often nuanced and intersectional, at times treats sexism and racism as theoretically analogous. See Rebecca Whisnant (2016) for a discussion of intersectionality in Dworkin's work.

Dworkin's perspective on sex work (which she terms "prostitution")—a job she had experience of—was that she was in favour of decriminalisation (1988, 133). However, she generally regarded it as an expression of male domination and believed it was a job that people entered out of necessity rather than opportunity. Therefore, she opposed arguments which emphasised women's agency in choosing the profession.

commitment to a humanism grounded not in an ontology of the European sovereign individual which, following Sylvia Wynter, is always already racialised (Scott and Wynter 2000), but a humanism understood as the end of coercive categorisations with everyone free to live their lives on their own terms. Her experiential knowledge was mined in the service of a complex commitment to theorising how otherness comes about and ending it. And she believed in the power of words, and her words, to effect such change.

ANDREA DWORKIN ON HETEROSEXUALITY AND GENDER

Dworkin occupies a narrative function within the story of second wave feminism as the arch essentialist. She is a "straw-person not just for gender conservatives, but also for the feminist third wave—a place where post-structural and sex-positive feminists can hang their critiques of radical feminism" (Cameron 2018, 38). Closer engagements with her work (e.g. Grant 2006; Brecher 2015; Jenkins 2018) have challenged her equation with essentialism, and read her as a social constructionist on the topics she is most widely remembered for: intercourse and pornography. To briefly summarise Dworkin's arguments on intercourse and pornography as they are commonly understood: Dworkin presents intercourse and pornography as the reflection and root of women's oppression (a circularity in her analysis that has been the source of much criticism). Intercourse is the lynchpin of heterosexuality (Fateman 2019, 30) and "intercourse in *reality*[7] [under conditions of male supremacy] is a use and an abuse simultaneously" (2019, 155). Dworkin doesn't say that all sex, or all intercourse, is rape. She is careful to cushion her piercing sentences with caveats like "often" and "frequently". However, she gets remarkably close: "Intercourse *often* expresses hostility or anger as well as dominance. Intercourse is *frequently* performed compulsively; and intercourse *frequently* requires as a precondition for male performance the objectification of the female partner" ([1987] 2007, 159). Pornography, she writes, is "the bible" of sexual violence ([1981] 1989, 68), "the DNA of male dominance" ([1981] 1989, xxxix). Pornography is understood as an authoritative speech act (McGowan 2009). It normalises certain sexual behaviours, and more often than not these are violent and woman hating.

---

[7] Catharine MacKinnon (2006) points out the "metaphysical distinction" between "truth" and "reality" in Dworkin's arguments: reality is social, whereas truth is ontological.

These arguments have seen her dismissed as both too radical (the logical conclusion is the end of intercourse) and too conservative (she has no analysis of women's pleasure) when it comes to the politics of heterosexuality. Dworkin, in the words of Ellen Willis, "reified the sex-class paradigm, defining it as a closed system in which the power imbalance between men and women is absolute and all-pervasive. Since the system has no discontinuities or contradictions, there is no possibility of successful struggle against it—at best there can be more resistance" (1984, 105). Dworkin's framework also offers no clear way for gender to signify outside of heterosexuality, therefore reinscribing the centrality of heteronormativity to gendered relationality. At the same time then, as Leo Bersani writes, the logical conclusion of Dworkin's views would be "the criminalisation of sex itself until it has been reinvented" and that until this happens, and until gender as we know it has been dismantled, Dworkin seems to argue for "the rejection of intercourse itself" (1987, 214). And therefore, whether reading her arguments as tending towards the promotion of politically correct (egalitarian, tender) sex, or the end of sex, for most feminists and queer scholars, the political application of Dworkin's arguments has been found wanting.

The focus on Dworkin's arguments on heterosexual intercourse and violence against women, however, tend to assume a cisnormative lens. Binary genders and embodiments are assumed and Dworkin's more radical arguments about the social construction of the categories "male" and "female" in the first place are typically overlooked. Yet throughout Andrea Dworkin's corpus, she wrote extensively on the social construction of not just sexuality, but sex, taking the naturalisation of a sex binary to be a central and distinct ingredient in the discursive scaffolding of patriarchy. Dworkin's theorisation of the male/female sex binary as socially constructed is a central component of her critique of heterosexual intercourse. Thus whilst she has been recognised (even if not positively) as a second wave theorist of [hetero] sexuality she also deserves to be recognised as a second wave theorist of cisnormativity. What I seek to propose here is that Dworkin's understanding of sex, gender and sexuality is one that advances key trans feminist insights: that sex is not determined on the basis of anatomy, that the imposition of gendering on us by others is a violence, and that embodiment for all people who do not have access to the always fragile security of white, cisgender, male privilege is, more often than not, hell. Dworkin was working in the second wave radical feminist tradition in which "to be human was considered by definition fluid, and therefore it was human not to fit into inhumane constraints and labels" (Mackay 2021,64). Sex, gender and sexuality cannot be separated in Dworkin's analysis and therefore her ultimate belief, that sex is fluid (i.e. her critique of cisnormativity) derives from her contention that sexuality and gender are too. Her utopia, as I will demonstrate, is one where everyone is free from the constraints of coercive categorisation, wherein there are a multiplicity of sexes, sexualities and desires.

For Dworkin "womanhood" is an internally diverse category, and what unites the category of "women" is not a shared experience (experiential essentialism) or biological features (biological essentialism) but a lack of bodily autonomy. Her feminism is clear that the central conceit of male supremacy is that women have neither categorical self-determination nor physical bodily autonomy: "I think that women's fundamental condition is defined literally by the lack of physical integrity of our bodies" (1988, 139). As such not only her philosophy, but her political priorities, share a trans feminist vision. There are oversights at every stage of her discussion; she ties femininity to subordination, making no space for femme politics, and has no analysis of unconscious desire or attachment; why it is that people want the things they do, essentially elevating political principle over unconscious investments. Nonetheless, as a theorist of the violence at the heart of compulsory sex, gender and sexuality, her work deserves a second look.

In recent years, these arguments about the violence of heterosexuality have been subject to valuable reassessments which release her from "the shackles of 'paranoid reading' that have befallen her writing" (Dymock 2018, 355). Katharine Jenkins (2018) and Jessica Joy Cameron (2017, 2018) have argued that Dworkin sees heterosexual violence not as innate, but ideological. Both argue that Dworkin needs to be read through the Marxist philosophical tradition of ideology critique, and that her analysis is not about men's biologically encoded aggression but amounts to "an interrogation of male supremacist ideology" (Jenkins 2018, 146). Cameron, likewise, explains that the radical feminist project, of which Dworkin was a part, is invested in exposing the "false set of ideas used to conceal unjust material relations […] in the interests of the ruling gender" (Cameron 2018, 7). Both, therefore, read Dworkin as understanding the "politically problematic nature of intercourse" (Jenkins 2018, 148) to lie in social rather than biological facts and see her project to be the exposing of otherwise mystified, naturalised relations of gendered, heterosexualised domination. These arguments demonstrate that hetero-sex is socially constructed, the product of a "particularly troubling representational strategy, not an essential truth" (Cameron 2018, 23). Instead of reading Dworkin as a "a victim feminist" (Henry 2004, 88)—who presented all women as overdetermined by their relationally subordinate position to men, and seemingly lacking the capacity for meaningful agency, pleasure or resistance (Segal 2015), reading Dworkin as offering a critique of the ideology of heterosexuality clarifies that her argument is the second wave insight that what we do in our intimate lives is not immune from the reproduction of social structures. Moreover, what is overlooked in Dworkin's work, and what a trans feminist reading illuminates, is that the naturalisation of heterosexual intercourse as the beginning and end of sexual normalcy is inseparable from the way that anatomical sex and dimorphic embodiment are constructed as the beginning and end of gendered intelligibility.

Dworkin's arguments about the social construction of heterosexuality and intercourse are intended to reach beyond an audience of heterosexual readers and include early discussions of the violence of compulsory heterosexuality for those existing outside of its logics (heteronormativity) as well as of the reproduction of heterosexual norms within otherwise queer relationships (homonormativity). The overlap between sexuality and gender in her analysis means that she reads heterosexual dynamics onto otherwise queer relationships and encounters. On the one hand, this contributes to accusations that she was a cultural feminist who argues for "politically correct" and egalitarian sexual practices (e.g. Echols 1983, 36). Whilst this, as I will discuss shortly, is a simplification, her rejection of all power dynamics in sex is what led to her critique of fellow feminists who engaged in sexual subcultures. However, she also argues that the violence of the heterosexuality (straight men over straight women) is inseparable from the violence of the hetero*norm* (to be a man is to not only dominate, but desire women; to be a woman is not only to be subordinate to men, but to desire that subordination). The compulsory, coercive character of heterosexuality is built into the very meaning of gender.

That Dworkin sees heterosexuality as an object of concern for all sexualities, makes her radical feminism more closely aligned with Queer Theory than conventionally presumed. In fact, her first published work of nonfiction, *Woman Hating* (1974) contains one of the earliest published instances of the term "hetero norm", well before the concept of heteronormativity became popularised within queer theory at the turn of the

1990s (e.g, Warner 1991; Cohen 1997; Berlant and Warner 1998).[8] Critiquing what she reads as the, heterosexualised power dynamics represented in supposedly counter-cultural sex newspaper, *Suck,* Dworkin writes: "but in *Suck,* as in the parent culture which maligns any deviation from the ole hetero norm, the hatred attached to the queer is very apparent" (1974, 86–7). Dworkin is using "hetero norm" here to delineate the constructed, compulsory and institutionalised character of heterosexuality, and "queer" to signal the abjection that attends practices and relationships that fall outside of the norm's legitimising purview—describing the same problematic that went on to become an object of vital and sustained critique in queer theory (Wiegman and Wilson 2015, 1).[9] Dworkin is interested not only in what the ideology of heterosexuality means for violence against women, but for the violence of gendering more broadly.

[8] Here is Lauren Berlant and Michael Warner's definition of "heteronormativity": "By heteronormativity we mean the institutions, structures of understanding practical orientations that make heterosexuality seem not only coherent-that is, organised as a sexuality-but also privileged. Its coherence is always provisional, and its privilege can take several (sometimes contradictory) forms: unmarked, as the basic idiom of the personal and the social; or marked as a natural state; or projected as an ideal or moral accomplishment. It consists less of norms that could be summarised as a body of doctrine than of a sense of rightness produced in contradictory manifestations-often unconscious, immanent to practice or to institutions. Contexts that have little visible relation to sex practice, such as life narrative and generational identity, can be heteronormative in this sense, while in other contexts forms of sex between men and women might *not* be heteronormative. Heteronormativity is thus a concept distinct from heterosexuality. One of the most conspicuous differences is that it has no parallel, unlike heterosexuality, which organizes homosexuality as its opposite. Because homosexuality can never have the invisible, tacit, society-founding rightness that heterosexuality has, it would not be possible to speak of "homonormativity" in the same sense" (1998, 548 n2, italics in original)
[9] There are also queer currents in Dworkin's "anti-social" writing style, and her visions for a future beyond gender. Alex Dymock argues that she deserves consideration within Halberstam's category of "shadow feminisms"—in which "negativity, rejection and failure mark a feminist resistance to patriarchal modes of becoming woman, and instead encourage modes of "unbecoming"" (2018, 357). Leah Clare Allen builds on this, contending that Dworkin is an "unexpected ancestor of queer theory" thanks to her "subversive challenges to mainstream culture" including her advocacy for androgyny and her attempts to write outside of standard typography and without capital letters (2016, 67). See also Dworkin 1974, 197–203). Finally, Dworkin's ultimate belief that heterosexuality is beyond rehabilitation also aligns her with certain currents of queer theory (e.g. Edelman 2004)—and these are valuable insights for reading the binary-resistant ontologies in Dworkin's arguments.

Connecting violence against women with the violence of all gendering practices begins to unravel the trans feminist potential in Dworkin's arguments. Dworkin, then, advances a conception of sex which is in line with Heaney's materialist trans feminism according to which "the actual provocation of trans femininity" is that "genitals do not ground sex in the way that cis people imagine, and all bodies can be penetrated and are thus vulnerable to social feminisation" (Heaney 2017, 6). Like Heaney, Dworkin's view is that gendering is a process which arises from the construction of sexed bodies into sexual subject positions, and within this social system, femininity is subordinate. In short, for Heaney, a materialist trans feminism recognises that it is the social symbolism of genitals that grounds a cisgender ideology composed of rigidly dichotomised sex roles. Reading Dworkin via Heaney's materialist trans feminism, therefore, offers a more illuminating interpretation of her critique of sex roles than queer theory and feminism alone have provided. Dworkin's critique of sexual intercourse through this lens becomes a critique of an identification (on the part of society, but also individuals) with genital difference as the sole source and site of sexed and gendered subjectivity. Heaney's materialist trans feminism, in asking about the power relations that accrue around symbols of sex difference, becomes instructive for expanding Dworkin's discussions of "sex" beyond a discussion of (hetero)sexuality.

"The Culture of Male-Female Discreteness", or Cisnormativity

Reading Dworkin outside of a binary frame, her arguments go further than taking aim at the ideology of heterosexuality and actually indict cisgender ideology. She uses the terms "patriarchy" and "male dominance" interchangeably, which has led her to been typically interpreted as exemplary of what Janet Halley calls "subordination feminism" (Halley 2006, 113), a view that fixes binary gender in order to present patriarchy as a problem of (M>F). However, this overlooks Dworkin's fundamental challenge which is to the order of the binary itself. Dworkin critiques "the culture of male-female discreteness" (1974, 186) and argues that "once we do not accept the notion that men are positive and women are negative, *we are essentially rejecting the notion that there are men and women at all*" ([1976] 1981, 110, italics mine). Dworkin's radical assertion is that changing relationships of sexuality will change the meaning of "men" and "women" altogether. In short, whilst her arguments start from a critique of sexuality as we know it, they extend to cover a critique of both sex and gender as we know them too. As Grant notes: "often overlooked is the fact that Dworkin called for the creation of a truly human being who moves beyond gender completely" (2006, 969). For Dworkin's feminism, the end of sexual dominance is also the end of sex difference. Her goal isn't just the eradication of violence against women. Whilst this was certainly proof of women's subordinate status, she rejected liberal aspirations to equality, noting that "a commitment to sexual equality with males [...] is a commitment to becoming the rich instead of the poor, the rapist instead of the raped, the murderer instead of the murdered" ([1976] 1981, 12). Her concern then is not only with gender hierarchy, but the gender binary itself and her goal is the end of the structures that create the categories of male and female in the first place.

Dworkin repeatedly characterises male dominance as a system "with an ideology and a metaphysics" ([1981] 1989, 203); the ideology is polarity, the metaphysics is the belief systems of religion, biology and heteronormative romance which authorise the very concept of the sexes. For example, she writes that "both conceptual systems—the theological and the biological—are loyal to the creed of male dominance and maintain that intercourse is the elemental (not socialised) expression of male and female, which in turn are the elemental (not socialised) essences of men and women" ([1987] 2007, 80). Here, Dworkin is going beyond the radical feminist argument that heterosexual intercourse is functional for reproductive futurism, to critique the notion that biological arguments about womanhood have any ontological grounding at all. "The attempt here" she writes in her first book *Woman Hating* "however modest and incomplete, is to discern another ontology, one which discards the fiction that there are two polar distinct sexes" (1974, 174–5). Dworkin's target is "the male sexual model" which is "based on a polarisation of humankind into man/woman, master/slave, aggressor/victim, active/passive" ([1976] 1981, 11). Her theorisation of male dominance does not reify or rely on the gender binary as critics such as Halley would presume; it takes this to be patriarchy's most fundamental ruse. Rather, as Judith Grant explains, Dworkin's analysis is directed at the "binary sex-gender-sexuality system in which all humans are divided into male and female and then hierachicalised" (2006, 969). A trans feminist critique of the normalisation and naturalisation of binary division is at the heart of Dworkin's analysis of the social construction of sex and gender. As a system, socially created and upheld, sex and gender have no ontological grounding. As such, Dworkin's analysis combines a critique of heterosexual violence, the violence of the hetero norm, and the violence of oppositional and hierarchical categorisation that precedes this. This demonstrates that her feminist and trans feminist priorities (opposing the violences of heterosexuality *and* cisnormativity) are inseparable.

Despite the discovery "that 'man' and 'woman' are fictions, caricatures, cultural constructs" (1974, 174), Dworkin explores the biopolitical mechanisms by which these sex/gender "fictions" are reproduced. Throughout her work, she highlights the role of the state and the law in regulating what is supposedly the most natural act in the world: intercourse. "Laws create nature—a male nature and a female nature and natural intercourse—by telling errant, unnatural human beings what to do and what not to do" ([1987] 2007, 187–8). For Dworkin, if the gender binary were "true", rather than just "real", it wouldn't need to be surrounded by a carefully enforced system of cultural scaffolding, and it wouldn't need to be to be so rigidly, consistently reinstated and defended: "Though some folks keep getting it wrong, law helps nature out by punishing those who are not natural enough and want to put the wrong thing in the wrong place" ([1987] 2007, 188). Dworkin traces the prohibitions against sodomy, the legitimisation of rape in marriage and the criminalisation of cross-dressing as all examples of the might of the state being called in to protect the fragile sex/gender system within which opposition and hierarchy are central to the social meanings of male and female ([1987] 2007, 197). As Fateman acknowledges, Dworkin's argument that "intercourse is socially and legally regulated to create and enforce sex difference and male supremacy" is one that many contemporary readers will have already reached "through Foucault or Butler" (2019, 30). That for Dworkin at the root of the sex/gender system is neither biology, or experience, but law—"these laws—great and small—work. They work by creating gender itself" ([1987] 2007)—reinforces the trans feminist potential in her arguments.

Given that Dworkin does not believe that there is any ontological basis to the categories of "male" and "female", how have they come to be so pervasive? Dworkin's account of how bodies are interpreted as "male" or "female" in the first place is remarkably similar to Judith Butler's well-known account of the performative utterance: "it's a girl!" (2011, 176)[10], an observation that is historiographically notable in itself given

[10] I discuss Butler's performative theory of gender, as well as it's canonical significance, in the following chapter.

how diametrically opposed their approaches are imagined to be. Whilst Dworkin is typically presumed to hold a characteristically second wave "coat rack view of sex and gender"—which holds sex as foundational, and gender as constructed—in fact it is the principle of division that is accorded ontological and epistemic primacy. Dworkin writes in *Woman Hating* "The culture predetermines who we are, how we behave, what we are willing to know, what we are able to feel. We are born into a sex role which is determined by visible sex, or gender" (1974, 34). For Dworkin, like Butler, "sex roles" ("male" or "female") are ultimately arbitrary assignations that are made at birth on the basis of "visible sex, or gender"—i.e. the possession of a penis or a vagina. Sex roles are binary, and like the contributors to the *Journal of Male Feminism,* Dworkin critiques the arbitrary carving-up of "human" characteristics into two, half designated to "men" and the other to "women"—with roles in sex, in the family and in social life being divided accordingly. Both "sex" and "gender" emerge as the ideological commitment to a binary world—the imposition of two options, two paths, two modes of behaviour—which must be completely opposite.

However, where Dworkin departs from Butler's influential argument about the performativity of gender, is in her assertion that gender performativity does not simply produce the truth of anatomical or biological sex, but that sex *acts* are an equally important aspect of this relationship. Dworkin agrees with Butler that masculinity (gender) is not innate, and does not reveal any inner truth, characterising it instead as an inherently relational, fragile subject position constantly dependent upon a subordinate Other for its existence. However, for Dworkin, this is why heterosex, or intercourse, comes to have a such a central place in her analysis. Dworkin writes that "fucking is the most gender reifying act" ([1981] 1988, 91). As Jacqueline Rose also argues, it is it "the great male performative" (2018, 3)—the way in which in a phallocentric economy the male confirms his similarity with other men and distance from, indeed disavowal of, the feminine. This quickly extends in Dworkin's analysis to sexual violence. If intercourse (sex acts) are necessary to confirm gender, which in turn is necessary to confirm anatomical sex, then particularly when masculinity is under attack, sexual violence becomes the means by which both sex and gender re-established, the vehicle through which a man confirms "that he is not her and that he is like other hims" [*sic*] ([1981] 1989, 107). Where Butler proposed that sex is an effect of gender, Dworkin's controversial argument is that sexuality also has a constitutive role to play in the successful performance (and

therefore cultural intelligibility) of gender. As Jessica Joy Cameron elucidates, it is not just that sex acts determine how bodies become gendered but
also that "the codification of bodies into discrete sexes and genders works to
codify sex acts themselves" (2018, 29). If a man is distinguished from a
woman by possession of a penis, and his social standing is inseparable from
the symbolic power it bestows, then "sex roles" refer not only to gendered
behaviours, but also to sex acts. Sex, gender and sexuality are thus com-
plexly enmeshed within Dworkin's analysis and her argument regarding the
social construction of sex is so difficult to accept because it requires a reconsideration of "the meaning of the act most of us take to be fundamental to
sex, fundamental to human existence" (Levy [1987] 2007, xv): intercourse.
It is therefore not surprising that her arguments have been so difficult to
accommodate. Accepting Dworkin demands nothing less than a transformation of gendered relationality itself. Her world is impossible to imagine
as it requires an overhaul in not just sexuality, but subjectivity.

Far from being a man-hating argument—a position which would have
her firmly wedded to a gender binary, Dworkin's point is to resist the idea
that genital attributes can imply anything about identity. To experience
oneself outside an ideology of cisness then, the symbolic reification of the
penis as determiner of sex role needs to be abandoned: "For men" she
writes, "I suspect that this transformation begins in the place they most
dread—that is, in a limp penis [...] I am saying that men will have to
renounce their phallocentric personalities, and the privileges and powers
given to them at birth as a consequence of their anatomy" ([1976] 1981,
13). Whilst biologically essentialist, trans-exclusionary, readings have
taken arguments such as these to propose that anyone born with a penis
and assigned male at birth is necessarily and always in a position of power
and privilege over anyone assigned female at birth—such a reading overlooks Dworkin's constant refutation of biologically based arguments.
Dworkin makes clear, in a statement that aligns her with vital arguments
for intersex rights (e.g. Morland 2014), that she believes "biologically
fixed, genetically or hormonally or genitally (or whatever organ or secre-
tion or molecular particle they scapegoat next) absolute" definitions of
gender to be one of the most reprehensible tools of "social and political
discrimination"(1988, 114). For Dworkin, identification with phallic
power—cis maleness—is contingent and a choice. If those assigned male
at birth interpret their own bodies differently, rather than relying on what
Heaney refers to as "the prop of sexual difference" (2017, 72) and what
Dworkin would add is also the prop of sexual dominance, then the sex/

gender system as we know it would begin to unravel. By focussing on the interpretation and social valuation of the body as the source of sex differ-ence, rather than genital status, Dworkin is outlining an alternative to the binarised, overdetermined cisgender order.

Both sex and gender are regarded as the cultures attempt to divide what "is clearly a multi-sexed species which has its sexuality spread along a vast continuum where the elements called male and female are not discrete" (1974, 183). Yet, for Dworkin, this is counter-knowledge that remains at the margins. As she sees it, the radical implications of this for the organisa-tion of society are such that they cannot be permitted and "the fictive dichotomy of absolute male and female sexual natures rooted in anatomi-cal differences must be maintained" ([1981] 1989, 149), with medical knowledge organised accordingly. Dworkin regards intersex characteristics as a natural expression of human continuity, rather than—as was common in her day—an error in the order of things, to be corrected by violent, coercive surgery. She finds proof in the emerging sexological literature on intersex—the same studies that would go on to inform Anne Fausto Sterling's widely cited challenge to sex dualism in 1993, and that I discuss in light of sexology's conflicted, yet undeniably trans, history in the fol-lowing chapter—that the categories of "male" and "female" are fictions as sex characteristics can't be tidily separated into two discrete categories.[11] Citing six different aspects of sexed embodiment, Dworkin is clear that there is no good reason to defend a sex binary concluding instead that humans are "clearly a multisexed species" (1974, 183).[12] The

---

[11] Dworkin appealed to the same research of John Money, which I discuss in the following chapter, to make the feminist case for "sex" being a spectrum, that Anne Fausto-Sterling (1993) would popularise within feminist theory two decades later. Moreover, Dworkin avoids the pathologised interpretations of sex and gender diversity that the clinical texts she consulted advanced, instead seeking to normalise, indeed universalise "cross-sexed phenom-ena" (1974, 181)

[12] The six dimensions of sex that Dworkin lists on the basis of John Money's findings are: "1. *Genetic or nuclear sexuality* as revealed by indicators like the sex-chromatin or Barr-body, a full chromosomal count and the leucocytic drumstick; 2. *Hormonal sexuality* which results from a balance that is predominantly androgenic or estrogenic; 3. *Gonadal sexuality* which may be clearly ovarian or testicular, but occasionally also mixed; 4. *Internal sexuality* as dis-closed in the structure of the internal reproductive system; 5. *External genital sexuality* as revealed in the external anatomy, and finally; 6. *Psychosexual development* which through the external forces of rearing and social conditioning along with the individual's response to these factors directs the development of a personality which is by nature sexual" (1974, 182, italics in original).

work of the American sexologist John Money, who I discuss in the following chapter, is among those she cites. However, in contrast to Money's
pathologising interpretations of intersex bodies, Dworkin presents the
existence of sexed variation as normal. For Dworkin, it is not that intersex
individuals need "correction" (i.e. surgical intervention). To the contrary,
the existence of intersex individuals should serve as a correction to culture.
What is pathological, and an expression of patriarchal reasoning, is the
denial of gender and sexed fluidity. She writes: "whatever we choose to
make out of the data of what is frequently called intersex, it is clear that sex
determination is not always clear cut and simple" (1974, 182). Whilst the
depth of "the commitment to human sexual discreteness and polarity"
makes instances of hermaphroditism "conceptually intolerable", in time
"we can presume then that we will discover cross-sexed phenomena in
proportion to our ability to see them" (1974, 181). For Dworkin, it is a
refusal to see beyond the binary that reinforces the exceptionalism of
intersex subjects, and once this ideological ruse is abandoned, intersex
embodiment will become increasingly recognised and accepted.

In *Queer Embodiment, Monstrosity, Medical Violence, and Intersex
Experience*, Hil Malatino critiques the medicalisation of non-dimorphic
sex and in particular the way that intersex bodies have been treated as disorders by the western medical establishment in order to naturalise a binary
sex/gender system (2019). For Malatino, doing justice to intersex and
trans lives requires thinking embodiment beyond sexual dimorphism and
therefore challenging the authority of medial discourses which problema-
tise such bodies. I read Dworkin as committed to a similar project.
Malatino writes that both the essentialist and constructionist views of sex
and gender are "unable to think beyond dimorphism, either as biological
truth or teleological manifestation". Both, he argues, are underpinned by
"a conception of gender as a stable, relatively static, durable, dimorphic
phenomenon that provides the fundamental scaffolding of selfhood: gender as being" (2019, 192)—and both these views enact quotidian violence
on trans, intersex, and gender-nonconforming subjects by proposing a
foundational conception of gendered realness. I have argued that, contrary to dominant misreadings, Dworkin is a constructionist—not only
with respect to the category of gender, but to sex. For her there is no
bodily foundation for sex, it is a political and legal mandate rather than an
enduring ground. Both sex *and* gender emerge as the product of a social
commitment to dividing bodies in the name of patriarchal domination,
which includes not only the domination of "men" over "women", but

also the division of the population into two mutually exclusive categories, fixed from birth. Dworkin's critique of sex and gender is located firmly at the level of the culture's commitment to binarisation rather than at the level of the body. As such, it is in line with Malatino's proposal to recognise gender as becoming and to think the sex/gender distinction anew (2019, 193).

Not only was Dworkin early among US feminists, and practitioners, to depathologise intersex embodiment, but her arguments present trans and intersex bodies as of unexceptional ontological status. She argues, for example, that "sexual freedom and freedom for biological women, or all persons "female", are not separable" (1974, 153), employing the modifier "biological" (1974, 67) when referring to what is now more commonly referred to as '"cisgender" women. This is an important distinction which resists the notion that those assigned female at birth have a monopoly on access to that category. Instead, "female" emerges in Dworkin's texts as a sign under which those who are "called into female embodiment by an experience that one understands to be feminising" (Heaney 2017, 294) can assume. Dworkin takes a universalising approach to gender construction (see Malatino 2015) understanding gendering processes to be applied to all bodies and her goal is a world where this is no longer done through violent interpellation (including violence against women) and the arbitrary restriction of half of humanity's attributes to half the population (normative gender violence).

What Dworkin presents as the distinction between "biological" and "trans" embodiment, is the vulnerability to violence that trans bodies endure in a society committed to a binary sex/gender order. In "the culture of male-female discreteness" (which I have been arguing can be translated as cisnormativity) "transsexuality is a disaster for the individual transsexual" (1974, 186). Although Dworkin writes that all women are oppressed as women, "every transsexual, white, black, man, woman, rich, poor, is in a state of primary emergency as a transsexual" (ibid.). For Dworkin, this means that trans people are *especially* or *urgently* oppressed on the basis of their trans identity. An identity "which brings with it as part of its definition death, is the identity of primary emergency" (1974, 23). And the urgency of trans people's struggle is what leads her to the conclusion, discussed at the beginning of this chapter, "that every transsexual is entitled to a sex-change operation, and it should be "provided by the community as one of its functions. This is an emergency measure for an emergency condition" (1974, 23). Dworkin is clear not only that recognition is essential for a liveable life, but also that this needs to be sustained by a material foundation—including free access to gender affirming medical care.

DWORKIN: UTOPIA AND "REALITY"

Dworkin was a gender abolitionist. She believed in the end of binary sex and gender at every level, from the personal to the institutional. This has made her arguments hard to stomach for most people who retain an attachment to gender at the most fundamental, often unconscious, level. Moreover, her proposal for how such a system comes about requires abandoning some of the aspects of existence; intercourse and identity, that people get most pleasure from.

During her lifetime, Dworkin's dogmatism led to further distancing from her arguments by feminists. Her contention that sex acts are always already encoded with the social, and violent, meaning of compulsory hetero-gender, was heavily resisted by "sex-positive" feminist scholars who argued that such a view overdetermines sexual intercourse, and leaves little room for meaningful sexual agency and pleasure. Whilst Dworkin offers a valuable outline of the connection between the social meanings of gender and fucking, it appears that she's so preoccupied with "getting fucked" and "fucking" as subordinate/dominant subject positions, she can't engage fully with practices of "genderfucking" through non-normative performances of sex and sexuality.

Dworkin was wrong that gender is overdetermined by heterosexuality, and this misguided argument demonstrates the limits to her rigid structuralism and the value of poststructuralist notions of resignification. She was wrong in her own time—when she chastised fellow feminists on account of their participation in sexual subcultures, and she is wrong now—when the rise of identities like "non-binary lesbian" demonstrate the resignification of historically gendered desires (see Hord 2020). Her gender abolitionism has also aided her weaponisation by TERFs, who argue that if gender is a social construct and the feminist goal is its eradication, then anyone who identifies as "transgender" is a dupe of "gender ideology". However, Dworkin's argument against gender was an argument against cis people, not trans people. Quoting James Baldwin, she argues: "It really is quite impossible [...] to be affirming about anything which one refuses to question" ([1987] 2007, 60). Questioning the norms that govern sex, gender and sexuality—in their hegemonic iterations, and the multiple violence's they induce, was both Dworkin's abiding offering; and where she left both her most enduring and regrettable marks.

Dworkin's vision is a future characterised by a multiplicity of sexes, sexualities and genders. Whilst she is both "anti-gender" and "anti-sex" as they currently exist, she looks to an alternative world characterised by pleasures going far beyond the heteronormative, ableist and, for many, ultimately unsatisfactory, if not simply downright boring, fuck. In this, she is aligned not with queer theory's investment of the subversiveness of fucking, but with trans and crip scholars' contributions to thinking desire beyond anatomy (McRuer 2006, Gill-Peterson in Aizura et al. 2020). Sex for Dworkin has radical ethical possibility, with the capacity to overhaul social relationality as we know it. What she proposes is a recognition of sexuality's multiplicities, its excess—an embrace of "erotic sensitivity all over the body (which needn't—and shouldn't—be localised or contained genitally" ([1976] 1981, 13). In *Intercourse* (1987) for example, Dworkin presents sex as containing pre-linguistic relational possibility. Like Lévinas' account of the "face-to-face" relation ([1969] 2013), sex is equated with ethical potentiality. Outside of the constraints of signification, before we are traversed by social categories, sex contains the possibility of non-egoic connection. "Sex" she writes in *Intercourse* "is the dim echo of that original nakedness, primal before anything else that is also human; later, isolated in an identity, hidden by it, insensate because of it, one is a social being ruled by conformity and convention, not naked" ([1987] 2007, 27). Sex contains the possibility of embodiment outside of the violence of identity categories and part of the problem of cisgender ideology, and the heterosexual scaffolding that maintains it, is that "it is built on polar role definition" and therefore not "authentic" (1974, 184–5).[13] Here Dworkin's arguments align with Marquis Bey's black trans feminist proposal that:

> Inasmuch as sex-as-act very often collapses erogenous pleasure to genitalia, trans with its troubling of genitalia as a primary site of erogenous activity and axiomatic designation of "true" sexed/gendered subjectivity, grows such a practice into at least a little bit of turmoil […] what possibilities for sex are opened up when transness unfixes genitalia as a privileged, fetishized,

---

[13] This argument can be read alongside Judith Butler's comments regarding the resignificatory potential of sex: "The construction of stable bodily contours relies upon fixed sites of corporeal permeability and impermeability. Those sexual practices in both homosexual and heterosexual contests that open surfaces and orifices to erotic signification or close down others effectively reinscribe the boundaries of the body along new cultural lines" (Butler [1990] 2006, 180).

site from which to derive a legible sexuality and definition of "proper" sexual acts"? (Bey in Aizura et al. 2020, 138–9)

Deconstructing both sex as anatomy and gender as role, and arguing for the end of both, Dworkin sets out a vision of desiring differently; outside of the structures of heteronormativity, cisnormativity, moving beyond a masculinist, ableist and unimaginative emphasis on fucking as the beginning and end of sexual pleasure and identity.[14] Once we desire differently, gender and embodiment will be transformed and Dworkin places intersex and trans embodiments at the vanguard of her political project. She writes, for example, that "transsexuality can be defined as one particular formation of our general multisexuality [which I take to refer to sexed embodiment rather than sexuality] which is unable to achieve its natural development because of extremely adverse social conditions" (1974, 186). What needs to change then is the cultural interpretation of transsexuality as exceptional. "By changing our premises about men and women, role-playing, and polarity, the social situation of transsexuals will be transformed, and transsexuals will be integrated into community, no longer persecuted and despised" (1974, 186). Dworkin's arguments are problematically allegorising here; she appears to take a universalising approach to transsexuality, proposing that trans experiences are epistemically valuable not in themselves, but for what they reveal about the fictitiousness of "the culture of male-female-discreteness"—cisnormativity.[15] She also

---

[14] See Jules Gill-Peterson's assertion in *Thinking With Trans Now* that "One of the allures of t4t as a mode of desire is the possibility—not a guarantee, mind you—of unlinking sex and intimacy from sex-as-anatomy, gender-as-role, and the obligation to be especially well formed as a subject or body" (Gill-Peterson in Aizura et al. 2020, 138).

[15] Universalising arguments don't have to elide the specificity of trans experience and can be important for de-stabilising distinctions that obscure inter-relationalities and uphold violent identities. Bailey Kier for example proposes that "everybody on the planet is now encompassed within the category of transgender" (2010, 189) and argues that recognising this is a step towards recognising our constitutive interdependence on each other, animals and the ecosystem. Julia Serano (2007, 51) writes, that "most of us are only a hormone prescription away from being perceived as the 'opposite' sex". As discussed, the collapsing of an ontological distinction between "trans" and "cis" embodiment and subjectivity is both philosophically and politically important. For Hil Malatino, a universalising approach to teaching gender construction (i.e. the idea that all bodies, all genders are made) is one way of teaching past the presumed conflicts between feminism and "trans" (2015). However, allegorising arguments on the other hand flatten and homogenise trans experiences and tend to reinscribe the division between "trans" and "cis", by framing discussions in terms of what "trans" can illuminate about "the norm"—with discrete boundaries between the norm and its reinforcing corollary maintained.

appears to hold the belief that most people are non-binary, noting that androgyny might be the "one road to freedom open to women, men and that emerging majority, the rest of us" (1974, 154). Dworkin's assertion of "the rest of us" as a growing, politically significant constituency, chimes with trans feminist (not TERF) gender abolitionist arguments (e.g. Bornstein 1994; Bey 2022); indeed it is the subtitle of Kate Bornstein's influential book: *Gender Outlaw* (1994). However, Dworkin was not the only second wave feminist thinker to present androgynous gender expression as the solution to the problems of patriarchy without success. Leslie Feinberg recalls the misgivings underlying this promising panacea: "as the women's movement in the seventies examined the negative values attached to masculinity and femininity in this society, some thought that liberation might lie in creating a genderless form of self-expression and dress. But of course androgyny was itself just another point on the spectrum of gender expression" (1996, 114). Moreover, as Feinberg alludes to, a championing of androgyny can be read as obscuring transsexual subjectivities—a critique regularly levelled at queer theorists (e.g. by Prosser 1998; Namaste 2011).

Revolutionary visions can be difficult to square with the constraints of culture. Yet, what remains valuable in Dworkin's utopia is its fundamental challenge not to binary identification as such, but to the assumption and anxious attachment to a mutually exclusive gender on the basis of a compulsory, unchosen and arbitrary assignation. Seeking a beyond to compulsory norms, coercive interpellation and identitarianism, Dworkin's vision is a world where difference—far from being the antithesis of radical feminism—becomes its essential element. Dworkin's post-patriarchal vision, arising from her materialist trans feminist challenge to a stable ontology of sexed and sexual truth, is of role-free, queer sexual possibility. Dworkin is committed to a world where everyone is free to live gender on their own terms, outside the restrictions of socially imposed expectations, and where categorical and bodily self-determination are the principal aims of feminism ([1981] 1989, 139). She writes that "the essence of oppression is that one is defined from the outside by those who define themselves as superior by criteria of their own choice" (1981, 1989, 149). As a result, taking control of language and meaning making systems such as religion and biology is a key means of challenging the imposition of identities from the outside.

Dworkin's understanding of the category of "woman" emerges as an *effect* of embodiment and the social meanings that the body accrues. It is both a category that one can be interpellated into, potentially violently, or—with the necessary conditions for self-determination—assume on one's own basis. Gender-based violence and normative violence cannot be so easily separated from the violence of being unfree to live one's body on one's own terms. Whilst socially, on Dworkin's view, women are *valued* on the basis of their reproductive potential, what united the social class of "women" is not a shared biology or set of experiences, but rather the lack of control over one's body—a shared priority for a trans feminist politics.

"Each life," Dworkin writes, "including each woman's life—must be a person's own, not predetermined before her birth by totalitarian ideas about her nature and her function, not subject to guardianship by some more powerful class, not determined in the aggregate but worked out by herself, for herself" (1983, 190–191). Through such a focus, Dworkin's priorities align with trans liberation which, as Emi Koyama writes, "is about taking back the right to define ourselves from medical, religious and political authorities" (2003, 250). Rape, sexual violence and transphobia, are each the consequence of a system in which bodily autonomy is denied to feminised and marginalised groups. As a result, "the basic claim of radical feminism" she writes is that "*all* freedom, including sexual freedom, begins with an absolute right to one's own body—physical self-possession" (1983, 59). For her, the opposite of oppression is not equality (which remains tied to a binary order and can be fought for by some at the expense of others) but freedom. According to her world view, in an act of genius tautology, under male domination, difference is turned into genetic inferiority which in turn is used to justify disadvantage. She highlights how "every racially despised group is invented with a bestial sexual nature" ([1981] 1989, 147) and describes as "reproductive imperialism" (1983, 150) the global state of nationalist necropolitics whereby "racist population programs [...] provide the means and ideological justifications for making masses of women extinct because their children are not wanted" (ibid.). Dworkin's feminist revolution begins at the level of taking control over naming ([1981] 1989, 17) in pursuit of bodily autonomy: "frankly, no one much knows what feminists mean; the idea of women not defined by sex and reproduction is anathema or baffling. It is the simplest revolutionary idea ever conceived, and the most despised" (1983, 190–191). This priority of universal self-determination united her political concerns:

from her (lesser known) commitment to prison abolition, to anti-pornography, from trans healthcare to abortion.[16]

Over the course of Dworkin's life, she also became increasingly frustrated with the pace of change and turned to more reformist routes in order to enact her politics. Along with her friend and colleague the legal scholar Catherine MacKinnon, in the 1980s Dworkin ostracised herself from much of the feminist movement through her perceived collaboration with the Right-Wing Regan Administration who had organised a commission led by Edwin Meese to investigate pornography. MacKinnon and

[16] Dworkin's prison abolitionism has gone unnoticed in dominant characterisations of her anti-pornography ordinance as a legal remedy (it was, as she and MacKinnon constantly reiterated a civil remedy—designed to enable individuals who had been harmed by pornography to be able to sue the pornographers. It was not, they contend, designed to embolden the carceral system e.g. Dworkin and MacKinnon (1988), Dworkin (1989, xxviii–xxxiv). Dworkin (2006, 165–166) explains in her memoir that she only contingently came to write a book on pornography after her proposal for a book on prisons received no uptake. I quote at length because it is a valuable complication to receptions of her as *only* concerned with violence against [cis] women, pornography and sexual violence "Perhaps because I came from the pacifist left, I had an intense and abiding hatred for prisons (even though the US prison system was developed by the Quakers). After the publication of *Our Blood*, I wrote a proposal for a book on prisons. I was struck by the way prisons stayed the same through time and place: the confinement of an individual in bad circumstances with a sadistic edge and including all the prison rites of passage. I was struck by how prisons were the only places in which men were threatened with rape in a way analogous to the female experience. I was struck by the common sadomasochistic structure of the prison experience no matter what the crime or country or historical era. That proposal was rejected by a slew of publishers. I found myself at a dead end.

But an odd redemption was at hand. I had noticed that in all pornography one also found the prison as leitmotif, the sexualisation of confining and beating women, the ubiquitous rape, the dominance and submission of the social world in which women were literally and metaphorically imprisoned.

I decided to write on pornography because I could make the same points—show the same inequities—as with prisons. Pornography and prisons were built on cruelty and brutalisation; the demeaning of the human body as a form of punishment; the worthlessness of the individual human being; restraint, confinement, tying, whipping, branding, torture, penetration, and kicking as commonplace ordeals. Each was a social construction that could be different but was not; each incorporated and exploited isolation, dominance and submission, humiliation, and dehumanisation". That Dworkin says that she came to write on pornography by way of a critique of prisons, is an important counter to categorisations of her as a "governance feminist" (Halley 2006) or a "carceral feminist" (Bracewell 2020) who supports an emboldened criminal justice system, and therefore lacks an intersectional analysis of the inherently racialised and classed dimensions of the prison-industrial complex.

Dworkin authored a civil rights ordinance which sought legal protection for women, children and trans people who had been harmed by pornography.[17] Despite passing briefly in Minneapolis and Indianapolis, pro-sex feminists warned that given the context of the repressive Christian New Right, such legislation would only be used to further police marginal sexualities (Duggan and Hunter 1995). Despite the criticism this judicial turn drew, it is important to highlight that this short-lived legislation saw "transsexuals" distinctly recognised in and protected by the law; an important nuance given the existing paucity of protection for trans individuals in the US.[18]

I began this chapter noting that Dworkin's body of work comprises an ambivalent archive, and this is apparent in the disjunct between her championing of individuals' entitlement to embodiment on their own terms, and her anti-pornography position that violent sex was necessarily both reflective of and reproductive of violent social relations. Dworkin took an uncompromising position that there could be no separation between fantasy and reality in the realm of sexuality, leading her to advance personal attacks against fellow feminists like Gayle Rubin and Amber Hollibaugh

[17] The anti-pornography ordinance defined pornography as follows: "Pornography is defined as the graphic, sexually explicit subordination of women in pictures and/or words that also includes women presented dehumanised as sexual objects, things, or commodities; or women presented as sexual objects who enjoy pain or humiliation; or women presented as sexual objects who experience sexual pleasure in being raped; or women presented as sexual objects tied up or cut up or mutilated or bruised or physically hurt; or women presented in postures or positions of sexual submission, servility, or display; or women's body parts—including but not limited to vaginas, breasts, buttocks—exhibited such that women are reduced to those parts; or women presented as whores by nature; or women presented being penetrated by objects or animals; or women presented in scenarios of degradation, injury, torture, shown as filthy or inferior, bleeding, bruised, or hurt in a context that makes these conditions sexual. If men, children, or transsexuals are used in any of the same ways, the material also meets the definition of pornography" (Dworkin 1989, xxxiii). It is important to note that "transsexuals" were explicitly protected by the legislation (Dworkin and MacKinnon 1988, 1997, 429), a distinction which recognises trans people as in need of specific protections in a legal context which would not guarantee this.

[18] At the time of writing in the US there have been sparse protections for trans people at a federal level. In 2020, Bostock v Clayton County, Georgia ruling designated transgender people as a protected class in matters of employment, but there is still no federal law designating transgender people as specifically requiring equal treatment, or to prohibit discrimination on the basis of housing, healthcare, adoption, education and other public programmes. Meanwhile, at a state level, there has been a raft of anti-transgender legislation, including 155 anti-transgender bills introduced in state legislatures in 2022 (Branigin and Kirkpatrick 2022).

for their participation in S/M practices and leather dyke radical groups. This attribution of false-consciousness, or worse patriarchal collaboration, to the sexual practices of fellow feminists led her to become repudiated by the growing "sex-positive" feminism of the 1980s that was increasingly finding its way into the academy. For her, no woman could freely choose to engage in submissive sexual behaviour. She thought that women were invisible to themselves, so internally "colonised" that they experienced their oppression and subordination as normal or aspirational.[19] Part of the aim of her writing was to bring readers to consciousness, to show people the world as she saw it. And when people did not share her position, she had no way of engaging in productive dialogue.

Dworkin's greatest insight then, that "each life—including each woman's life—must be a person's own" (1983, 191) and that relinquishing controls (linguistic, economic, social) over how an individual defines, and what an individual does with their body, is the necessarily foundation for meaningful liberation, is also the one that she did not follow through on in her own life. By seeking to police what queer feminists were doing in their own sex lives and with their own bodies, Dworkin's insightful critiques of the sexualised effects of power became too tightly enmeshed with a politics that sought to sanitise sex. What began as a pioneering investigation of the social construction of sex, became a rule-book for political

---

[19] Dworkin's writing is highly problematic in its use of the language of slavery and racism to emphasise her arguments about the severity of women's oppression. In *Intercourse,* she has a chapter entitled "Occupation/Collaboration" which employs the language of colonisation extensively: "The political meaning of intercourse for women is the fundamental question of feminism and freedom: can an occupied people—physically occupied inside, internally invaded—be free; can those with a metaphysically compromised privacy have self-determination...?' (2007, 156). Drawing commonalities between sexism and racism was a rhetorical strategy employed by white feminists who had been active in civil rights and anti-Vietnam war organising, and transferred the language that had been politically appropriate in that context across to feminism, in order to draw attention to the politics of gender. Yet it also build on the problematic tendency of first-wave white feminism in the United States to use the inhuman condition of black slaves as containers for the experiences of white women. As bell hooks writes, "No other group in America has used black people as metaphors as extensively as white women involved in the women's movement" ([1981] 2015, 141). Instrumentalising and inappropriate, Dworkin's analysis had a tendency to flatten out the distinctive characters of racism and sexism, operationalising the sensational capacity for metaphor at the expense of attending to the specificities of oppression. Whilst her vision then, is one of a society free from *all* forms of oppression, she has a tendency to treat race and gender as theoretically analogous in a way that is representative of much of second wave white feminism's shortcomings.

action, leading Dworkin and many second wave feminists to over-invest in sex itself as the site of political change itself. As Gayatri Spivak explains, "The good insistence that "the personal is political" often transformed itself into something like "only the personal is political"" (Spivak and Rooney 1997, 358) and suddenly new prescriptions of politically correct behaviour were being established. However, whilst Dworkin's life and work do not permit of a cohesive whole, and her record on the regulation of sex is found wanting, this is not, I have argued, a good reason to dismiss Dworkin's philosophical contributions wholesale. Dworkin's discussion of the social construction of sex the act and sex the assignment offers valuable insights into the violence of embodiment for all women, all trans people and all those for whom coercive gendering practices work to restrict and impoverish becoming.

CONCLUSION: ANDREA DWORKIN'S CHALLENGE TO CISGENDER IDEOLOGY

Andrea Dworkin's contribution to second wave feminism has been over-determined by her position on the losing side of the sex wars and her role in co-authoring the anti-pornography ordinances. This chapter has argued that Dworkin deserves to be revisited, not only for her contributions to theorising sexual violence and heterosexuality—but for the relevance of her analysis for a critique of cisnormative reasoning. For Dworkin, the ability to define what one does with one's body is her abiding concern—and the project to which she dedicated her life. Whilst the vilification she directed towards fellow feminists, as well as her structuralist shortcomings, are cause for caution, and reflect the risks of politicising the personal that second wave feminism faced, they are not straightforwardly a reason for rejection. As Johanna Fateman concludes "right or wrong—right *and* wrong—Dworkin's oracular voice helped to shape the historic grassroots feminist organising of the late '70s and '80s" and left behind a "complex, experimental body of work" that deserves to be read (2019, 39). As with contributors to the *Journal of Male Feminism*, Dworkin's mining of her own life experiences not only reproduced the world she was living in but went some way to transforming it.

By reading Dworkin through Heaney and Malatino's critiques of cis-gender ideology, I have sought to demonstrate that Dworkin's philosophy offers an example of a second wave challenge to cisnormativity. Rather than depart from a sex/gender distinction which naturalises the former, for Dworkin both are the product of the culture's commitment to duality, and her feminist vision is a complete abolition of a sex/gender order, with individuals free to define their bodies, their subjectivities and their erotic selves outside the restrictive language of male/female, gay/straight. Akin to Marx's theory of history, for Dworkin the end of male dominance would yield an end of "sex" and "gender" as we know them. Categories of male and female would wither away, and the exceptional ontological status of non-cis subjects would no longer hold.

My argument is not that Dworkin was a sophisticated trans feminist theorist. The overdetermination of gender by sexual subject positions reinforces a fictitious alignment of sexuality and gender which, as detractors have pointed out, elided the possibility of gendered self-determination. Far from all of Dworkin's contributions have not stood the test of time, and there is much in her critique of heterosexual power relations that obscures and denies queer and trans (and of course, heterosexual) subjectivities. However, revisiting Dworkin's account of the social construction of sex offers a surprising alignment between second wave radical feminism and contemporary trans epistemologies. Dworkin's philosophy of sex and gender includes relevant insights in which transgender and cisgender are equally constructed, and wherein protection, bodily autonomy and the ability to live one's live on one's own terms emerge as inalienable rights.

These were priorities that extended beyond theory, and that Dworkin took forward in her co-authored anti-pornography civil rights ordinances. They also offer an important counter to stories which naturalise a separation between the bodies of trans people and cisgender women on account of Dworkin-esque priorities of taking violence against women seriously. Cristan Williams writes that "something intrinsic to radical feminism is lost when we characterise "radical feminism" as being locked in a bitter battle against trans people" (2016, 257). In the progress narrative wherein second wave feminism is always and only essentialist and exclusionary, radical feminism's "long and courageous trans inclusive history gets lost (Williams 2016, 255). The past life of trans radical feminists as well as trans inclusive radical feminists such as Andrea Dworkin are written out of history, whilst meaningful alliances between second wave and trans feminist analyses of woman hating and trans misogyny, sexism and cissexism, and freedom from compulsory gender roles, are precluded.

BIBLIOGRAPHY

Ahmed, Sara. 2017. *Living a Feminist Life*. Durham: Duke University Press.

Aizura, Aren Z. et al. 2020. Thinking with Trans Now. *Social Text*, 38 (4): 125–147.

Allen, Leah Claire. 2016. The Pleasures of Dangerous Criticism: Interpreting Andrea Dworkin as a Literary Critic. *Signs: Journal of Women in Culture and Society* 42 (1): 49–70.

Antler, Joyce. 2018. *Jewish Radical Feminism: Voices from the Women's Liberation Movement*. New York: New York University Press.

Berlant, Lauren, and Michael Warner. 1998. Sex in Public. *Critical Inquiry* 24 (2): 547–566.

Bersani, Leo. 1987. Is the Rectum a Grave? *October* 43: 197.

Bey, Marquis. 2022. *Black Trans Feminism*. Durham: Duke University Press.

Bornstein, Kate. 1994. *Gender Outlaw: On Men, Women and the Rest of Us*. New York: Routledge.

Bracewell, Lorna. 2020. "Sex Wars, SlutWalks, and Carceral Feminism." *Contemporary political theory*, 19 (1): 61–82.

Branigin, Anne, and N. Kirkpatrick. 2022. Anti-Trans Laws Are on the Rise. Here's a Look at Where—and What Kind. *The Washington Post*. WP Company, October 20. https://www.washingtonpost.com/lifestyle/2022/10/14/anti-trans-bills/.

Brecher, Bob. 2015. Andrea Dworkin's Pornography: Men Possessing Women—a Reassessment. In *Women and Violence: The Agency of Victims and Perpetrators*, ed. H. Marway and H. Widdows, 145–161. London: Palgrave Macmillan.

Butler, Judith. [1990] 2006. *Gender Trouble: Feminism and the Subversion of Identity*. New York; London: Routledge.

———. [1993] 2011. *Bodies that Matter: On the Discursive Limits of "sex"*. Abingdon, Oxon; New York: Routledge.

Cameron, Jessica Joy. 2017. Dworkin's Subjects: Interpellation and the Politics of Heterosexuality. *Feminist Theory* 18 (1): 3–16.

———. 2018. *Reconsidering Radical Feminism: Affect and the Politics of Heterosexuality*. Vancouver: UBC Press.

Chesler, Phyllis. 2021. Andrea Revised: Andrea Dworkin: The Feminist As Revolutionary by Martin Duberman, *Dignity. A Journal of Analysis of Exploitation and Violence* 6 (1): 7.

Cohen, Cathy J. 1997. Punks, Bulldaggers, and Welfare Queens: The Radical Potential of Queer Politics? *GLQ: A Journal of Lesbian and Gay Studies* 3 (4): 437–465.

Doyle, Jennifer. 2015. *Campus Sex, Campus Security*. South Pasadena, CA: Semiotext(e).

Duberman, Martin. 2020. *Andrea Dworkin: The Feminist as Revolutionary*. New York: The New Press.

Duggan, Lisa, and Nan D. Hunter. 1995. *Sex Wars: Essays on Sexual Dissent and American Politics*. New York: Routledge.

Dworkin, Andrea. 1974. *Woman Hating*. New York: Dutton.

———. [1976] 1981. *Our Blood: Prophecies and Discourses on Sexual Politics*. New York: Perigee Books.

———. 1983. *Right-Wing Women: The Politics of Domesticated Females*. New York: Pedigree Books.

———. 1988. *Letters from a War Zone: Writings 1976–1987*. London: Secker & Warburg.

———. [1981] 1989. *Pornography: Men Possessing Women*. New York: E.P. Dutton.

———. 1997. *Life and Death: Unapologetic Writings on the Continuing War Against Women*. New York: Free Press.

———. 2000. *Scapegoat: The Jews, Israel, and Women's Liberation*. London: Virago.

———. 2006. *Heartbreak: The Political Memoir of a Feminist Militant*. London: Continuum.

———. [1987] 2007. *Intercourse*. New York: Basic Books.

Dworkin, Andrea and MacKinnon, Catharine.1988. Pornography & Civil Rights: A New Day for Women's Equality. Organising Against Pornography, Minneapolis, Minn.

Dymock, Alex. 2018. Anti-Communal, Anti-Egalitarian, Anti-Nurturing, Anti-Loving: Sex and the 'Irredeemable' in Andrea Dworkin and Catharine MacKinnon. *Paragraph* 41 (3): 349–363.

Echols, Alice. 1983. Cultural Feminism: Feminist Capitalism and the Anti-Pornography Movement. *Social Text* 7 (7): 34–53.

Edelman, Lee. 2004. *No Future: Queer Theory and the Death Drive*. Durham: Duke University Press.

Fateman, Johanna. 2019. Introduction. In *Last Days at Hot Slit: The Radical Feminism of Andrea Dworkin*, ed. Johanna Fateman and Amy Scholder, 9–42. South Pasadena, CA: Semiotext(e).

Fateman, Johanna, and Amy Scholder, eds. 2019. *Last Days at Hot Slit: The Radical Feminism of Andrea Dworkin*. South Pasadena, CA: Semiotext(e).

Fausto-Sterling, Anne. 1993. The Five Sexes. *The Sciences* 33 (2): 20–24.

Feinberg, Leslie. 1996. *Transgender Warriors: Making History from Joan of Arc to Dennis Rodman*. Boston: Beacon Press.

Glaser, Dana. 2021. Andrea Dworkin, Last Days at Hot Slit. *Chicago Review*, July 28. https://www.chicagoreview.org/andrea-dworkin-last-days-at-hot-slit/.

Grant, Judith. 2006. Andrea Dworkin and the Social Construction of Gender: A Retrospective. *Signs: Journal of Women in Culture and Society* 31 (4): 967–993.

Halley, Janet E. 2006. *Split Decisions: How and Why to Take a Break from Feminism*. Princeton, NJ: Princeton University Press.

Heaney, Emma. 2017. *The New Woman: Literary Modernism, Queer Theory, and the Trans Feminine Allegory*. Evanston, IL: Northwestern University Press.

Henry, A. 2004. *Not My Mother's Sister: Generational Conflict and Third-wave Feminism.* Bloomington: Indiana University Press.

hooks, bell. [1981] 2015. *Ain't I a Woman: Black Women and Feminism.* Boston, MA: South End Press.

Hord, Levi C.R. 2020. Specificity without Identity: Articulating Post-Gender Sexuality through the 'Non-Binary Lesbian'. *Sexualities* 25 (5–6): 615–637.

Jenkins, Katherine. 2018. Who's Afraid of Andrea Dworkin? Feminism and the Analytic Philosophy of Sex. In *The Bloomsbury Companion to Analytic Feminism*, ed. Pieranna Garavaso, 144–168. London: Bloomsbury Academic.

Kier, Bailey. 2010. Interdependent Ecological Transsex: Notes on Re/production, 'Transgender' Fish, and the Management of Populations, Species, and Resources. *Women & performance* 20 (3): 299–319.

Koyama, Emi. 2003. The Transfeminist Manifesto. In *Catching a Wave: Reclaiming Feminism for the 21st Century*, ed. Rory Cooke Dicker and Alison Piepmeier, 244–262. Boston: Northeastern University Press.

Levinas, Emmanuel. 2013. *Totality and Infinity: An Essay on Exteriority.* Pittsburgh, PA: Duquesne University Press.

Levy, Ariel. 2007. Foreword. In Dworkin, Andrea. *Intercourse*. New York: Basic Books: xi–xxvii.

Mackay, Finn. 2021. *Female Masculinities and the Gender Wars the Politics of Sex.* London: I.B. Tauris.

MacKinnon, Catharine. 2006. Catharine MacKinnon Speaks on the Work of Andrea Dworkin. *Feminist Reprise*, April 7. https://feminist-reprise.org/library/resistance-strategy-and-struggle/catharine-mackinnon/.

MacKinnon, Catharine, and Andrea Dworkin. 1997. *In Harm's Way: The Pornography Civil Rights Hearings.* Cambridge, MA: Harvard University Press.

Malatino, Hil. 2015. Pedagogies of Becoming. *TSQ: Transgender Studies Quarterly* 2 (3): 395–410.

———. 2019. *Queer Embodiment: Monstrosity, Medical Violence, and Intersex Experience, Expanding Frontiers: Interdisciplinary Approaches to Studies of Women, Gender, and Sexuality.* Lincoln: University of Nebraska Press.

McGowan, Mary. 2009. On Pragmatics, Exercitive Speech Acts and Pornography. *Lodz Papers in Pragmatics* 5 (1): 133–155.

McRuer, Robert. 2006. *Crip Theory Cultural Signs of Queerness and Disability.* New York: New York University Press.

Morland, Iain. 2014. Intersex. *TSQ: Transgender Studies Quarterly* 1 (1–2): 111–115.

Namaste, Viviane K. 2011. *Sex Change, Social Change: Reflections on Identity, Institutions, and Imperialism.* Toronto: Women's Press.

Palmer-Mehta, Valerie. 2016. A "suitably dead" woman: Grieving Andrea Dworkin. *Communication and Critical/Cultural Studies* 13 (3): 287–304.

Phipps, Alison. 2016. Whose Personal Is More Political? Experience in Contemporary Feminist Politics. *Feminist Theory* 17 (3): 303–321.
Pollitt, Katha. 2015. Andrea Dworkin, 1946–2005. *The Nation*, June 29. https://www.thenation.com/article/archive/andrea-dworkin-1946-2005/.
Prosser, Jay. 1998. *Second Skins: The Body Narratives of Transsexuality*. New York: Columbia University Press.
Provitola, Blase A. 2022. TERF or Transfeminist Avant La Lettre? *TSQ: Transgender Studies Quarterly* 9 (3): 387–406.
Raymond, Janice G. 1979. *The Transsexual Empire: the Making of the She-Male*. Boston: Beacon Press.
Rose, Jacqueline. 2018. I am a Knife. *London Review of Books*, February 22. https://www.lrb.co.uk/the-paper/v40/n04/jacqueline-rose/i-am-a-knife.
Schotten, C. Heike. 2022. Terfism, Zionism, and Right-Wing Annihilationism. *TSQ: Transgender Studies Quarterly* 9 (3): 334–364.
Scott, David, and Sylvia Wynter. 2000. The Re-Enchantment of Humanism: An Interview with Sylvia Wynter. *Small Axe* 8 (September): 119–207.
Segal, Lynne. 2015. *Straight Sex: Rethinking the Politics of Pleasure*. London: Verso.
Serano, Julia. 2007. *Whipping Girl: A Transsexual Woman on Sexism and the Scapegoating of Femininity*. Emeryville: Seal Press.
Serisier, Tanya. 2013. Who Was Andrea? Writing Oneself as a Feminist Icon. *Women* 24 (1): 26–44.
Spivak, Gayatri, and Ellen Rooney. 1997. 'In a Word' Interview. In *The Second Wave Feminism Reader: A Reader in Feminist Theory*, ed. Linda J. Nicholson, 356–378. London: Routledge.
Stoltenberg, John. 2020. Andrea Dworkin Was a Trans Ally. *Boston Review*, April 7. https://www.bostonreview.net/articles/john-stoltenberg-andrew-dworkin-was-trans-ally/.
Walters, Suzanna. 2016. "Introduction: The Dangers of a Metaphor—Beyond the Battlefield in the Sex Wars." *Signs*, 42 (1): 1–9.
Warner, M. 1991. Introduction: Fear of a Queer Planet. *Social Text* 29: 3–17. http://www.jstor.org/stable/466295.
Whisnant, R. 2016. Our Blood: Andrea Dworkin on Race, Privilege, and Women's Common Condition. *Women's studies international forum* 58: 68–76.
Wiegman, Robyn, and Elizabeth A. Wilson. 2015. Introduction: Antinormativity's Queer Conventions. *Differences* 26 (1): 1–25.
Williams, Cristan. 2016. Radical Inclusion: Recounting the Trans Inclusive History of Radical Feminism. *TSQ: Transgender Studies Quarterly* 3 (1–2): 254–258.
Willis, Ellen. 1984. Radical Feminism and Feminist Radicalism. *Social Text* 3 (3): 91–118.

CHAPTER 5

The Category of "Sex" Before the Sex Wars

The imbrications of gender and sexual aberrance require that one does not read "the question of sex" as exclusively concerned with sexual acts or object choice but as also indicative of gendering practices and trans ways of being
—C. Riley Snorton, *Black on Both Sides*

"The time has come to think about sex" announced Gayle Rubin in the stirring opening line to her landmark 1984 essay *Thinking Sex: Notes for a Radical Theory of the Politics of Sexuality* (2011c, 137). She was, of course, talking not about sex the assignment, but sex the act—sexuality.[1] The essay was first presented as a workshop paper at the fabled Barnard Conference on Sexuality in 1982—the "flashpoint" (Comella 2008, 202) of the sex wars in the US, a series of heated divisions in the US and UK

---

[1] Rubin notes the "two very different meanings" of sex later in the essay. However, it is the impact of her arguments for the development of "sexuality" and "gender" as distinct analytical objects that I am interested in.

© The Author(s), under exclusive license to Springer Nature   147
Switzerland AG 2023
E. Cousens, *Trans Feminist Epistemologies in the US Second Wave*,
Breaking Feminist Waves,
https://doi.org/10.1007/978-3-031-33731-4_5

over the politics of pornography, S/M and butch/femme.[2] The Barnard conference has gone on to attain many accolades. It cemented divisions between "sex-positive" and "sex-negative" feminists,[3] aired perspectives such as Rubin's—whose paper has been called "the inaugural act of queer theory" (Wiegman 2012, 96)—and validated academic discussions of sexual pleasure with texts such as *Pleasure and Danger* (Vance 1984) and *Powers of Desire* (Snitow et al. 1983) becoming "coveted books for even the hippest of young scholars" (Walters 2016b, 4). What this chapter

[2] Whilst divisions between anti-pornography feminists and pro-sex/anti anti-pornography feminists, with the former often "calling-out" the latter, had been around for a while, the Barnard conference saw these tensions come to a head. Anti-pornography feminists accused conference organisers of promoting patriarchal, politically incorrect, sexual practices and had significant leverage on the university administration, as well as in the feminist press at the time. A response letter in *Feminist Studies* (see Abelove, H. et al. 1983), arguing against what the co-signees felt amounted to censorship and accusing "one segment of the feminist movement" of using "McCarthyite tactics to silence other voices", was signed by 285 academics and included prominent names that have subsequently become key theorists of gender and sexuality: Henry Abelove, Dorothy Allison, Ros Baxandall, Judith Butler, Patrick Califia, John D'Emillo, Ellen DuBois, Alice Echols, Zillah Eisenstein, Kate Ellis, Barbara Epstein, Estelle Freedman, Faye Ginsberg, Donna Haraway, Susan Harding, Lind Hoagland, Amber Hollibaugh, Judith Levine, Cherrie Moraga, Joan Nestle, Esther Newton, Judith Newton, Gayle Rubin, Sara Ruddick, Eve Kosofsky Sedgwick, Ann Snitow, Carole Vance, Daniel J Walkowitz, Judith R Walkowitz and Ellen Willis.

The Barnard conference has been "undertheorised" yet it is nonetheless "frequently referenced" within feminist historiographies (Corbman 2015, 52). In 2016, *Signs: Journal of Woman and Culture in Society,* published a special issue "Pleasure and Danger: Sexual Freedom and Feminism in the Twenty-First Century" revisiting the sex wars, the conference and their impact on the development of feminism.

[3] I use "sex-positive" to refer to discourses which championed women's sexual agency and the avoidance of shame. I use "sex-negative" to refer to positions such as Dworkin's which prioritised opposing violence against women. Essentially, these two positions reflect different interpretations of sexual liberation. "Sex-positive" or "pro-sex" feminists tend to follow a positive interpretation as freedom *to* whereas "sex-negative" or "anti-sex" feminists tend to ascribe to a negative conception of freedom: freedom *from* unwanted sexual advances. Clearly these are not separable, however as priorities they can collide. Recent years have seen challenges to the polarisation contained under these two labels (e.g. Glick 2000; Clare 2015) Whilst I find the "sex-positive"/"sex-negative" binary to be an unhelpful way of doing justice to the complexity of sexual politics for feminists, and to collapse very different versions of feminism (anti sex work and trans-exclusionary feminists get lumped together with anti-violence feminists), when I reproduce these categorisations here, it is for the purpose of indicating how the Barnard conference has been historicised as a clash between "pro-sex" and "anti-porn" feminists (Corbman 2015) and for signalling the continuation of this oppositional framework within feminist thinking thereafter.

explores however, is how the historicisation of the conference, and canoni-sation of Rubin's arguments, have impacted understandings of the tempo-rality of trans feminism. I am interested in how the conference has become a place holder for a "before" and "after" in feminist approaches to sex (and gender) and how the conferences role as a "turning point" has con-tributed to a narrative in which "sex" (the assignment) in the second wave was always already "cis", with the effect that the contributions of trans individuals to the developments and debates of feminism are ignored.

C. Riley Snorton's epigraph at the opening of this chapter points to the significance for trans studies of clarifying between the multiple interpreta-tions of "sex"—an argument that has also subtended many of the discus-sions throughout this book. In this chapter, however, I propose that an unacknowledged impact of the scholarly story of the sex wars, is that trans interpretations of "the question of sex" in the second wave have been sidelined. I will argue that it was trans people in the 1960s whose labour laid the groundwork for the emergence of "sex" and "gender" as distinct categories, and that this in turn allowed "women's studies" (second wave feminism's academic instantiation) to achieve academic credibility. Yet, within feminist genealogies, this dependence on trans knowledges is rarely acknowledged and instead it is more regularly Judith Butler's performa-tive theory of gender, that is credited with creating the conditions for a more trans positive feminism to emerge in the 1990s.

SECOND WAVE FEMINISM, SEX AND GENDER

Stella Sandford writes that "for some, it was the sex/gender distinction that allowed second wave feminism to get off the ground and few feminist scholars would disagree on the fact, if not the nature, of its historical importance" (1999, 18). As Sandford alludes to, feminist philosophy in the 1970s hinged upon the "woman question"; taking up Simone de Beauvoir's famous notion that one is not born, but rather becomes, a woman ([1949] 1997) to theorise the complex mechanics through which "womanhood" was constructed. The sex/gender distinction catalysed much of the scholarly output within the newly emerging field of "Women's Studies", providing a framework through which feminists could argue that gender was socially constructed, and allowing them to apply a philosophi-cal analysis to exploring how and through what social processes gender construction took place (e.g. Jaggar 1983).

Kate Millett was one of the first feminists to make use of the sex/gender distinction in her landmark text, *Sexual Politics*. Published in the women's liberation movement's "watershed" (Hesford 2013, 3) year of 1970, and skyrocketing Millett to become one of the public faces of second wave feminism, the book's argument, revolutionary at the time, was that there is no evidence that "the present social distinctions of patriarchy (status, role, temperament) are physical in origin" ([1970] 1977, 29).[4] Instead, Millett puts forward the relatively new notion of socialisation as central to our understandings of "masculinity" and "femininity", before offering a critical reading of canonical American male writers: D.H. Lawrence, Norman Mailer and Jean Genet, exposing their misogyny and sexualised objectification of women. A central piece of evidence that she leverages against what she writes is the widely held belief that "patriarchy is endemic in human social life" ([1970] 1977, 26) is the—at the time little known—concept of gender.

> Important new research not only suggests that the possibilities of innate temperamental differences seem more remote than ever, but even raises questions as to the validity and permanence of psyco-sexual identity. In doing so it gives fairly concrete positive evidence of the overwhelmingly *cultural* character of gender, i.e.—personality structure in terms of sexual category (1977, 29 italics in original).

For Millett then, the concept of gender provides the necessary scaffolding to argue for the equal treatment of women, on the grounds that observed differences between the sexes are most likely in the realm of gender and therefore cultural and social, not biological.

The "important new research" that Millett is referencing, is the work of John Money and Robert Stoller. These American sexologists, or "the gender scientists" (Califia 2003, 52) pioneered "developments" in understandings of sex, gender and sexuality in the mid-twentieth century through their studies on and work with trans and intersex patients. Money is attributed with creating the concept of "gender" meanwhile Stoller built on this to propose the sex/gender distinction (Gill-Peterson 2018; Dahms 2021). Millett became among the first of many feminists throughout the second wave who "increasingly borrowed the language of gender and distinguished gender from biological sex and also from sexual desire"

---

[4] Kate Millett, against her wishes, appeared on the cover of *Time* magazine later that year.

(Meyerowitz 2004, 263) in order to build on the Beauvoirian sentiment that observed differences between men and women were acquired not innate. As we saw in the last chapter, Dworkin (1974) also appealed to John Money's recent research and Vernon A. Rosario (2004, 280–287) notes how Money's conception of "gender" became central analytical leverage within feminism. "Though battered over time, it was a building block of feminist theory from the 1960s on. [...] The dichotomy was productive and politically expedient" (2004, 283).

Whilst many feminists gladly accepted the sex/gender framework, most did "not pay such close attention to the work of the researchers who studied transsexuality, and most accepted the categories of female and male as self-evident" (Meyerowitz 2004, 263). Millett, for example, fails to interrogate the fact that Money's concept was introduced to justify coercive surgeries on intersex patients, uncritically accepting that his research was based on "cases of genital malformation" ([1970] 2000, 30). In fact, Money's notion of "gender" had been established in the treatment of intersex patients not as a way not of deconstructing the binary of male/female but securing it at a time of epistemological crisis. "Sex had become an unwieldy biological category, now composed of genotype, gonads, hormones, genitals, internal organs, secondary anatomical features, and psychology with none of them externing what amounted to a determinate influence" (Gill-Peterson 2018, 97). Whilst this was a period characterised by an intensification of attention directed towards fixing the definition of sex, as Meyerowitz notes, none of the "doctors, scientists, reporters, lawyers, judges, feminists and gay liberationists, among others" [...] "could settle the question of the interconnections among sex, gender and sexuality" (2004, 285). Money, who was looking for a justification for performing "corrective" surgeries on intersex patient to "fix" their ambiguous sex, therefore introduced "gender" (i.e. sex socialisation) in 1955 and advised that a clinicians' job was to determine "a *best* sex for each of their patients" and to ensure they were raised accordingly (Germon 2009, 24). Money created the concept of "gender" which "would make nonbinary morphology into underdevelopment, allowing medicine to claim that sex assignment was merely its normal completion" (Gill-Peterson 2018, 99). "Gender" thus emerged precisely to ground a basis for the indeterminacy of "sex" and the detethered categories of "male" and "female".

Money, however, did not argue for a sex/gender *distinction*. For him, gender was the principal category of clinical significance. It was Robert Stoller, one of John Money's colleagues at the John Hopkins Gender

Identity Clinic, the first clinic in the United States to perform sexual reassignment surgeries on children and adults,[5] who advanced the analytic separation of sex and gender in the 1960s.[6] Stoller "was a prominent figure in United States psychoanalytic circles from the 1960s onward" whose "work determined to a significant degree, gender's history as an ontological concept" (Germon 2009, 63). He built on and complexified Money's initial theory, distinguishing between gender identity and gender role and entrenched gender into "the binary logic of dimorphic sexual difference" by "returning to and reinforcing an imagined nature/nurture divide, rendering sex the property of the former and gender the property of the latter" (ibid., 64). However, these insights were developed via Stoller's pathologising view of the trans and intersex patients he worked with.[7] He opposed surgery for trans people, instead regarding transsexuality, transvestism and homosexuality as psychological disorders—opinions he set out to prove (Meyerowitz 2004, 126). As such, the origins of the "sex/gender" distinction are equally conservative; whilst feminists adapted the idea to argue in favour of less prescriptive modes of socialisation, Stoller created it in order to defend traditional gender roles.

Whereas for Stoller and Money, transsexuality was a matter of psychological maladjustment and therefore, whilst coercive surgeries on intersex bodies were supported, gender affirmative ones were not, Harry

---

[5] The Clinic was established in 1965 by a grant from the Erickson Foundation, and performed its first "sex reassignment surgery" in 1966 (Bullough and Bullough 1993, 259).

[6] Robert Stoller's book *Sex and Gender* was published in 1968. The second volume, published in 1975, was called *The Transsexual Experiment*.

[7] Highly influential on the development of Stoller's thought was a patient named Agnes. Stoller had been searching for an endocrine theory of biological sex and when, in 1958, he started working with "Agnes", a white, feminine presenting woman who also had a penis and testicles. Savvy to the availability of "sex-change" surgery for intersex patients, Agnes did not tell the doctors that she had been taking her mother's oestrogen pills and she managed to convince Stoller, along with Harold Garfinkel and Dr Alexander Rosen, to prescribe her surgery, as a solution to her sexed indeterminacy but strong gender presentation. Agnes confirmed Stoller's endocrine theory: she had a biological defect that feminised her, a "core gender identity" and it was her *sex* that needed to be changed not her *gender*. This confirmation fed into Stoller's distinction between sex and gender, and it wasn't until 1968 that he learned of Agnes' self-administration of oestrogen. Paul Preciado reads Agnes' "deception" of Robert Stoller as evidence that gender identity is "nothing other than script narration, performative fiction, rhetoric" (2013, 386). Agnes' story has provided the basis for a full-length, semi-fictional, semi-dramatised film: *Framing Agnes* (Joynt 2022). Kessler and McKenna (1978) were early feminist theorists to argue that not only gender, but sex, too, is socially constructed—and they drew on Agnes' experience to make these conclusions.

Benjamin, who was working with trans patients at his private clinic on Park Avenue in New York City, was developing a more "sympathetic" understanding of transsexuality to his colleagues. Benjamin "wondered if it wouldn't be more effective to simply give transsexuals what they kept saying they wanted: a chance to live in the gender they preferred" and became a "pioneer in the development of the process of sex reassignment, and the author of the standards of care that would underlie ethical guidelines for the treatment of transsexuals for the coming years (Califia 2003, 15).[8] After having worked with189 trans patients at his private practice, he published the *Transsexual Phenomenon* in 1966—a book that both mounted a "polemic in favour of legitimising gender confirmation surgery" and also "veers into an armchair-slumming account of perversion and tragedy restricted to a small minority of the population, as if to violently undo the prospect" (Gill-Peterson 2018, 140–141). The "core idea championed by Benjamin, was that while the gender identities of transsexuals were pathological, they was impervious to alteration. If the mind cannot be changed according to this logic, the body must be changed to alleviate the suffering of the patient" (Bettcher 2016, 409). He also "staked a relatively unambiguous claim to analytical separation of gender from object choice [i.e. transsexuality necessitating heterosexuality] that would become integral to the medical gatekeeping around transsexuality" (Gill-Peterson 2018, 142).[9] However, as the bible for medical gatekeeping, the *Transsexual Phenomenon* "was passed from hand to hand within the transsexual communities, whose members were often willing to follow the necessary scripts that led to acceptance for surgery" (Stone 1992, 161). Many trans individuals seeking gender affirming interventions would, understandably, repeat the "wrong body narrative", with its heteronormative assumptions, that Benjamin had created the standard for.[10] Benjamin, like Stoller, also built on Money's new concept of gender in order to shape the sexual science developments that feminists would then adopt.

Isabel Dahms writes that these "father figures", of gender science provided "the origins of gender" before the "appropriation of the concept for

---

[8] In 1979, the Harry Benjamin Standards of Care were refined and standardised and in 1980 "transsexualism" was added to the DSMIII as a mental disorder (Bettcher 2016, 410).
[9] Discusses the Harry Benjamin standards of care, 1979.
[10] For more on the "wrong body discourse" see Kimi Dominic "The *True Transsexual* and Transnormativity" (2021).

feminist purposes" (Dahms 2021. 41).[11] Certainly, the research of Money, Stoller, Benjamin and their colleagues as forerunners in the field of US sexology at the time provided the conceptual scaffolding for some of the most influential developments in western feminist theory. For instance, feminist psychologists Susan Kessler and Wendy McKenna whose 1978 book *Gender: An Ethnomethodological Study* was a ground-breaking theorisation of gender—and sex—as socially constructed, anticipating by a decade Butler's popularisation of the argument that sex is an effect of gender, based their arguments on the studies of "transsexualism" that were taking place at John Hopkins. By appealing to the management of gender by transsexuals, Kessler and McKenna drew the conclusion that all gender is managed by people living within the constructs of "male" and "female" and argued against the binary view of biological sex. In doing so, they returned, as Meyerowitz writes, "without seeming to know it, to an early twentieth century model of biological sex as a continuum" (2004, 263). Dworkin drew on Money's findings regarding intersex embodiment, Millett used Stoller and Money's research as foundational for her theory of sexual politics and, as Dahms highlights, Anne Oakley (1972) and Gayle Rubin ([1975] 2011b) both depended on and credited Money with the advancement of their own theories of sex and gender.[12] For Rubin, Money's concept of "gender" "was one of the resources at hand with which to build feminist frameworks" (quoted in Dahms 2021, 46). Whilst gender, and the sex/gender distinction has often been credited with being one of (white, western) second wave feminism's major inventions, as genealogies of the concept have demonstrated, it was sexologists—particularly Money and Stoller—that initiated the concept of gender which was then "appropriated from the sexual sciences by a number of early academic feminists and put to work to argue against women's inferior social, politi-

---

[11] The study of sex has a much longer history. Jules Gill-Peterson discusses the earliest figures in European endocrinology in the mid nineteenth century, who worked with a theory of life's natural bisexuality (2018, 40–41). Among these was Darwin for whom: "in every female all the secondary male characters, and in every male all the secondary female characters, apparently exist in a latent state, ready to be evolved under certain conditions [...] we see something of an analogous nature in the human species" (quoted in Gill-Peterson 2018, 41). In Europe in the 1920s, Magnus Hirschfeld's sexological community was shaping understandings of transvestism and intersexuality, and provided medical transition for trans people (Gill Peterson 2018, 59).

[12] These feminists were often critical of the reproduction of gender stereotypes by the doctors and scientists.

cal, and economic standing" (Germon 2009, 19).[13] It is significant, then, that the origins of gender are not in the challenge to sex dimorphism, but its maintenance.

SEX AND GENDER BEHIND THE SCENES0

Whilst Dahms and Germon credit the "gender scientists" with pioneering "gender" and the "sex/gender distinction", Benjamin, Stoller and Money were only able to develop the theories that they did due to their interactions with trans women and men at the time. Not only did trans patients have far greater knowledge of their own "condition" than the doctors they approached (both through experience and extensive research)[14]—and were therefore educating the doctors on the impact of hormones and new surgical techniques, for example (Meyerowitz 2004, 153–4), but it was a close network of well-connected and influential trans lecturers, colleagues and philanthropists that provided the informational and financial backing that would shape the evolving understandings of "sex" and "gender". The self-knowledge and tireless research of many self-identified transsexuals and transvestites was integral to the development the gender research taking place in the mid-twentieth century. From sending carefully compiled bibliographies to scientists, exposing them to more longstanding research from Europe, and introducing researchers to their networks, trans individuals provided the intellectual and epistemic foundations for many of the ensuing "advancements" in sex and gender research (and theory) in the United States in the second half of the twentieth century. Three whose contributions were particularly integral to the research of Stoller, Benjamin and Money are Louise Lawrence, Reed Erickson and Virginia Prince.

---

[13] Jules Gill-Peterson argues that Money's role in the creation of "gender" as a category has been granted too much historical weight and "we should locate the emergence of gender in work with intersex children with adrenal conditions before Money arrived at Hopkins" (2018, 99).
    [14] This included sourcing and reading anything published on the subject of sex/gender variance. Francine Logandice was not the only trans person in the US to compile extensive bibliographies of the available literature, and to share these with public libraries and gender research institutes in order to provide a foundation for the institutionalised study of sex and gender. However, her correspondences with the Indiana University Institute for Sex Research, the Gender Services of Chicago and with Johnathan Katz and Vern Bullough demonstrate how highly demanded her advanced knowledge and commitment to collecting all available information on transsexuality and transvestism was. These correspondences were accessed in Francine Logandice collection, Carton 1.

Louise Lawrence contributed immensely to gender related developments in both scientific, and community circles in the mid twentieth century. A trans woman, she "devoted herself to teaching medical authorities
and scientists about transvestites and transsexuals" (Meyerowitz 2004,
154). She had compiled clippings and books, the "obligatory transsexual
file" (Stone [1987] 1992), and shared these with Alfred Kinsey—using
her extensive research, and network of cross-dressers to convince him to
understand the significance of transvestism (Meyerowitz 2001, 76).
Lawrence was a highly influential and well-connected figure in the transgender community in the United States, which she had played a big role
in bringing together. Before living full-time as a woman in 1942, she had
been cross-dressing most of her life and had amassed an extensive correspondence network with transgender people across the world.[15] Lawrence's
network became invaluable for the other sexual researchers she assisted,
including Alfred Kinsey who was collecting data on transvestites and transsexuals as part of the research for his now infamous "Kinsey scale".
Lawrence sent Kinsey letters, photos, books and manuscripts to bolster his
own research materials. Lawrence also frequently lectured on transgender
topics to Karl Bowman, director of the Langley Porter Clinic which
became a major centre of research on variant sexuality and gender in the
1940s and 1950s, introducing transness to the clinical establishment.[16]

When Lawrence met Benjamin, who was in the process of researching
the *Transsexual Phenomenon*, she introduced him to the writings of David
O. Cauldwell—who had pioneered the use of the term transsexual in his
1949 essay *Psychopathia Transsexualis* and championed sex reassignment
surgery (Meyerowitz 2004, 154). Prior to this, Benjamin had had no
word for "transsexual". Lawrence's network was also invaluable to
Benjamin's research. Benjamin's status as a forerunner in transsexual
knowledge production and medicine was therefore made possible on the
back of Lawrence's longstanding expertise, patient education and thanks
to her role as a "sounding board for...many of his ideas" (Meyerowitz
2004,154). Yet whilst Benjamin's preface to the *Transsexual Phenomenon*

[15] This would then become the basis for Virginia Prince's *Transvestia* mailing list (Stryker
2005, xv).
[16] Bowman's own research, as was the case with much of the sexual science of the day, had
questionable motivations and outcomes. Bowman conducted research on homosexuality by
using as test subjects gay men whose sexuality had been discovered whilst they were serving
in the military, and his experiments involved castrating them in order to see if this would alter
their sexual behaviour (Stryker 2008, 41–2; Largent 2008, 21).

acknowledges the influence of Christine Jorgensen's unsought celebrity for focussing "attention on the problem as never before. Without her courage and determination, undoubtedly springing from a force deep inside her, transsexualism might be still unknown" Lawrence's professional guidance remains uncredited. It was "the help and labor of well-connected trans community members like [Christine] Jorgensen and Lawrence [that] made [Benjamin's] clinical research possible" writes Jules Gill-Peterson (2018, 139), and which facilitated the gender research that would become a bedrock of second wave feminism. However, "while doctors were far from the only labor force behind the discourse on transsexuality, they received nearly all of the credit and recognition" (ibid.).

Virginia Prince, who I discussed in Chap. 3 as one of the initiators of a trans community print culture in North America (thanks to Lawrence's correspondence network), was another influence on Kinsey, Benjamin and Money. She identified as a heterosexual transvestite and made a clear distinction between sex, gender and sexuality, in order to argue that crossing *gender* was normal and not pathological, unlike the real sex deviants who crossed sexuality (homosexuals) or who crossed sex (transsexuals). She sought to distance transvestism (purely about gender expression) from homosexuality and transsexuality (both, for her, associated with *sexual* deviance—even though the meaning of "sex" in each is very different). Prince formulated a notion of the "true transvestite", who was heterosexual and had no desire, or need, for surgery. As Robert Hill explains, "Prince would cast the transvestite's personal struggles into a larger story of every man's need for emancipation from limited, restrictive, oppressive, and completely arbitrary *gender* roles" (2007, 309). She presented this philosophy as a panellist at professional conferences, wrote scientific papers on the topic, authored widely consulted essays and books such as *The Transvestite and His Wife* (1967)—the second edition of which was dedicated to Harry Benjamin and Karl Bowman-, *How To Be a Woman Though Male* (1971) *and Understanding Cross-Dressing* (1976). Not only was her sheer output of significance, but so was her influence on the clinical discourse. Robert Stoller conducted interviews with Prince which extended over 29 years (Docter 2004). It was Prince's definition of transvestism which had informed Benjamin's perception of transvestism and transsexuality as heterosexual (Hill 2007, 73), and that became the adopted by the *Diagnostic and Statistical Manual* of the American Psychiatric Association in 1987 (Bullough and Bullough 1993, 302).[17] The manual's deeply embedded association of "gender dysphoria" with heterosexuality, which became a long-lived element of the clinical script and "seriously delayed the wider recognition that trans men could be gay" (Gill-Peterson 2020, 137), reflected Prince's arguments in her paper "sex vs. gender" ([1973] 2005) which had been presented at the second interdisciplinary symposium on gender dysphoria syndrome at Stanford university.[18]

Whilst Prince's own philosophy was biased against homosexuality, her influence on the development of theories of sex and gender, as well as the sexological research that informed the foundations for gatekept medicine, was immense. Susan Stryker argues that "Prince's sexological writings on transgender phenomena should be as widely known, and as well regarded, as Benjamin's. And yet, because she was openly a transvestite, Prince could speak 'only' as a transvestite, and not as a medical expert whose professional knowledges and competencies were respected by her professional peers" (Stryker 2005, xvi). This is, as Stryker writes, "an injustice is buried in that construction of knowledge and authority" (ibid). Trans epistemologies shaped the contents of sex and gender knowledges in the mid-twentieth century, yet these integral influences on the development of both science and feminism remain almost entirely overlooked.

Financing and moulding these developments from behind the scenes was Reed Erickson, another well-connected patient of Benjamin's. In 1964, Erickson, a wealthy Louisiana businessman who had transitioned a year earlier, launched the Erickson Educational Foundation (EEF) as a philanthropic organisation with the mission of providing "assistance and support in areas where human potential was limited by adverse physical, mental or social conditions, or where the scope of research was too new, controversial or imaginative to receive traditionally oriented support" (quoted in Devor and Matte 2004, 185). The EEF, which ran until 1984, provided support for trans individuals offering services such as peer support groups, lists of sympathetic and knowledgeable professionals and a wide range of educational resources. It sponsored medical research, conferences, and symposia on transsexuality, and subsidised scholarly

[17] See also Zagria "Harry Benjamin in Transvestia Magazine" (2022) for a discussion of the intellectual influence of Prince on Benjamin.
[18] See Nicholas Matte "Historicising Liberal American Transnormativities" (2014) for the place of the Stanford conference in the development of clinical understandings of gender.

publications. Erickson also funded the National Transsexual Counselling Unit that radical trans feminist Suzy Cooke joined in 1971,[19] homophile movements such as ONE INC "that contributed to the social acceptability of marginalised people that was grounded in fact not prejudice" (Devor and Matte 2004, 201) and put money into new age spirituality research.

Crucially, however, it was Erickson's vision and financing that was behind the development of trans medicine as a legitimate field of study in the United States. It was EEF grants that enabled John Money to open the John Hopkins Gender Identity Clinic in 1965 in the first place. The EEF funded the research of Harry Benjamin and his associates, financing the Harry Benjamin Foundation—the first formal network of doctors and psychologists starting to recommend surgery for trans individuals. For a while, Erickson and Benjamin had a good working relationship, combining their financial and medical processes in the shared aim of "a future in which trans people were recognised, understood, respected and could access medical services and support" (Devor and Matte 2007, 50). At the time, before the negative impacts of clinical gatekeeping had been widely felt, Erickson, like Louise Lawrence, had a "faith in science" and believed in its positive potential for improving the lives of trans people (Meyerowitz 2004, 211). Whilst the relationship between Benjamin and Erickson fell through after a few years, it was this period of research that got Benjamin's profile established and saw the publication of *The Transsexual Phenomenon*. In the late 1960s, the EEF provided funds to Richard Green and John Money for the publication of a major volume on transsexualism. Green and Money edited the volume, Erickson wrote the foreword, and Benjamin wrote the introduction (Meyerowitz 2004, 223). *Transsexualism and Sex Reassignment* would dislodge Benjamin's earlier text to become the leader in the field of gender research.[20] Therefore, "without the backing of Erickson, a trans man, it is unlikely that transsexual medicine would have grown and professionalized in the 1960s" (Gill-Peterson 2018, 139). His philanthropy largely informed every aspect of work being done on transsexualism, sex and gender in the 1960s and 1970s, in the US and beyond,

---

[19] This was shortly before it changed its name to Transexual Counselling Unit—with the one 's' marking a departure from the medical discourse deployed by the likes of Money and Benjamin (Meyerowitz 2004, 234).

[20] *Transsexualism and Sex Reassignment* was dedicated to Harry Benjamin as "the pioneer of transsexual research" (Califia 2003, 62)

and therefore many of the concepts that second wave feminism then adapted from this research had Erickson's imprint on them.

Erickson's contribution to the development of trans medicine in the United States was profound. Erickson himself, and the EEF more broadly, were instrumental in improving healthcare and services for trans people. His influence, however, went much further. Not only was Erickson funding the scientific developments in trans and intersex medicine that second wave feminists later drew upon, but he was actively shaping them too. As Joanne Meyerowitz explains, the EEF directed the research agendas and "to a certain extent the science followed the money" (2004, 224). Erickson retained a high-level of engagement with, and influence over, the social, political and scientific implications of the work the EEF was funding. As Stoller, Benjamin and Money were becoming recognised as some of the pioneers of the new medical frontier the US, their escalating output and influence was inseparable from the provisions of the EEF.[21] The EEF also "cosponsored the first International Symposium on Gender Identity" and "accelerated the research agendas, enabled some of the publications, and promoted the clinical practice of the doctors and scientists who endorsed sex-reassignment surgery" (ibid.).

The EEF also directly influenced second wave feminism. Having realised the importance of social education, Erickson and the EEF developed print resources including a newsletter and EEF information pamphlets and utilised speaking engagements and mainstream media—including TV and radio to fight for public acceptance for trans people. The speaker events played a significant role in changing perceptions of transsexualism, including amongst feminist researchers such as Kessler and McKenna, who used the outputs produced by the EEF to introduce their classes to "transsexualism" (see Devor and Matte 2007, 55).[22]Not only was Erickson's funding and vision essential to supporting trans individuals, he "provided essential financial and structural support to a fledgling movement" (Devor

[21] Aaron Devor and Nicholas Matte note that "Many of the professionals who would come to play important roles in the field of transsexual medicine in particular were initially funded in part (if not wholly) by the EEF, including Harry Benjamin, John Money, Richard Green, Milton Diamond, Roger Gorski, Don Laub, Ira Pauly, Anke Erhardt, and June Reinisch, among others. Likewise, the EEF funded many non-medical research grants, including to social scientists such as historian of sexuality Vern Bullough, sociologist Harold T. Christenson, and criminologist Marie Mehl" (2007, 60).
[22] Nicholas Matte (2014) discusses the rise of the "professional transsexual" as a result of the EEF's approach.

and Matte 2007, 48) and also contributed to the dissemination of trans epistemologies that would become the cornerstone of gender theory taken up in early second wave classics such as *Sexual Politics.*

While the significance of Money and Stoller's contributions to the concepts of "gender" and the "sex/gender distinction" for the development of second wave feminist theory is beginning to be recognised (e.g. Germon 2009; Dahms 2021), what is still rarely acknowledged is who was steering the development of this research. Shaping the research agenda and findings around sex and gender in the second half of the twentieth century were influential trans people, motivated by a commitment to human liberation and with a belief that science could be a vehicle for this. Not only does second wave feminism's intellectual development have an overlooked sexual science history, it has an overlooked trans history too.

THE RACIAL HISTORY OF SEX AND GENDER

Whilst the US medical model that second wave feminists were drawing on had been shaped by the research, situated knowledges and funding of influential trans people in the twentieth century, this was also a model which was based on histories racial violence and technologies of biopolitical control. Maria Lugones' discussion of the "coloniality of gender" (2007) draws our attention to the way that naturalised ideas of "sex" and "gender" are inseparable from their origins within a colonising, binary gaze. This is echoed by Oyèrónké Oyěwùmí who highlights the western particularity of assuming that biology dictates distinct social relationalities. Offering the example of pre-colonial Yoruba, where social relations such as seniority rather than anatomy, determined the roles people had in relation to one another (1997, 12–14), Oyěwùmí demonstrates the Eurocentrism in the concept of "women" with its grounding in biological characteristics.

Both Lugones and Oyěwùmí' highlight that sex and gender are distinctly western formulations and speak to the inextricability of sex and gender binarisms from histories of race and racialisation. As historians have discussed, this has a particular valence in the clinical setting. The work of Siobhan Somerville (2000), C. Riley Snorton (2017) and Jules Gill-Peterson (2018) demonstrates that not only were sex and gender used as biopolitical tools to categorise and control colonised bodies, but the history of European and American sexology is a violent legacy of using "native" gendered embodiments to produce whiteness, and rank cultural development in accordance with race. Somerville (2000) highlights how in the early twentieth century, sexologists used practices of comparative anatomy to locate the boundaries of race through the sexual and reproductive anatomy of the African female body. Black women's genitalia and reproductive capacities were seen to be central to the establishment of the "proper" contours of sex difference [read white masculinity and femininity]. Black women's bodies, the size of their buttocks, labia minora and vagina, were all investigated and colonial sexologists judged them to exceed to the boundaries of the "normal"—and fully developed—female. For Snorton, not only were enslaved Black women measured and investigated, then made to index undeveloped womanhood, they were degendered, de-sexed, and "thingified" (2017, 5). Building on Hortense Spillers' notion of the black body as "flesh" (1987), Snorton vividly documents how "father of modern gynecology", James Marion Sims, conducted gynecological experiments on enslaved Black women in plantations demonstrating precisely how deep this de-gendering, the "thingification" of black life, ran. Black women's bodies were therefore central both to the invention of sex and gender, but also the *study* of sex and gender in the laboratories of western scientists. As Meyerowitz reminds us, "biological sex has a history" (2004, 21) and this history is highly racialised.

These legacies were inherited in the work of Benjamin, Money and Stoller. Benjamin, who had begun his medical career in Germany, bought much of the European interest in eugenics and plasticity, "the inherent indeterminacy of sex as a biological form" (Gill-Peterson 2018, 35) to America. He was "actively involved with eugenics research and institutions" and "helped to import the European racialisation of plasticity as the eugenic alterability of sex as phenotype" (Gill-Peterson 2018, 66–67). This then influenced John Money's work with intersex patients. He appealed to notions of racialized plasticity to argue for the primacy of sex rearing (i.e. socialisation) over any biological attribute; proposing anatomical sex changes as a form of medical treatment. Gill-Peterson points out that it was the whiteness of the patients Money was working with, and the humanism that they therefore had access to, that made their nonbinary bodies in need of medical intervention. "Nonbinary children *needed* to be forcibly normalised because their whiteness precluded the social stigma they might otherwise endure". Thus, Money's invention of gender, "*was* a form of race" (Gill-Peterson 2018, 122). This approach was disastrous for many of the patients on whom Money performed invasive, often non-consensual surgeries and highlights the interlacing of intersex surgery with the development of transgender medicine.

Binary sex and binary gender, therefore, both emerged as racial cate-gorisations. The concept of gender that trans people were shaping, and with which feminists were working with, was thus a recent sexological intervention designed to naturalise a racialised cisnormative scientific frame, one which was particularly concerned with the medicalisation of intersex embodiments, and which had its roots in colonial and eugenicist practices.

Focussing on the backdrop to the emergence of second wave femi-nism's animating concepts is not as we have seen a necessarily subversive history. Louise Lawrence and Virginia Prince were able to play a leading role in shaping the scientific landscape due to their own educational back-grounds and white middle-class respectability. Meanwhile Reed Erickson was supremely wealthily on the back of his family's property portfolio and smelting business.[23] On the one hand, these individuals—particularly Lawrence and Erickson—did contest the "ontological problem" of bio-logical sex, and thus contributed to efforts to address ideologies not only of cissexism, but whiteness too. They worked to "decouple anatomical medicalized markers of gender (e.g., genitalia) from sociogenically gen-dered subjects" which, in light of the racial history of sexology, Marquis Bey formulates as a central goal of Black feminism (2022, 52). However, Virginia Prince reinforced the sex/gender distinction without concern for the pathologisation of transsexualism and homosexuality that her arguments endorsed. She sought social acceptance for white, middle-class transvestites at the expense of other sex/gender marginals and used her class and race privilege to effect her liberal politics of inclusion. Sexology has a conflicted history, and the intertwinement of trans individuals with this is no exception. Moreover, revisiting the direction of travel between second wave feminism's key concepts and mid-twentieth century trans medicine offers a reminder that the "woman question" as it was being formulated by cisgender, white feminists, dovetailed with the research of racist, eugenicist sexologists—highlighting the longstanding intertwine-ment of feminism with state sanctioned racism.[24]

---

[23] See Meyerowitz, *How Sex Changed* (2004, 210).

[24] See Serena Bassi and Greta LaFleur (2022) for a discussion of contemporary TERF poli-tics and their alignment with the global new right. See Vron Ware ([1996] 2015) for white women's role in British imperialist histories.

SEX, GENDER AND DISCIPLINARY DEVELOPMENT

Thus far, I have argued that the sex/gender distinction—which became one of second wave feminism's animating frameworks—has an unacknowledged trans history, thereby reversing the story according to which "trans" arrives "after" feminism, rather than being integral to the development of western feminism from the start. I now return to the historiography of the Barnard conference, with which I opened this chapter. The scholarly story of the Barnard conference is one which set the stage for analytical divisions and distinctions between "feminism", "queer theory" and "transgender studies", and in doing so, has contributed to a story in which "sex" in the second wave is presumed to be always already "cis". Victoria Hesford has discussed the "profoundly disorienting" rift between feminism and queer theory, which took place in the 1990s (2013, 6) in response to a coalescence of factors, including the fallouts from the Barnard conference.[25] A key ingredient in this rift is in the perceived divergence in "proper objects" for each field, which had the effect of carving up sex, gender and sexuality such that sex became less of a significant category in its right. Within feminism, gender became a central category of analysis (e.g. Lorber 1994) and sex became subsumed to gender. Likewise, within queer studies, sexuality became one of the discipline's core categories with the effect that distinctions between sex as desire, sex as act, and sex as assignment became overlooked.[26]

There is an argument here about how this carving up of disciplinary "proper objects" (gender *or* sexuality), a carving up that became a generative object in its own right,[27] buttressed the elision of trans subjectivities in

[25] Another important factor was the AIDS crisis, which was met with an "in your face" form of resistance to state neglect—providing the basis for queer theory's oppositional tendencies (see Amin 2016).

[26] See Berlant and Warner (1998), Dean (2000), Edelman (2004) for examples of canonical queer theory texts which prioritise "sex" (meaning sexuality) as a privileged category for analysis.

[27] For more on debates over the relationship between feminism and queer theory as academic fields see the 1994 special issue of *differences*: Naomi Schor and Elizabeth Weed (eds.) More Gender Trouble: Feminism Meets Queer Theory, especially Butler, Judith. 1994. "Against Proper Objects." More recently, Tuija Pulkkinen (2016) has argued that "issues of women/gender and sexuality/queer, however much they appear to diverge, in fact belong together in the academy, both institutionally and in terms of scholarly tradition". For Victoria Hesford (2005), the lesbian feminist complicates clear divisions between second wave feminism and queer theory. Meanwhile for Clare Hemmings "in the sexual division of theoretical labor, queer theorists and not feminist theorists still appear to be having all the fun" (2016, 87).

1990s queer theory and feminism (Keegan 2020) and if you follow this footnote,[28] I consider it briefly. What I am interested in pursuing in the rest of this chapter, however, is how Rubin's intervention, as part of a broader narrative wherein feminism moves towards being a discipline primarily suited to the study of gender, contributes to an understanding of "sex" in the second wave as "cis" and elides the contributions of trans people to the period's intellectual development; affirming a temporality in which anti-essentialist, trans-inclusive feminism is a 1990s development.

Thinking Sex went on to achieve the canonical status it has, in part due to Rubin's challenge to feminism's disciplinary authority on the study of "sex":

> I want to challenge the assumption that feminism is or should be the privileged site of a theory of sexuality. Feminism is the theory of gender oppression. To automatically assume that this makes it the theory of sexual

---

[28] For Cáel Keegan (2020), both queer studies and women's studies have sidelined "transgender" and "transsexuality". Within "queer studies", Keegan argues that this was the effect of the assumption that gender means sexuality, and therefore is not a sufficiently interesting object of investigation in itself. Keegan follows Janet Halley (2006) in arguing that feminism/women's studies is attached to a "subordination model" of gender which relies on a fixed binary and therefore is incompatible with transgendered and transsexual fluidity and mobility. These are big overarching claims to make about disciplines, on the basis of little evidence except for one special issue of *Social Text* in the case of "queer studies" and Janet Halley's polemical and heavily challenged characterisation of feminism (see Wiegman 2012). However, it is patently true that "trans" perspectives have a history of being sidelined to a "special guest" (Malatino 2015) model of inclusivity within women's studies. Meanwhile, queer studies has been widely criticised for allegorising trans experiences. Both approaches have fared particularly poorly with respect to accomodating transsexuality, particularly heterosexual transsexuality. Whilst I want to avoid making large generalisations about internally and cross-culturally diverse "fields" of study, I think it is worth highlighting the elision of the category of "sex" as a valuable category in its own right that the distinction between sexuality and gender as objects of analysis gave rise to. A dominant trend that emerged in American feminism and queer theory in the 1990s, was to treat "sex" as synonymous with either gender or sexuality, and therefore not an axis of oppression (or analysis) in itself. For instance, the 2004 *GLQ* forum titled "Thinking Sex/Thinking Gender", which presented 19 takes on the epithet and culminated in a 102 page special "GLQ forum" issue of *GLQ*, discusses the relationship between gender and sexuality (Jagose and Don Kuluck eds. 2004), with only two of the contributions substantially theorising sex as distinct from sexuality (see Spade and Wahng 2004: 240–253 and Rosario 2004: 280–287). When sex/gender/sexuality gets reduced to gender/sexuality, the experiences of trans people, especially transsexuals, for whom sex is an important dimension of subjectivity and embodiment gets elided.

oppression is to fail to distinguish between gender, on the one hand, and erotic desire, on the other" (Rubin [1984] 2011c, 177–178).[29]

The essay did more than just intervene in the feminist discussions of the period. In providing the political justification for a waning of feminism's authority as the privileged lens through which to study sex,[30] the arguments in *Thinking Sex* went on to reshape critical engagements with the nexus of sex, gender, and sexuality (Love 2011). Clarifying feminism as a field suited to the study of "gender" but not (or to a lesser extent) "sexuality", Rubin's influential argument heterosexualises feminist arguments up until this point; sexuality "was proposed as not gender, not only gender, and not gender in its heteronormative modes" (Hemmings 2016, 84). It also, as I will demonstrate, cisgenders second wave feminist arguments, sidelining "sex" as a significant category of analysis in its own right, an important element of trans-inclusive feminism, as illuminated in Snorton's epigraph.

If sexuality is analytically divorced from gender, what happens to "sex" as a category of embodiment? Indeed, whilst this was not the meaning of "sex" that Rubin's essay focussed on, in distinguishing between "sexuality" and "gender" as privileged objects for feminism and queer studies respectively, the fact that second wave feminism was also a lively source of knowledge production on all aspects of "sex"—embodiment and subjectivity as well as desire—is overlooked. Instead, according to dominant narratives of feminism's *intellectual* development "third wave feminists tend to consider second wave feminism as triangulated in essentialism, universalism and naturalism" (Gillis et al. 2004, xxiv) and dependent on an "untheorised female body" (Stryker 2007, 63) as its philosophical foundation. These characterisations lead to the overwhelming association of the period's philosophical output as "cis"; attached to an understanding of sex as the uncritically accepted biological foundation for gender's socialised effects.

Judith Butler's citation is central to this storytelling. Clare Hemmings argues that in western feminist progress narratives, Butler is accorded

---

[29] See Heather Love (2011), Rachel Corbman (2015) and Kadji Amin (2016), for discussions of the influence of the sex wars on the direction of the academic study of sexuality in the US, and particularly for the formation and appeal of queer theory at the turn of the 1990s.

[30] Rubin has resisted interpretations of her essay as dismissing feminism: "I certainly never intended "Thinking Sex" as an attack on feminism [...] it "assumed a largely feminist readership. It was delivered at a feminist conference, aimed at a feminist audience, and written within the context of a feminist discussion. I do not consider it an attack on a body of work to say that it cannot do everything equally well" (2011a, 303).

feminism's "narrative momentum" (2011, 175). Butler's performative theory of gender in *Gender Trouble* is regularly paraphrased as having "collapsed the sex/gender distinction" (Salih 2002, 55)—whether or not they did has been taken up elsewhere[31]—and as a result, they are regularly narrated as being "the *first* to challenge feminism's foundational category, 'woman'" (McBean 2016 9, italics mine).[32] It is the following line from Butler' *Gender Trouble* (2006, 9–10) that has been taken up as proof of this collapse and become elementary in introductory textbooks, lectures and courses in gender studies:

perhaps this construct called 'sex' is as culturally constructed as gender; indeed, perhaps it was always already gender, with the consequence that the distinction between sex and gender turns out to be no distinction at all.

This abstracted argument typically gets juxtaposed to a "before" when feminism relied on a "coat rack view of sex and gender" where sexed bodies are like coat racks and "provide the site upon which gender [is] constructed" (Nicholson 1994, 81).[33] For Butler, it is a "stylised repetition of acts" (2006, 191) that performatively creates the illusion of a gendered

[31] See for example, Stella Sandford, "Contingent Ontologies: Sex, Gender and 'Woman' in Simone de Beauvoir and Judith Butler" (1999), Samuel Chambers, "'Sex' and the Problem of the Body: Reconstructing Judith Butler's Theory of Sex/Gender" (2007) and Samatha Pergadia "Geologies of Sex and Gender: Excavating the Materialism of Gayle Rubin and Judith Butler" (2018).

[32] Equally in return narratives it is in a post-Butler, theoretically enriched, world that we can now return to the activist seventies, armed as we are with the necessary philosophical insights to make good on earlier ambitions. Meanwhile loss narratives, either explicitly or by reference to deconstruction or queer theory, take aim at the density and abstraction of Butler's work to mourn a time when feminism was concerned with pressing political issues.

[33] Clare Hemmings' detailing of the dominant narratives of western feminism's storytelling highlight the differing mobilisations of an overall consensus that feminism developed from relying on a unified subject, "woman" as it's necessary foundation in the 1970s, to the postmodern fragmentation of this category in the 1990s. Focussing on the "gloss paragraphs" (2016, 18) that repeat themselves in key feminist journals, she demonstrates that the "*dominant narratives* that emerge in the telling of feminist stories" (2011, 16 italics in original) rely on common sense views and shared understandings that require little by way of interrogation or evidence. Whilst the key nodes in this historiography are the same; from activist utopianism to theoretical complexity; from unified "women" to difference and deconstruction, the affective currency of the story varies depending on the storyteller. Either it is one of progress (goodbye to the unsophisticated bad old days), loss (a lament at feminism's perceived de-politicisation) or return (we can synthesise today's theoretical sophistication with yesterday's activist urgency and materialism).

reality and sexed foundation. Moreover, "that gender reality is created through social performances means that the very notions of an essential sex and a true or abiding masculinity or femininity are also constituted as part of the strategy that conceals gender's performative character" (ibid.). By bringing deconstruction to bear on feminism, Butler is typically credited with being "the first" to deconstruct sex.

What I am interested in, is how this narrative of the sex/gender distinction as evolving from understanding sex as fixed, to sex as an effect of gender (both reductive characterisations of more nuanced perspectives) and the corresponding citation convention regarding Butler's "collapse of the sex/gender distinction" contributes to a story in which the category of "sex" in the second wave was always already "cis". It is common, for example, to see accounts of the genesis of trans feminism rehearse the progress narrative that Hemmings (2011; 2016) identifies, tying second wave feminism to a biologically essentialist and therefore trans-exclusionary definition of womanhood—without any evidence that this was the case. To offer just a few examples, Emi Koyama's *Trans feminist Manifesto*, appeals to the same story of second wave feminism that Butler's narrative function evokes:

> Though second wave of feminism popularised the idea that a person's gender is distinct from her or his physiological sex and is socially constructed, it largely left unquestioned the belief that there was such a thing as true physical (biological) sex. The separation of gender from sex was a powerful rhetorical move used to break down compulsory gender roles, but it allowed feminists to question only half of the problem, avoiding the question of the naturalness of essential female and male sexes (Koyama 2003, 249).

Sally Hines' overview of the development of trans feminist perspectives of sex and gender likewise characterises second wave feminism as overwhelmingly essentialist:

> Conceptualisations of the differences between sex—as biological—and gender—as cultural—were crucial to second wave feminist thought. The sex/gender binary thus became principal. Through the 1960s and 1970s studies of gender—as separate from sex—materialised through feminist work. Gender, it was stressed, was a social category, which was imposed and internalised across multiple sites...(Hines 2020, 702)

And more recently, and in the context of trans studies, Howard Chiang draws on a similair pre/post-Butler trajectory in his review of Afsaneh Najmabadi's *Professing Selves:*

A growing body of literature in the history of transsexuality, intersexuality, and transgender communities now gives historical weight to Butler's famous claim that "'sex' is as culturally constructed as gender. (Chiang 2016, 158).

Whilst more nuanced genealogies are available,[34] the progress narrative that Hemmings identifies remains a readily available and recyclable story which excuses failing to undertake more detailed engagement with feminist philosophies of the 1970s (and 1980s). When Butler is granted a seminal position in the story of "sex" and "gender", such that "sex" in the second wave remains "cis"—as Koyama, Hines and Chiang's own glosses allude to—the vast and varied trans feminist epistemologies circulating during the second wave are written out of feminist theory. Moreover, the influences of trans epistemologies that shaped the categories of "sex" and "gender" in the second wave are nowhere to be seen. Instead, these citations homogenise second wave feminism as theoretically trans-exclusionary, politicising "gender" whilst taking for granted a stable foundation of "sex". An obvious contribution of [many] trans feminist epistemologies is that sex too is mutable.[35] Where do these bodies go in a story in which Butler was to challenge the fixity of sex?

The degree to which Butler is regarded as shifting the terms of feminist enquiry, then, not only obfuscates the dynamic engagements with the categories of "woman" and "sex" long being foregrounded by trans feminists, Black feminists, feminists of color and radical feminists throughout the second wave, but also authorises accounts of trans feminism, as

---

[34] Mary Hawkesworth's 1997 essay "Confounding Gender" gives a useful overview of the state of "gender" as an analytical concept within feminism at the time of the 1990s. It also makes the relevant argument that gender has been overly invested and advises that "it will be helpful to enrich our conceptual terminology, taking advantage of crucial distinctions such as sexed embodiedness, sexuality, sexual identity, gender identity, gendered divisions of labor, gendered social relations, and gender symbolism, rather than collapsing such diverse notions into the single term *gender*" (1997, 682, italics in original).

[35] Virginia Prince's philosophy of transvestism by contrast relies on the immutability of sex for her notion of "true transvestism" (see Hill 2007, 57, also Chapter 2, footnote 65).

discussed at the start, as a "third wave sensibility".[36] The association of second wave feminism with essentialism and exclusionarity naturalises a separation between "women" and trans people in the development of feminism and facilitates the elision of the contributions of trans people to feminist knowledge production prior to 1990.

According to Robyn Wiegman, the transition from "women" to "gender" as feminism's principal object of analysis, represented a rescue effort for feminism. "Gender" became invested with the theoretical sophistication and capaciousness that "women" had become symbolically antagonistic to (Wiegman 2012).[37] This investment in "gender" to make good of "women's" categorical failure was complimented by feminism's embrace of postmodernism and differences within the category of woman, over and against the intellectual narrowness of feminism's earlier universalising understanding of woman (Hemmings 2016). *From* women, *to* gender is thus, as Wiegman illustrates, a promise, containing a whole host of institutional and academic investments: from exclusion to inclusion, from white feminism to intersectional feminism and—most importantly for my argument—from sex and gender essentialism (or cisnormativity) to

---

[36] The idea that Butler was the first to challenge the category of "woman" not only writes out the contributions of trans people to the development of feminism but also second wave Black feminist thought, which drew on long legacies of Black women's challenges to dominant definitions of womanhood, since Sojourner Truth's historic 1851 speech: "Ain't I a woman?". In addition, as Rachel Corbman points out, Butler's argument about the ways in which the sex/gender binary is reproduced through compulsory heterosexuality had already been made by black lesbian feminists including Barbara Smith 'in her influential speech to the National Women's Studies Association: Racism and Women's Studies, when she explained: enforced heterosexuality is the extreme manifestation of male domination and patriarchal rule' (Corbman 2015, 72). In "Uses of the Erotic", Audre Lorde similarly denaturalises heterosexual imperatives, locating them in a specifically "European-American male tradition" ([1984] 2017, 29).

[37] As Black feminists have pointed out, Black women and women of colour have always functioned in excess of that category (Truth 1851, hooks [1981] 2015; Green and Bey 2017). The Santa Cruz Feminist of Color Collective highlight the coalitional rather than essentialist understanding of "women" that grounds their feminist of color organising: "the concept 'of colour' does not so much function to demarcate an inside and an outside, an "us" versus "them" but instead creates the possibility of a larger "we" (Dotson 2014, 27). A coalitional approach to the category of "women" resists what Robyn Wiegman describes as the "categorical essentialism" embedded in the idea that "women" is necessarily a "scene of exclusion". As she writes, this "tends to situate critiques by "women of colour and lesbians" as ends in themselves and not as powerful critical investments in the possibility of making *women* adequate to the political aspiration that the founding paradigm ascribed to it" (2012, 63, italics in original).

fluidity.[38] Butler's citation is therefore central to this promise and offers a valuable response to feminism's own crisis of "sex" that was permeating in the aftermath of the sex wars, and was codified in Rubin's influential distinction between the study of sex and the study of gender.

What I want to suggest, then, is that Butler's citation plays two key roles in the story of the category of "sex" before the sex wars. First, they are both invested with "queering" feminism and moving feminism away from the "sex negativity"[39] of the sex wars. And, second, they are credited with deconstructing sex, therefore offering a theoretically sophisticated, less trans-exclusionary alternative to the essentialist philosophies of "the past". Yet whilst cisnormativity was certainly present in some second wave radical feminism, this book has demonstrated that the archive of trans feminist print culture, as well as more canonical texts such as Andrea Dworkin's corpus, point to a far more complex picture regarding the epistemologies of sex that were circulating in the second wave. As this chapter has discussed, the emergence of feminism's key concepts in the second wave had trans feminism as their foundations. Moreover, "gender", far from being a necessarily more inclusive, fluid category that could replace woman, has—as its origins—the racist, biopolitical roots of the clinic

---

[38] This follows from my point in Chap. 2, where I argued that whilst the "woman question" became installed as a question of ontology (what *is* a woman) via the institutionalisation of feminism in the second half of the 1970s. However, it began in the women's liberation movement as a far more open question of collective identity, where for women of colour, queer and trans women, "women" signified both a horizon to be fought for and an object of generative contest against patriarchally imposed expectations.

[39] Sex-negativity was a term initiated by self-defined "pro-sex" feminists to critique anti-pornography feminists during the sex wars. It has since assumed the status of a shorthand for forms of feminism that are: anti-pornography, anti-sex-work, and anti-S/M. However, it has been contested in recent years for its grouping of often vastly different sexual practices together, and it's reductive binarised characterisation of these various practices as simply "good" or "bad" (Glick 2000). That Butler has been received as "rescuing" feminism from its sex-negative excesses, is exemplified in quotes such as the following: In a book dedicated to legal applications of Butler's thought, Elena Louzidou argues that Butler's "intervention introduced a refreshing perspective in feminist thought. Women were not any more to be viewed as passive, repressed by power and waiting for the regime of power to alter, recognise and "represent" them in order to be able to transform their conditions of liveability" (Louzidou 2007, 4). This is exemplary of Butler's apparent reconciliation of the animosity of the sex wars, through the Foucauldian insight that power/knowledge cannot be fully escaped (and therefore that the anti-pornography ambitions of "liberating" woman as a group was doomed to fail) but *can* be subverted—granting transgressive potential to previously marginalised sexual practices.

which sought precisely to reinscribe a foundation for cis, white woman-hood (the categories of "male" and "female"), as it was increasingly clear that sex attributes were too unwieldy for the task.

Conclusion: From "Trans" to Feminism: The Direction of Travel of Feminism's Key Concepts

The idea that second wave feminism depended on an untheorised female body as its ground has contributed to idea that the second wave was not only demographically, but philosophically, "cis". Trans feminism is then positioned as arriving "after" second wave feminism. Such an assumption is embedded in citation conventions which posit second wave feminism as attached to an essentialising sex/gender distinction, prior to Judith Butler's performative theory of gender in the 1990s. When Butler's con-tribution to the sex/gender debate is taken as a unique challenge to a past life of political and philosophical exclusionarity, they are positioned as not just queering feminism (by challenging the alignment of gender with het-erosexuality) but also "transing" feminism, putting in place the conditions for a feminism that no longer appeals to an untheorised biological basis as its ground.[40]

Resisting this temporality, this chapter has demonstrated that rather than arriving "after" second wave feminism, it was a network of influential trans labourers in the mid-twentieth century, that provided second wave feminism with its conceptual scaffolding. Louise Lawrence, Virginia Prince and Reed Erickson were among the many trans figures whose knowledge

[40] It is widely recognised that Butler's contribution to feminist theory "queered feminism", putting into circulation the philosophical foundations for queer theory's key concepts at the turn of the 1990s. Eve Sedgwick captures the historic significance of *Gender Trouble* for the emerging field of queer theory, in the first essay to the inaugural issue of the field's journal *GLQ*: "Anyone who was at the 1991 Rutgers conference on Gay and Lesbian Studies and heard *Gender Trouble* appealed to in paper after paper, couldn't help being awed by the pro-ductive impact this dense and even imposing work has had on the recent development of queer theory and reading" (Sedgwick 1993, 1). For a discussion of the queer precedents in second wave feminism see Lisa Downing and Lara Cox's 2018 special issue of *Paragraph* "Queering the Second Wave" (Downing and Cox 2018). Butler's reception within trans studies has been more mixed. Whilst the notion of gender as performative (*Gender Trouble*, 2006) or citational (*Bodies that Matter*, 2011) is decidedly anti-foundationalist and anti-essentialist, in reducing all operations of power to norms, Butler's arguments were met with sustained criticism for underplaying attachment to norms, leading to critiques that Butler's work allegorises trans lives (Prosser 1998; Heaney 2017).

laid the groundwork for the sexological developments of John Money, Robert Stoller and Harry Benjamin, that second wave feminists would then centre in their own theories of patriarchy and socialisation. The key concepts of "sex" "gender and "gender roles" that US feminism in the second wave sourced from recent sexological studies were directly informed by the lives and labour of a community of trans intellectuals and activists. These concepts have their own murky histories, and the past life of sexology includes racialised biomedicine and the development of medical gatekeeping. The backdrop to feminism's key concepts then is as ambivalent as the rest of the second wave and it has not been my intention to occlude this. However, returning to Stryker's argument about doing justice to processes of knowledge production, this chapter has argued feminist historiographies need to acknowledge second wave feminism's trans feminist influence. Not only is trans feminism not a recent development, it was trans feminism that enabled academic feminism in the second wave to get off the ground.

BIBLIOGRAPHY

Abelove, Henry, et al. 1983. The Barnard Conference. Letter to the Editor. *Feminist Studies* 9 (1): 177–182.

Amin, Kadji. 2016. Haunted by the 1990s: Queer Theory's Affective Histories. *Women's Studies Quarterly* 44 (3/4): 173–189.

Bassi, Serena, and Greta LaFleur. 2022. Introduction. *TSQ: Transgender Studies Quarterly* 9 (3): 311–333.

Beauvoir, Simone de. [1949] 1997. *The Second Sex*. London: Vintage.

Benjamin, Harry. 1966. *The Transsexual Phenomenon*. New York: Julian Press.

Berlant, Lauren, and Michael Warner. 1998. Sex in Public. *Critical Inquiry* 24 (2): 547–566.

Bettcher, Talia Mae. 2016. Intersexuality, Transgender, and Transsexuality. In Lisa Disch, and Mary Hawkesworth (eds), *The Oxford Handbook of Feminist Theory*, 407–427. Oxford University Press.

Bey, Marquis. 2022. *Black Trans Feminism*. Durham: Duke University Press.

Bullough, V. L. (Vern L.), and B. Bullough. 1993, *Cross Dressing, Sex, and Gender*. Philadelphia: University of Pennsylvania Press.

Butler, Judith. 1994. Against Proper Objects. *Differences* 6 (2–3): 1–26.

———. [1990] 2006. *Gender Trouble: Feminism and the Subversion of Identity*. New York; London: Routledge.

———. [1993] 2011. *Bodies that Matter: On the Discursive Limits of "sex"*. Abingdon, Oxon; New York: Routledge.

Califia, Patrick. 2003. *Sex Changes: Transgender Politics*. San Francisco: Cleis Press.

Cauldwell, David. 1949. Psychopathia Transsexualis. *Sexology* 16: 274–280.

Chambers, Samuel A. 2007. 'Sex' and the Problem of the Body: Reconstructing Judith Butler's Theory of Sex/Gender. *Body & Society* 13 (4): 47–75.

Chiang, Howard. 2016. The Axiom of Sex. *Journal of Women's History* 28 (4): 158–163.

Clare, Eli. 2015. *Exile and Pride: Disability, Queerness, and Liberation*. Duke University Press.

Comella, L. 2008. Looking Backward: Barnard and its Legacies. *The Communication Review* 11 (3): 202–211.

Corbman, Rachel. 2015. The Scholars and the Feminists: The Barnard Sex Conference and the History of the Institutionalization of Feminism. *Feminist Formations* 27 (3): 49–80.

Dahms, Isabell. 2021. Isabell Dahms—Always Trouble: Gender before and after Gender Trouble (2020). *Radical Philosophy*. https://www.radicalphilosophy.com/article/always-trouble.

Dean, Tim. 2000. *Beyond Sexuality*. Chicago: University of Chicago Press.

Devor, Aaron H., and Nicholas Matte. 2004. One Inc. and Reed Erickson. *GLQ: A Journal of Lesbian and Gay Studies* 10 (2): 179–209.

Devor, Aaron, and Nicholas Matte. 2007. Building a Better World for Transpeople: Reed Erickson and the Erickson Educational Foundation. *The International Journal of Transgenderism*. 10 (1): 47–68.

Docter, Richard F. 2004. *From Man to Woman: The Transgender Journey of Virginia Prince*. Northridge, CA: Docter Press.

Dominic, Kimi. 2021. The *True Transsexual* and Transnormativity: A Critical Discourse Analysis of the Wrong-Body Discourse. PhD Dissertation. Accessed 03 March 2023. http://dspace.library.uvic.ca/bitstream/handle/1828/13627/Dominic_Kimi_PhD_2021.pdf

Dotson, Kristie. 2014. Building on "the Edge of Each Other's Battles": A Feminist of Color Multidimensional Lens. *Hypatia* 29 (1): 23–40.

Downing, Lisa, and Lara Cox. November 2018. Queering the Second Wave: Anglophone and Francophone Contexts. *Paragraph. A Journal of Modern Critical Theory* 41 (3). Edinburgh: Edinburgh University Press.

Dworkin, Andrea. 1974. *Woman Hating*. New York: Dutton.

Edelman, Lee. 2004. *No future: Queer Theory and the Death Drive*. Durham: Duke University Press.

Ekins, Richard, and Dave King. 2005. Introduction. *The International Journal of Transgenderism* 8 (4): 1–4.

Germon, Jennifer. 2009. *Gender: A Genealogy of an Idea*. New York: Palgrave Macmillan.

Gillis, Stacy, Gillian Howie, and Rebecca Munford. 2004. *Third Wave Feminism: A Critical Exploration*. Basingstoke; New York: Palgrave Macmillan.

Gill-Peterson, Jules. 2018. *Histories of the Transgender Child*. Minneapolis: University of Minnesota Press.

———. 2020. in Aizura, Aren Z. et al. 2020. Thinking with Trans Now. *Social Text* 38 (4): 125–47.

Glick, Elisa. 2000. Sex Positive: Feminism, Queer Theory, and the Politics of Transgression. *Feminist Review* 64 (1): 19–45.

Green, Kai M., and Marquis Bey. 2017. Where Black Feminist Thought and Trans* Feminism Meet: A Conversation. *Souls* 19 (4): 438–454.

Halley, Janet E. 2006. *Split Decisions: How and Why to Take a Break from Feminism*. Princeton, NJ: Princeton University Press.

Hawkesworth, Mary. 1997. Confounding Gender. *Signs: Journal of Women in Culture and Society* 22 (3): 649–685.

Heaney, Emma. 2017. *The New Woman: Literary Modernism, Queer Theory, and the Trans Feminine Allegory*. Evanston, IL: Northwestern University Press.

Hemmings, Clare. 2011. *Why Stories Matter: The Political Grammar of Feminist Theory*. Durham: Duke University Press.

———. 2016. Is Gender Studies Singular? Stories of Queer/Feminist Difference and Displacement. *Differences* 27 (2): 79–102.

Hesford, Victoria. 2005. Feminism and Its Ghosts. *Feminist Theory* 6 (3): 227–250.

———. 2013. *Feeling Women's Liberation*. Durham: Duke University Press.

Hill, Robert S. 2007. *'As a man I exist; as a woman I live': Heterosexual Transvestism and the Contours of Gender and Sexuality in Postwar America*. PhD dissertation. University of Michigan.

Hines, Sally. 2020. Sex Wars and (Trans) Gender Panics: Identity and Body Politics in Contemporary UK Feminism. *The Sociological Review* 68 (4): 699–717.

hooks, bell. [1984] 2015. *Ain't I A Woman: Black Women and Feminism*, 2nd edn. New York: Routledge.

Jaggar, Alison M. 1983. *Feminist Politics and Human Nature*. Lanham: Rowman & Littlefield.

Jagose, Annamarie, and Don Kulick. 2004. Thinking Sex/ Thinking Gender. *GLQ: A Journal of Lesbian and Gay Studies* 10 (2): 211–212.

Joynt, Chase. 2022. *Framing Agnes*. Film. Canada: Fae Pictures and Level Ground.

Keegan, Cáel M. 2020. Getting Disciplined: What's Trans About Queer Studies Now? *Journal of Homosexuality* 67 (3): 384–397.

Kessler, Suzanne J., and Wendy McKenna. 1978. *Gender: An Ethnomethodolgical Approach*. New York: Wiley.

Koyama, Emi. 2003. The Transfeminist Manifesto. In *Catching a Wave: Reclaiming Feminism for the 21st Century*, ed. Rory Cooke Dicker and Alison Piepmeier, 244–262. Boston: Northeastern University Press.

Largent, Mark A. 2008. *Breeding Contempt: The History of Coerced Sterilization in the United States*. New Brunswick, N.J.; London: Rutgers University Press.

Logandice, Francine. *Fancine Logandice Collection*. Carton 1 and Carton 2, Collection Number 2002–04, The Gay and Lesbian Historical Society Archives, San Francisco CA.

Lorber, Judith. 1994. *Paradoxes of Gender*. New Haven, CT: Yale University Press.

Lorde, Audre. 2017. *Your Silence Will Not Protect You*. London: Silver Press.

Louzidou, Elena. 2007. *Judith Butler: Ethics, Law, Politics*. New York: Routledge-Cavendish.

Love, Heather. 2011. Introduction. *GLQ: A Journal of Lesbian and Gay Studies* 17 (1): 1–14.

Lugones, María. 2007. Heterosexualism and the Colonial/Modern Gender System. *Hypatia* 22 (1): 186–219.

Malatino, Hil. 2015. Pedagogies of Becoming: Trans Inclusivity and the Crafting of Being. *TSQ: Transgender Studies Quarterly* 2 (3): 395–410.

Matte, Nicholas. 2014. *Historicizing Liberal American Transnormativities: Medicine, Media, Activism, 1960–1990*. ProQuest Dissertations Publishing.

McBean, Sam. 2016. *Feminism's Queer Temporalities, Transformations: Thinking Through Feminism*. London: Routledge, Taylor & Francis Group.

Meyerowitz, Joanne. 2001. Sex Research at the Borders of Gender: Transvestites, Transsexuals, and Alfred C. Kinsey. *Bulletin of the History of Medicine* 75 (1): 72–90.

Meyerowitz, Joanne J. 2004. *How Sex Changed: A History of Transsexuality*. Cambridge, MA: Harvard University Press. ProQuest Ebook Central.

Millett, Kate. [1970] 1977. *Sexual Politics*. London: Virago.

———. 2000. *Sexual Politics*. Urbana: University of Illinois Press.

Nicholson, Linda. 1994. Interpreting Gender. *Signs* 20 (1): 79–105.

Oakley, Ann. 1972. *Sex, Gender and Society*. London: Temple Smith.

Oyěwùmí, Oyèrónkẹ́. 1997. *The Invention of Women: Making An African Sense Of Western Gender Discourses*. Minneapolis; London: University of Minnesota Press.

Pergadia, Samantha. 2018. Geologies of Sex and Gender: Excavating the Materialism of Gayle Rubin and Judith Butler. *Feminist Studies* 44 (1): 171.

Preciado, Paul B. 2013. *Testo Junkie: Sex, Drugs, and Biopolitics in the Pharmacopornographic Era*. New York: The Feminist Press at the City University of New York.

Prince, Virginia Charles. 1967. *The Transvestite and His Wife*. Los Angeles: Chevalier Publications.

———. 1971. *How to Become a Woman, Though Male*. Los Angeles: Chevalier Publications.

———. 1976. *Understanding Cross Dressing*. Tulare: Chevalier.

Prince, Virginia. [1973] 2005. Sex Vs. Gender. *The International Journal of Transgenderism* 8 (4): 29–32.

Prosser, Jay. 1998. *Second Skins: The Body Narratives of Transsexuality, Gender and Culture Series*. New York: Columbia University Press.

Pulkkinen, Tuija. 2016. Feelings of Injustice: The Institutionalization of Gender Studies and the Pluralization of Feminism. *Differences* 27 (2): 103–124.

Rosario, Vernon A. 2004. The Biology of Gender and the Construction of Sex? *GLQ: A Journal of Lesbian and Gay Studies* 10 (2): 280–287.

Rubin, Gayle. 2011a. Sexual Traffic: Interview with Gayle Rubin by Judith Butler. In *Deviations: A Gayle Rubin Reader*, 276–309. Durham: Duke University Press.

———. [1975] 2011b. The Traffic in Women: Notes on the 'Political Economy' of Sex. In *Deviations: A Gayle Rubin Reader*, 33–65. Durham: Duke University Press.

———. [1984] 2011c. Thinking Sex: Notes for a Radical Theory of the Politics of Sexuality. In *Deviations: A Gayle Rubin Reader*, 137–181. Durham: Duke University Press.

Salih, Sarah. 2002. *Judith Butler*. London: Routledge.

Sandford, Stella. 1999. Contingent Ontologies: Sex, Gender and 'Woman' in Simone de Beauvoir and Judith Butler. *Radical Philosophy* 97: 18–29.

Schor, Naomi and Weed, Elizabeth (eds.) 1994. More Gender Trouble: Feminism Meets Queer Theory. *Differences* 6 (2–3): 1-313

Sedgwick, Eve Kosofsky. 1993. Queer Performativity: Henry James's The Art of the Novel. *GLQ: A Journal of Lesbian and Gay Studies* 1 (1): 1–16.

Snitow, A., C. Stansell, and S. Thompson, eds. 1983. *Powers of Desire: The Politics of Sexuality*. New York: Monthly Review Press.

Snorton, C. Riley. 2017. *Black on Both Sides: A Racial History of Trans Identity*. Minneapolis, MN: University of Minnesota Press.

Somerville, Siobhan B. 2000. *Queering the Color Line: Race and the Invention of Homosexuality in American Culture, Series Q*. Amsterdam: Duke University Press.

Spade, Dean, and Sel Wahng. 2004. Transecting the Academy. *GLQ: A Journal of Lesbian and Gay Studies* 10 (2): 240–253.

Spillers, Hortense. 1987. Mama's Baby, Papa's Maybe: An American Grammar Book. *Diacritics* 17 (2): 65–81.

Stoller, Robert J. 1968. *Sex and Gender: On the Development of Masculinity and Femininity*. London: Routledge.

———. 1975. *Sex and Gender. the Transsexual Experiment*. London: Hogarth.

Stone, Sandy. [1987] 1992. The Empire Strikes Back: A Posttranssexual Manifesto. *Camera Obscura: Feminism, Culture, and Media Studies* 10 (2): 150–176.

Stryker, Susan, 2005. Foreword. *The International Journal of Transgenderism*. [Online] 8 (4): xv–xvi.

———. 2007. Transgender Feminism. In *Third Wave Feminism*, ed. S. Gillis, G. Howie, and R. Munford. London: Palgrave Macmillan.

———. 2008. *Transgender History: The Roots of Today's Revolution*. 1st ed. New York: Seal Press.

Truth, Sojourner. 1851. Ain't I A Woman? Available online. Sojourner Truth: Ain't I A Woman? (U.S. National Park Service). Accessed 4 July 2023. www. nps.gov/articles/sojourner-truth.

Vance, Carole, ed. 1984. *Pleasure and Danger: Exploring Female Sexuality.* Boston: Routledge and K. Paul.

Walters, Suzanna, ed. 2016a. Pleasure and Danger: Sexual Freedom and Feminism in the Twenty-First Century. *Signs* 42 (1): 1–297.

———. 2016b. Introduction: The Dangers of a Metaphor—Beyond the Battlefield in the Sex Wars. *Signs* 42 (1): 1–9.

Ware, Vron. [1996] 2015. *Beyond the Pale: White Women, Racism and History.* London: Verso.

Wiegman, Robyn. 2012. *Object Lessons.* Durham, NC: Duke University Press.

Zagria. 2022. Harry Benjamin in Transvestia Magazine. *Gender Variance Who's Who*, December 01. https://zagria.blogspot.com/2022/12/harry-benjamin-in-transvestia-magazine.html#.ZAG83uzP23I

CHAPTER 6

Conclusion

To be recognised as human, levelly human, is enough
—Combahee River Collective, A Black Feminist Statement

Sex, The Second Wave and Not Getting Stuck

Second wave feminism is a "sticky" object. It is temporally stuck- its arguments confined to the 1970s with little to offer twenty-first-century feminist debates or struggles. It is affectively sticky, "saturated with [negative]
affect" (Ahmed 2014, 11), if not, the definition of "bad" feminism altogether. And a seemingly ever-expanding list of [negative] associations
attach to it. More often than not a lesson in what not to think or how not
to do feminism, than an enduring dialogue partner for contemporary
issues, second wave feminism comes with a lot of heavy baggage.

This book has argued that reconsidering the temporality of second
wave feminism has a particular pertinence for our recognition of trans
feminisms past and present. Historians working on trans history are constantly challenging the framing of trans lives and labour as recent discover-
ies in order to counter "assertions of the putative 'newness' of transgender
experience" which are "consistently used to undermine the legitimacy of
nonbinary genders" (LaFleur et al. 2021, 4). Yet the longstanding presence of trans women and men within feminism, as well as the influence

© The Author(s), under exclusive license to Springer Nature
Switzerland AG 2023
E. Cousens, *Trans Feminist Epistemologies in the US Second Wave*,
Breaking Feminist Waves,
https://doi.org/10.1007/978-3-031-33731-4_6

that trans knowledges have had on the feminist movement, is only beginning to be subject to detailed reappraisal. Second wave feminism has a rich trans feminist history, and the trans feminist epistemologies that were circulating in that period are of historical and philosophical relevance today.

Rather than positioning the second wave chronologically, or defining the period as activist rather than academic, a trans feminist reading practice enables us to encounter the second wave as a genre, particular features of which include: questioning, collaboration, and the sharing of experience as a way of giving language to previously unspoken affects and embodiments. The second wave feminism that I have been considering here has been characterised by its utopianism and its contention that nothing less than an assault on ontology will do.

When women's studies became institutionalised as an academic field in the 1970s, the idea of a sex/gender distinction which ontologised the former became a central analytic device. However, the academically authored arguments that made their way into published books were far from representative of the contributions to knowledge production that were taking place at this time of social and political upheaval. This book has argued that the majority of second wave feminism circulated outside the academy; in print, in manifestoes and in consciousness-raising groups. Expanding the canon of second wave feminism to include the overlooked arguments taking place in independently produced community journals and the print culture from the period reveals a rich set of theoretical resources developed by trans women and the wider feminist movement in the 1970s, which can contribute to dialogues on sex and gender today. This is an urgent, intersectional move, drawing on the Black feminist principle that valuable theory exceeds institutionalised academic knowledge production and whilst my own use of source materials remains limited, is one with the capacity to transform citation practices going forward. Many of these contributions are theoretically valuable in themselves and demonstrate the confluence of theory and action, evidence collaborative forms of knowledge production, and provide pedagogical insights into how dissent and disagreement can be part of theoretical development.

The central argument of this book is that the widely received notion that US feminism's second wave was philosophically and demographically "cis" deserves a reassessment. In opening up second wave feminism to a trans feminist re-reading, this argument has been supported by three additional propositions. First, there is the philosophical argument that the "sex/gender debate" has not been settled and that second wave texts, including journals by those on the transfeminine spectrum, are valuable sources of theory on this topic. Second, there is a historiographical argument that the way that second wave feminism has been conventionally framed elides the existence of the trans people shaping the knowledges and activism of the day. And third, there is a disciplinary argument; that productive alliances can be forged between second wave feminist and trans studies literature, and that expanding the canon to include print culture has an important, intersectional role to play in enabling this.

The idea that sex and gender were ontologically distinct categories first entered the vernacular of western feminism via the emerging sexological literature being produced by American scientists such as John Money, Harry Benjamin and Robert Stoller. Whilst these researchers were pathologising, created the foundations for medical gatekeeping, and made careers on the back of the trans and intersex people they worked with, it is important to remember that trans and intersex individuals weren't just patients. They were also fellow practitioners, colleagues, academics and philanthropists- shaping the development of the sexual sciences, in more and less beneficial directions.

The development of taxonomies, like the history of feminism itself, is not linear, and the distinction between categories of "sex" and "gender" that had been established through the influence of Virginia Prince, Reed Erickson and Louise Lawrence on the "gender scientists" not only enabled second wave feminism to get off the ground. This framework also provided important means for negotiating and communicating sexed and gendered embodiment for Margo Schulter, readers of the *Journal of Male Feminism* and Andrea Dworkin who all reworked these notions outside biologically essentialist and pathologising frameworks. These authors advanced a trans feminist resistance to the violence of gendering as something imposed from outside- arguing instead for gendered self-determination as the first and foremost priority of radical, coalitional feminism. Kalaniopua Young writes that, that "The structural violence of gender oppression affects everyone, whether self-identified as men, women, asexual, and/or gender or sexual liminal" (in Boellstorff et al. 2014, 428–9) and I have argued that bringing second wave and trans feminist analyses together illuminates the structural violence of coercive gender for everyone. Demonstrating that gender-based violence affects everyone is an important lesson from the trans feminist epistemologies circulating during

US feminism's second wave, and one that offers an important rejoinder to the strategic weaponisation of [cisgender] women's vulnerability in contemporary transphobic discourses.[1]

A second lesson in the trans feminist perspectives encountered here which speaks to the present moment is a resistance to single-issue identity politics (Dean 1996). In Margo Schulter's *Second Wave* essay, she argues against a politics of "more oppressed than though" (1973, 41), instead holding on to a commitment to liberation understood as human liberation. In an article two years later for *Gay Community News*, she reiterates her exasperation at the identity politics of the period noting that "It is a curious quirk of human nature that people often spend 50% of the time fighting against their own oppression, and the other 50% passively ignoring or even actively justifying the equally painful oppression of others" (1974, 6). In many ways, her comments foreshadowed what Malatino has described as the subsequent decades "lack of attention to the oppression encountered by trans communities" (2021, 828) by both feminist and

---

[1] Over the course of writing this book, trans women have been subject to repeated moral panics which weaponise the vulnerability of (cis, white) women, or children (the two figuratively powerless groups in need of protection from the state) in order to curtail the rights and freedoms of trans people. These policies do not protect [most] women or children. As Katie Oliviero (2016) explains, such "precarity politics" license protectionist forms of violence, and shore up the illusion of security for some at the expense of naturalising or legitimising harms to others. This is particularly apparent in the UK, where trans-exclusionary discourses have positioned trans women as threats to other women, and trans children as threats to the social fabric. The last ten years have also witnessed a sustained, co-ordinated alignment of far-right nationalism with anti "gender-ideology" discourses. These have proliferated globally—with the far right and religious right framing "gender-ideology" (a wide umbrella that scapegoats gay and queer sexualities, post-modern feminism- Judith Butler in particular, and trans rights) as a threat to national stability (see Heinemann and Stern 2022; Korolczuk and Graff 2021). This has some of the same characteristics to a moral panic, "spreading paranoia and suspicion, and inciting demands for ever greater forms of state regulation and 'protection'" (Wiegman 2019, 4). However, it has a more sustained momentum to it- lacking the episodic and reactionary character of moral panics. As Judith Butler has argued "anti-gender movements are not just reactionary but fascist trends, the kind that support authoritarian governments" (2021, para 16). This is the backdrop for the current more reactionary attacks on trans rights and immigrant rights, and some commentators are arguing is more aptly characterised as a neo-fascist moment of neoliberalism (Fassin 2018; West 2016). For more on trans exclusionary radical feminism's and the far right see the special issue of *Transgender Studies Quarterly:* Trans-Exclusionary Feminisms and the Global New Right edited by Serena Bassi and Greta LaFleur (2022) and Alyosxa Tudor, "Decolonising Trans/Gender Studies: Teaching Race, Sexuality and Migration in Times of the Rise of the Global Right" (2021).

queer movements. As identity politics has thrived through the disciplinary devices of a political economy which rewards spectacularised individualised suffering, aspirations like Schulter's towards a non-exclusionary "human" as the basis for solidarity and resistance gesture towards an alternative. There are echoes of this vision in Dworkin's Jewish humanism, and in contributors to the *Journal of Male Feminism's* call for an end to the arbitrary restriction of feminine human expression from half of the population. The Combahee River Collective's second wave black feminist statement put forwards a similar proposal: "We reject pedestals, queenhood, and walking ten paces behind. To be recognised as human, levelly human, is enough" ([1978] 2014, 273–4). What would it mean to take forward this aspiration that we recognise everyone as "levelly human" today?

Cathryn Bailey cautions that "valuable resources may be lost by assuming that current problems and concerns have no historical precedents" (Bailey 1997, 23) and I propose that historicising and theorising trans contributions to feminist discussions is an important strategy that contests the divisive narratives that pit cis women against trans people today, and narrate histories of exclusion to do so.

BEFORE: TRANS STUDIES

Rather than revisit second wave feminism through a narrative of "loss" or "return", stories that predict in advance what we will find and what its significance for contemporary feminism is (Hemmings 2011), what if we look before second wave feminism to trans studies? If we presume that not only trans individuals, but many of the perspectives associated with trans studies came before second wave feminism, how do the philosophical and political developments of the period read differently? The oversights of queer theory and gender studies to do justice to trans perspectives are well-rehearsed in trans studies, which has reinstated the category of sex as an important category of analysis (see Keegan 2020, 393). However, without properly historicising gender studies, feminism, and queer theory's respective (and repeated) failures to incorporate trans subjectivities and embodiments, the origin story of trans feminism is destined to be forever after. Resisting the naturalisation of disciplinary divisions, and the narratives that sustain them, enables us to push at the borders identity knowledges and re-incorporate those whom disciplining inevitably marginalises.

In response to Andrea Long Chu and Emmett Harsin Drager's polemical acceptance of trans epistemologies as *after* and derivative of queer studies in their provocative, and highly generative article *After Trans Studies*, which begins: "Let's face it: Trans Studies is over. If it isn't, it should be" (Chu and Drager 2019, 103), Cassius Adair, Cameron Awkward-Rich, and Amy Marvin have proposed that in fact we are "before trans studies". Institutionalised marginality and precarity they argue, means that "the 'field' of trans studies has not yet happened" (2020, 306). As a means of highlighting the lack of material support for the field, their response is important. Writing from the UK, where there are no Transgender Studies departments and very little institutional support or recognition for the discipline, their presentation of trans studies as a utopian horizon is persuasive. However, this book also wants to argue for "before: trans studies" as trans feminist methodology, a way of disrupting the temporality of trans feminist epistemologies as an afterthought and instead to highlight the influence and longstanding presence of trans perspectives in the development of feminism itself. To argue for "before: trans studies" is to disrupt the temporal separation between second wave feminism and trans studies, and to propose that feminist histories need to undo their cisnormative assumptions, by affirming that trans labourers, thinkers and epistemologies have not only always been there, but that their existence is inseparable from the formation of feminism itself.[2]

"Before: trans studies" is also an important political move. This separation between (cis) women and trans people in feminism's historiography has become common in both academic discourses and in public feminism with worrying consequences. In reactionary public discourses, the equation of second wave feminism with essentialist feminism serves to pit an authentic, (cis) feminist second wave subject against the spectre of the threatening trans body who is invested with feminism's undoing. "Before: trans studies" reminds us that the threat is not from trans individuals, but from TERFs who use "harassment and violence to insert themselves into feminist spaces" (Williams 2020). Before: trans studies, reminds us "that the first seeds were down decades ago" (Adair et al. 2020, 306) and that resisting the marginalisation of trans labourers and trans perspectives past and present is not only politically important but theoretically valuable.

---

[2] V. Varun Chaudhry makes a similar argument with respect to queer studies. For Chaudhry, "queer studies must take the lead from transgender studies (and not the other way around): rather than being new, trendy, and theoretically sexy, trans studies has always been there, often lurking in the theoretical shadows, with little attention or resources to back up its importance" (2019, 49).

Sara Ahmed gestures towards the motivation which began this project when she writes "I would suggest that it is trans feminism today that most recalls the militant spirit of lesbian feminism in part because of the insistence that crafting a life is political work" (2017, 227). Highlighting foundational texts by Sandy Stone, Susan Stryker and Julia Serano, Ahmed points out that "these texts assemble a politics from what they name: showing not only how the sex-gender system is coercive, how it restricts what and who can be, but how creativity comes from how we survive a system that we cannot dismantle by the force of our will alone" (ibid.). This elegantly captures my proposition there is something about the affect and the style of second wave feminism that is particularly aligned with trans feminism; and that this revolutionary and embodied impulse remains valuable today. Each of the texts explored in this book take forward what I have argued is this second wave trans feminist sensibility, creating politics and possibilities through the naming and sharing of experience.

The second wave was, and remains, many things and disagreement and divisions ran rife. But by expanding the canon of second wave feminism to include print culture, I hope to begin the process of creating more usable histories. As a philosopher, my own turn to the archive has been a citation tactic, a means of intervening in the chronology of both trans feminism and second wave feminism, which places the former always in the future and the latter as firmly in the past. And whilst it is impossible to discern a representative story of second wave feminism, what I hope to have made clear in this book is that histories of second wave feminism can't be told without centring the presence of trans people in the movement and its related knowledge production. Foregrounding the trans feminist epistemologies in US feminism's second wave reinstalls trans people as one of feminism's central subjects and contests the monopolisation of feminism's recent history, in name of more liveable, levelly human, lives for all.

Bibliography

Adair, Cassius, et al. 2020. Before Trans Studies. *TSQ: Transgender Studies Quarterly* 7 (3): 306–320.

Ahmed, Sara. 2014. Introduction: Feel Your Way. In *The Cultural Politics of Emotion*, NED-New 2nd ed., 1–19. Edinburgh University Press.

———. 2017. *Living a Feminist Life*. Durham: Duke University Press.

Bailey, Cathryn. 1997. Making Waves and Drawing Lines: The Politics of Defining the Vicissitudes of Feminism. *Hypatia* 12 (3): 17–28.

Bassi, Serena, and Greta LaFleur. 2022. Trans-Exclusionary Feminisms and the Global New Right. *TSQ: Transgender Studies Quarterly* 9 (3): 228.

Boellstorff, Tom, et al. 2014. Decolonizing Transgender: A Roundtable Discussion. *Transgender Studies Quarterly* 1 (3): 419–439.

Butler, Judith. 2021. Why Is the Idea of 'Gender' Provoking Backlash the World Over? | Judith Butler. *The Guardian*. Guardian News and Media. October 23. https://www.theguardian.com/us-news/commentisfree/2021/oct/23/judith-butler-gender-ideology-backlash.

Chaudhry, V. Varun. 2019. Centering the 'Evil Twin': Rethinking Transgender in Queer Theory. *GLQ: A Journal of Lesbian and Gay Studies* 25 (1): 45–50.

Chu, Andrea Long, and Emmett Harsin Drager. 2019. After Trans Studies. *TSQ: Transgender Studies Quarterly* 6 (1): 103–116.

Combahee River Collective. [1978] 2014. A Black Feminist Statement. *Women's Studies Quarterly*, 42 (3/4): 271–280.

Dean, Jodi. 1996. *Solidarity of Strangers: Feminism after Identity Politics.* Berkeley: University of California Press.

Fassin, Éric. 2018. The Neo-Fascist Moment of Neoliberalism. *OpenDemocracy.* 10 August. https://www.opendemocracy.net/en/can-europe-make-it/neo-fascist-moment-of-neoliberalism/.

Heinemann, Isabel, and Alexandra Minna Stern. 2022. Gender and Far-Right Nationalism: Historical and International Dimensions. Introduction. *Journal of Modern European History* 20 (3): 311–321.

Hemmings, Clare. 2011. *Why Stories Matter: The Political Grammar of Feminist Theory.* Durham: Duke University Press.

Keegan, Cáel M. 2020. Getting Disciplined: What's Trans About Queer Studies Now? *Journal of Homosexuality* 67 (3): 384–397.

Korolczuk, Elżbieta, and Agnieszka Graff. 2021. *Anti-Gender Politics in the Populist Moment.* Taylor and Francis.

LaFleur, Greta, et al. 2021. Introduction: The Benefits of Being Trans Historical. In *Trans Historical: Gender Plurality before the Modern,* ed. Greta LaFleur et al., 1–24. Cornell University Press.

Malatino, Hil. 2021. The Promise of Repair: Trans Rage and the Limits of Feminist Coalition. *Signs: Journal of Women in Culture and Society* 46 (4): 827–851.

Oliviero, Katie. 2016. Vulnerability's Ambivalent Political Life: Trayvon Martin and the Racialized and Gendered Politics of Protection. *Feminist Formations* 28 (1): 1–32.

Schulter, Margo. 1973. Beyond Two-Genderism: Notes of a Radical Transsexual. *The Second Wave* 2 (4): 40–43.

———. 1974. Transsexophobia: Old Arguments Against New People. *Gay Community News,* 30 March: 6.

Tudor, Alyosxa. 2021. Decolonising Trans/Gender Studies: Teaching Race, Sexuality and Migration in Times of the Rise of the Global Right. *TSQ: Transgender Studies Quarterly* 8: 2.

West, Cornel. 2016. Goodbye, American Neoliberalism. A New Era Is Here. *The Guardian*. Guardian News and Media. 17 November. https://www.theguardian.com/commentisfree/2016/nov/17/american-neoliberalism-cornel-west-2016-election.

Wiegman, Robyn. 2019. Introduction. *Differences* (Bloomington, Ind.) 30 (1): 1–14.

Williams, Cristan. 2020. TERF Hate and Sandy Stone. *TransAdvocate.com*. Accessed 28 June 2022. https://www.transadvocate.com/terf-violence-and-sandy-stone_n_14360.htm.

INDEX[1]

[1] Note: Page numbers followed by 'n' refer to notes.

© The Author(s), under exclusive license to Springer Nature
Switzerland AG 2023
E. Cousens, *Trans Feminist Epistemologies in the US Second Wave*,
Breaking Feminist Waves,
https://doi.org/10.1007/978-3-031-33731-4

Printed by Printforce, United Kingdom